VISUAL QUICKSTART GUIDE

Excel

FOR WINDOWS 95

Maria Langer

 Peachpit Press

Excel for Windows 95
Visual QuickStart Guide
Maria Langer

Peachpit Press
2414 Sixth Street
Berkeley, CA 94710
510/548-4393
800/283-9444
510/548-5991 (fax)

Find us on the World Wide Web at:
http://www.peachpit.com

Peachpit Press is a division of Addison-Wesley Publishing Company

Editor: Jeremy Judson
Copy editor: Terry Wilson
Technical editor: Mark Budzyn
Cover design: The Visual Group
Production: Maria Langer

Colophon

This book was created with QuarkXPress 3.11 on a Macintosh 7100/66. The fonts used were Charlotte, Charlotte Sans, and Corinthian Bold from Letraset.

Notice of Rights

Notice of Liability

ISBN 0-201-88372-4

9 8 7 6 5 4 3 2 1

Printed and bound in the United States of America

♻ Printed on recycled paper

Dedication

To Tom, Kim, Angie, Steve, and the rest of
the red, white, and blue guys at the HP
PO. This one's for you.

Thanks!

To Jeremy Judson, Ted Nace, and the rest of the folks at Peachpit Press, for giving me the opportunity to share my Excel knowledge with Windows 95 users and for keeping me very busy for the past year and a half.

To Terry Wilson, for sharp-eyed copy editing and for meeting my nearly impossible deadlines.

To Microsoft Corporation, for continuing to refine and expand the capabilities of Excel.

To Ray and Jim at Apexx Technology, Inc. for helping me get my Mac-PC Network up and running in time to work on this book. Apexx has great support!

To Mike, for…well, he knows.

http://www.intac.com/~gilesrd/

TABLE OF CONTENTS

Table of Contents

Chapter 5:   **Using Functions in Formulas**

Chapter 7:   **Drawing and Formatting Objects**

Chapter 8: **Creating Charts**

Chapter 9: **Editing and Formatting Charts**

Chapter 10: Printing

Chapter 11: **Working with Databases**

Chapter 12: **Advanced Formula Techniques**

Chapter 13:   Add-ins and Macros

THE EXCEL WORKPLACE 1

Introduction

Excel is a powerful and often complex spreadsheet software package. With it, you can create picture-perfect worksheets, charts, and lists based on just about any data you can enter into a personal computer.

This Visual QuickStart Guide will help you take control of Excel's feature-rich work environment by providing step-by-step instructions and plenty of illustrations. A generous helping of tips show you how you can be more productive and avoid the "traps" that new, uninformed Excel users may encounter.

This book is designed for page-flipping. Use the thumb tabs, index, or table of contents to find the topics for which you need help. But if you're brand new to Excel, I recommend that you begin by reading at least the first two chapters. These chapters contain important information you'll need to fully understand the instructions presented in the rest of the book.

One last word of advice before you start: don't let Excel intimidate you! Sure, it's big, and yes, it has lots and lots of commands. But as you work with Excel, you'll quickly learn the techniques and commands you need to get your work done. That's when you'll be on your way to harnessing the real power of Excel.

The Excel screen

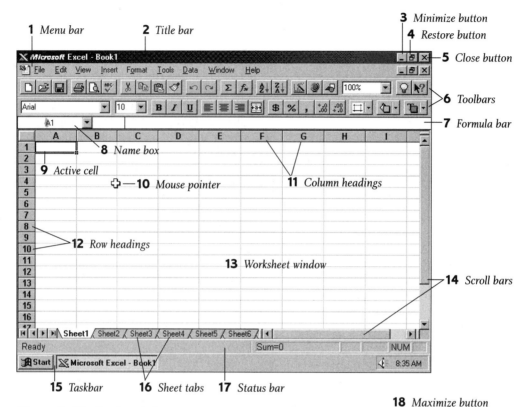

Figure 1. *The Excel workplace.*

18 *Maximize button*

Figure 2. *A minimized workbook window.*

Key to the Excel Screen

1 *Menu bar*

The menu bar gives you access to all of Excel's commands.

2 *Title bar*

The title bar displays the name of the current window. When the window is not maximized (as it is here), you can move it by dragging it by its title bar.

3 *Minimize button*

The minimize button reduces the window to an icon (see **Figure 2**). Once reduced, the button changes into the restore button.

4 *Restore button*

The restore button restores the window to its previous size and position. Once restored, the button changes into the maximize button.

Key to the Excel Screen (continued)

5 *Close button*

The close button closes the window.

6 *Toolbars*

Toolbars put a wide variety of menu commands within easy reach of your mouse pointer. You can show, hide, or customize any of Excel's toolbars.

7 *Formula bar*

The formula bar displays the contents of the active cell.

8 *Name box*

The name box displays the active cell's reference or name.

9 *Active cell*

The active cell is the cell in which text and numbers appear when you type. You can identify it by the dark or colored border that surrounds it.

10 *Mouse pointer*

When positioned within the worksheet window, the mouse pointer appears as a hollow plus sign. You can use the mouse pointer to select cells, enter data, choose menu commands, and click buttons.

11 *Column headings*

Each worksheet column is labeled with one or two letters of the alphabet. These are column headings.

12 *Row headings*

Each worksheet row is labeled with a number. These are row headings.

13 *Worksheet window*

The worksheet window is where you'll be doing most of your work with Excel. This window has a series of columns and rows which intersect at *cells*. You enter data and formulas in the cells to build your worksheet.

14 *Scroll bars*

Scroll bars let you shift the contents of the window so you can see information that does not fit in the window. To use a scroll bar, click an arrow at one end, click in the light area of the scroll bar, or drag the rectangular scroll box.

15 *Taskbar*

The Windows 95 taskbar gives you instant access to other programs or windows that are open. Click the name of an item to switch to it.

16 *Sheet tabs*

Each Excel document has one or more sheets combined together in a *workbook*. Sheet tabs let you move from one sheet to another within the workbook. Click on the tab for the sheet you want to view.

17 *Status bar*

The status bar provides information about your work and any buttons or commands you point to or select.

18 *Maximize button*

The maximize button (see **Figure 2**) enlarges a window to fill the screen. Once maximized, the button changes into the restore button.

The Excel Screen

To use the mouse

There are four basic mouse techniques:

■ Pointing means to position the mouse pointer so that its tip is on the item on which you are pointing (see **Figure 3**).

■ Clicking means to press the left mouse button once and release it. You click to make a cell active, position the insertion point, or choose a button or menu command.

■ Double-clicking means to press the left mouse button twice in rapid succession. You double-click to open an item or select text for editing.

■ Dragging means to press the mouse button down and hold it down while moving the mouse. You drag to reposition a window or select multiple cells.

Figure 3. *Pointing to the File menu.*

About Menus

All of Excel's menu commands are accessible through its menus. **Figures 4**, **5**, and **6** show examples of Excel's menus.

■ A menu command that appears in gray cannot currently be selected.

■ A menu command followed by an elipsis (…) displays a dialog box. I discuss dialog boxes later in this chapter.

■ A menu command followed by a triangle has a submenu. The submenu displays additional commands when the main command name is highlighted.

■ A menu command followed by keyboard keys (like Ctrl+X) can be chosen with a shortcut key.

■ A menu command preceded by a ✔ has been "turned on." To toggle the command from on to off or off to on, choose it from the menu.

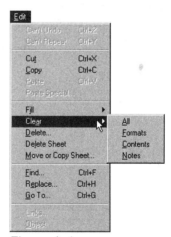

Figure 4. *An Excel menu with submenus.*

To use a menu

1. Point to the menu from which you want to choose a command and click the mouse button to display the menu.

   or

   Hold down the Alt key and press the keyboard key corresponding to the underlined letter of the menu name.

Figure 5.
Selecting a command from a menu.

Figure 6. *Selecting a command from a submenu.*

2. Move the mouse down the menu until the command you want is highlighted (see **Figure 5**) and click the mouse button. If the command is on a submenu, move the mouse down the menu until the submenu name is highlighted and the submenu appears. Then move the mouse down the submenu until the command you want is highlighted (see **Figure 6**) and click the mouse button.

   or

   Press the keyboard key corresponding to the underlined letter of the command you want.

To use shortcut menus

Excel's shortcut menus are hidden until you display them. Once displayed, they offer only those commands applicable to the current selection.

1. Point to the item for which you want to use a shortcut menu.

2. Hold down the Shift key and press the F10 key.

   or

   Click the right mouse button.

   A menu appears at the mouse pointer (see **Figure 7**).

3. Click the command you want.

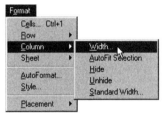

Figure 7. *Press Shift+F10 or click the right mouse button to display a shortcut menu of applicable commands.*

Using a Menu

To use a shortcut key

1. Hold down the modifier key for the shortcut (normally the Control key, which is abbreviated on menus as Ctrl).

2. Press the shortcut key.

For example, the shortcut key for the Save command (under the File menu; see **Figure 8**) is Ctrl+S. To use this shortcut key, hold down the Control key and press the S key.

Figure 8. *The Save command and its shortcut key.*

✔ Tip

■ Many shortcut keys are standardized from one Microsoft application to another. The Save, Print, and Copy commands are three good examples; they're usually Ctrl+S, Ctrl+P, and Ctrl+C.

To use toolbar buttons

Excel's toolbars offer another quick way to choose commands.

1. Point to the button for the command you want. A tiny box called a *ToolTip* appears, telling you what the button does (see **Figure 9**).

Figure 9. *The Bold button and its ToolTip.*

2. Click once on the toolbar button to activate the command.

✔ Tip

■ Buttons that have triangles on them are really menus. Click the triangle to display the menu (see **Figure 10**). Then click to select the button you want.

Figure 10. *The Borders button is really a menu in disguise.*

About Toolbars

By default, two toolbars are automatically displayed by Excel when you run it:

- The Standard toolbar (see **Figure 11a**) offers buttons for a wide range of commonly-used commands.
- The Formatting toolbar (see **Figure 11b**) offers buttons for commonly used formatting commands.

✔ Tip

- Other toolbars may appear automatically depending on the type of sheet or object you are working with. For example, when you work with a chart, the Chart toolbar appears.

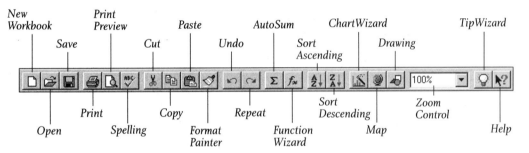

Figure 11a. *The Standard toolbar.*

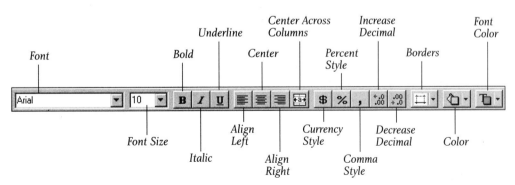

Figure 11b. *The Formatting toolbar.*

About Dialog Boxes

Excel uses dialog boxes to get information from you before it completes the execution of a command. Dialog boxes have many standard parts that work the same way to gather information about your choices.

To use a dialog box

■ Tabs (see **Figure 12a**), which appear at the top of some dialog boxes, let you move from one group of options to another. To switch to another group of options, click its tab.

■ Text boxes (see **Figure 12b**) let you enter information from the keyboard. Click in the text box to position an insertion point within it. Then enter a new value.

■ List boxes (see **Figure 12c**) offer a number of options to choose from. Use the scroll bar to view options that don't fit in the list window. Click an option to select it; it becomes highlighted.

■ Check boxes (see **Figure 12d**) let you turn options on or off. Click in a check box to toggle it. When a ✔ appears in the check box, its option is turned on. When a check box is gray, part of the selection has the option turned on while the rest of the selection has it turned off.

■ Option buttons (see **Figure 12e**) let you select only one option from a group. Click on an option to select it. If you click on an option that is not already selected, the one that was selected is turned off.

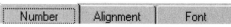

Figure 12a. *Tabs let you switch from one group of options to another within the same dialog box.*

Figure 12b. *Text boxes let you enter text or numbers.*

Figure 12c. *List boxes let you choose from a number of available options.*

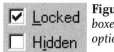

Figure 12d. *Check boxes let you turn options on or off.*

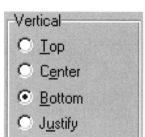

Figure 12e. *Option buttons let you select only one option from a group.*

Using Dialog Boxes

Figure 12f. *Drop-down lists offer another way to select one option from a group.*

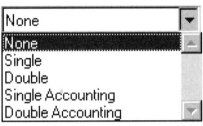

Figure 12g. *Click the triangle to display a list of options. Then click the option you want.*

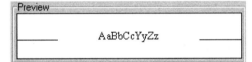

Figure 12h. *A Preview area shows you the effects of any changes you make before you close the dialog box.*

Figure 12i.
Command buttons let you accept or cancel changes or open other dialog boxes.

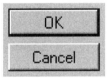

■ A dialog box with a title bar can be moved anywhere on screen by dragging it by its title bar.

■ Within a dialog box, you can press the Tab key to move from one option to the next. You can also use the Spacebar and arrow, letter, and Enter keys to toggle options and make selections without using your mouse.

■ Drop-down lists (see **Figures 12f** and **12g**) also let you select one option from a group. Click the triangle to display the list. Then choose the option you want by clicking it.

■ Preview areas (see **Figure 12h**), when available, illustrate the effects of your changes before you finalize them by clicking OK.

■ Command buttons (see **Figure 12i**) let you access other dialog boxes, accept changes and close the dialog box (OK), or close the dialog box without making changes (Cancel). To choose a button, click it.

✔ Tips

■ When a dialog box appears, you'll have to dismiss it by clicking OK or Cancel before you can continue working with Excel.

■ When the contents of a text box are selected, whatever you type will replace the selection.

■ Excel often uses text boxes and list boxes together (see **Figures 12b** and **12c**). You can use either one to make a selection.

■ In some list boxes (like the one in the Open dialog box), double-clicking an option selects it and closes the dialog box.

■ You can turn on any number of check boxes in a group, but you can select only one option button in a group.

■ The OK button is normally the "default" command button in a dialog box. This means you can often choose it by pressing the Enter key. Similarly, you can often choose the Cancel button by pressing the Esc key.

Using Dialog Boxes

Browsing Online Help

To browse Excel Help

1. Choose Microsoft Excel Help Topics from the Help menu (see **Figure 13a**).

    or

    Double-click the Help button on the Standard toolbar.

    A Help Topics window appears. If necessary, click the Contents tab to display a table of contents (see **Figure 13b**).

2. Click the topic that interests you and click Open.

    or

    Double-click the topic that interests you.

    The book icon to the left of the topic changes to look like an open book. Subtopics appear beneath it (see **Figure 13c**).

3. Repeat step 2 to zero in on the topic you want. When you open a topic with a question mark icon before it, a help window with information about that topic appears (see **Figure 13d**).

✔ Tips

■ To print the contents of a help window, click the Options button to display a menu of options. Then click Print Topic.

■ To return to the table of contents from a help window, click the Help Topics button.

■ Click any underlined word or phrase in a help window to display a box with more information about it. Click the box to dismiss it.

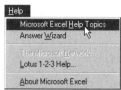

Figure 13a. *Accessing Microsoft Excel Help Topics from the Help menu.*

Figure 13b. *The Help Topics window's table of contents.*

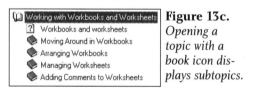

Figure 13c. *Opening a topic with a book icon displays subtopics.*

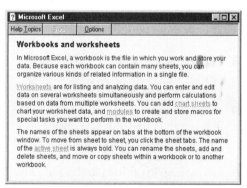

Figure 13d. *Opening a topic with a question mark icon displays information about that topic.*

Figure 14a. *The Help Topics index lists all help topics in alphabetical order.*

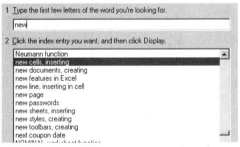

Figure 14b. *When you type a word or phrase in the text box, the list box contents shift in an attempt to match what you typed.*

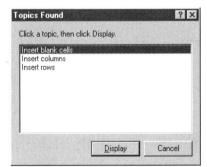

Figure 14c. *If an index topic has subtopics, they appear in the Topics Found window.*

To search Excel Help

1. Choose Microsoft Excel Help Topics from the Help menu (see **Figure 13a**).

   or

   Double-click the Help button on the Standard toolbar.

2. In the Help Topics window that appears, click the Index tab, if necessary, to display the Help Topics index (see **Figure 14a**).

3. In the text box at the top of the window, type the first few characters of the name of the topic that interests you. As you type, the contents of the list box shifts in an attempt to match the characters (see **Figure 14b**).

4. In the list box, click the topic that interests you to select it. Then click the Display button.

   or

   Double-click the topic that interests you.

5. A Topics Found window may appear (see **Figure 14c**). In its list box, click the topic that interests you and click Display or double-click the topic.

   Excel will either display a window containing information about that topic (see **Figure 13d**) or display an Answer Wizard window (see **Figure 15b**). I tell you about the Answer Wizard on the next page.

To dismiss Excel Help

When you are finished using Excel Help, click the window's close button to dismiss it and return to Excel.

Searching Online Help

To use the Answer Wizard

1. Choose Answer Wizard from the Help menu.

   or

   Double-click the Help button on the Standard toolbar and click the Answer Wizard tab in the Help Topics window.

2. In the text box at the top of the Answer Wizard window, type a phrase that describes what you want to do.

3. Click the Search button. Excel displays a list of topics that might provide the information you need (see **Figure 15a**).

4. Click a topic and click Display or double-click a topic.

   Excel will either display a window containing information about that topic (see **Figure 13d**) or display an Answer Wizard window that guides you, step by step, to complete the task (see **Figure 15b**).

To use ScreenTips

1. Click once on the Help button on the Standard toolbar or in a dialog box. The mouse pointer turns into an arrow with a question mark beside it (see **Figure 16a**).

2. Choose a menu command or click a window feature for which you want more information. A box containing information about the item appears (see **Figure 16b**).

3. To dismiss a ScreenTips box, click it.

✔ Tip

■ A brief description of any button or command you point to is always available in the status bar near the bottom of the screen (see **Figure 17**).

Figure 15a. *Use the Answer Wizard to ask for help in plain English.*

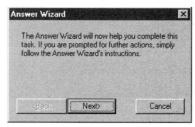

Figure 15b. *The Answer Wizard can guide you through the completion of a task.*

 Figure 16a. *Click the Help button once to get a help pointer.*

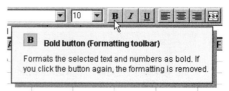

Figure 16b. *ScreenTips display information about items you click on with the help pointer.*

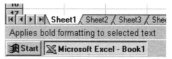

Figure 17. *The status bar displays a brief description of buttons and commands you point to.*

WORKSHEET BASICS 2

Numeric Values

Text Values — | Formula: =B1-B2

	A	B
1	Sales	$1,000.00
2	Cost	400.00
3	Profit	$ 600.00

Figure 1a. *This very simple worksheet illustrates how a spreadsheet program like Excel works with values and formulas.*

	A	B
1	Sales	$1,150.00
2	Cost	400.00
3	Profit	$ 750.00

Figure 1b. *When the value for Sales changes from $1,000 to $1,150, the Profit result changes automatically. Everything else remains the same.*

How Worksheets Work

Excel is most commonly used to create *worksheets*. A worksheet is a collection of information laid out in columns and rows. As illustrated in **Figure 1a**, each worksheet cell can contain one of two kinds of input:

■ A *value* is a piece of information that does not change. Values can be text, numbers, dates, or times. A cell containing a value usually displays the value.

■ A *formula* is a collection of values, cell references, operators, and predefined functions that, when evaluated by Excel, produces a result. A cell containing a formula usually displays the results of the formula.

Although any information can be presented in a worksheet, spreadsheet programs like Excel are usually used to organize and calculate numerical or financial information. Why? Well, when properly prepared, a worksheet acts like a super calculator. You enter values and formulas and it calculates and displays the results. If you change one of the values, no problem. Excel recalculates the results almost instantaneously without any additional effort on your part. (See **Figure 1b**.)

How does this work? By using cell *references* rather than actual numbers in formulas, Excel knows that it should use the contents of those cells in its calculations. Thus, changing one or more values affects the results of calculations that include references to the changed cells. As you can imagine, this makes worksheets powerful business planning and analysis tools!

Understanding Worksheets

To start Excel in Windows 95

If Excel is installed without other Microsoft Office components, click the Start button, click Programs, and click Microsoft Excel (see **Figure 2**).

or

If Excel is installed as part of Microsoft Office, click the Start button, click Programs, click Microsoft Office, and click Microsoft Excel.

To start Excel in Windows NT

In the Program Manager, double-click the Microsoft Excel icon.

✔ Tip

■ When you start Excel, a workbook window named *Book1* appears. This window is described in Chapter 1.

To create a new workbook file

Click the New Workbook button on the Standard toolbar.

or

1. Choose New from the File menu (see **Figure 3**).

   or

   Press Control+N.

   The New dialog box appears.

2. If necessary, click the General tab to display its options (see **Figure 4**).

3. Click the Workbook icon to select it.

4. Click OK.

✔ Tips

■ The icons shown in the New dialog box represent installed template files.

■ The New dialog box does not appear when you click the New Workbook button.

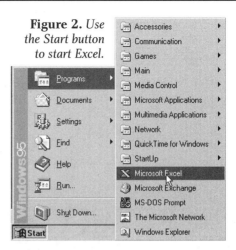

Figure 2. *Use the Start button to start Excel.*

Figure 3. *The File menu lets you create new files and open existing files.*

Figure 4. *The New dialog box lets you select a template for new documents.*

To open a workbook file

1. Choose Open from the File menu (see **Figure 3**).

   or

   Press Control+O.

   or

   Click the Open button on the Standard toolbar.

2. In the Open dialog box that appears (see **Figure 5**), locate the file you want to open.

3. Click the file name to select it and click Open.

   or

   Double-click the file name to select it and open it.

✔ Tips

■ If the document you want to open is one of the four most recently opened documents, it may appear in a file list near the bottom of the File menu (see **Figure 3**). If so, simply select it from the File menu to open it quickly.

■ You can use options at the bottom of the Open dialog box to search for files based on name, type, contents, or modification date. I tell you about finding files in Chapter 4.

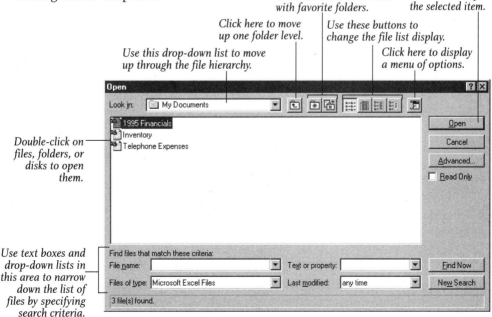

Use these buttons to work with favorite folders.

Click here to open the selected item.

Click here to move up one folder level.

Use these buttons to change the file list display.

Use this drop-down list to move up through the file hierarchy.

Click here to display a menu of options.

Double-click on files, folders, or disks to open them.

Use text boxes and drop-down lists in this area to narrow down the list of files by specifying search criteria.

Figure 5. *Use the Open dialog box to locate and open existing Excel files.*

About Cells

Worksheet information is entered into *cells*. A cell is the intersection of a column and a row. Each little "box" in the worksheet window is a cell.

■ Each cell has a unique *reference*. The reference uses the letter(s) of the column and the number of the row. Thus, cell *B4* would be at the intersection of column *B* and row *4*. The reference for the active cell appears in the name box (see **Figure 6**).

■ To enter information in a cell, you must make that cell *active*. A cell is active when there is a dark border around it. Anything you type is entered into the active cell.

To make a cell active

Use the mouse pointer to click in the cell you want to make active.

or

Use the arrow keys or other movement keys on the keyboard (see **Table 1**) to move the dark border to the cell you want to make active.

or

1. Choose Go To from the Edit menu

   or

   Press F5 or Control+G.

2. In the Go To dialog box (see **Figure 7**), enter the cell reference for the cell you want to make active in the Reference edit box.

3. Click OK. The cell you specified becomes active.

✔ Tip

■ Using the scroll bars does not move the cell pointer or change the active cell. It merely changes your view of the worksheet's contents.

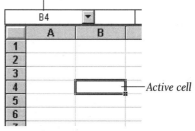

Cell reference in name box

Active cell

Figure 6. *The reference for an active cell appears in the name box.*

Key	Movement
Up Arrow	Up one cell
Down Arrow	Down one cell
Right Arrow	Right one cell
Left Arrow	Left one cell
Tab	Right one cell
Home	First cell in row
Page Up	Up one window
Page Down	Down one window
Control+Home	Cell A1
Control+End	Cell at intersection of last column and last row containing data

Table 1. *Keys for changing the active cell.*

Figure 7. *The Go To dialog box lets you activate any cell quickly.*

A
B
C
D
E
January
February
March
Sales
$1,000.00
$1,250.00
$1,485.00
Cost
400.00
395.00
412.00
Profit
$ 600.00
$ 855.00
$1,073.00

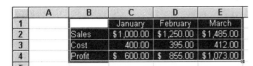

Figure 8. *In this illustration, the range* B1:E4 *is selected.*

Sales
$1,150.00
Cost
400.00
Profit
$ 750.00

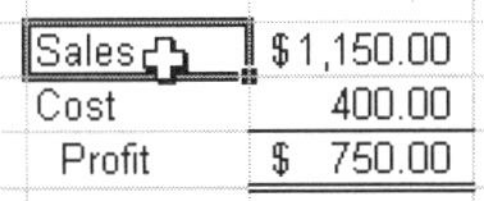

Figure 9a. *To select these cells, start here…*

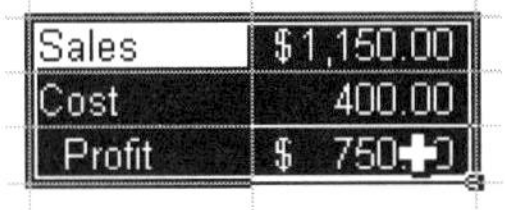

Sales
$1,150.00
Cost
400.00
Profit
$ 750

Figure 9b. *…then press down the mouse button and drag to here.*

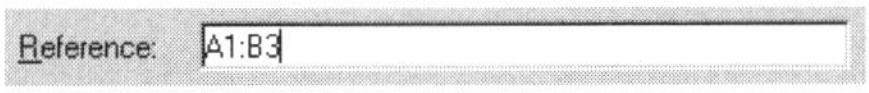

Reference:
A1:B3

Figure 10. *You can also use the Go To dialog box to select a range of cells.*

About Selecting Ranges

By selecting multiple cells or a *range* of cells, you can use commands on all selected cells at once. A range (see **Figure 8**) is a rectangular selection of cells defined by the top left and bottom right cell references.

To select a range of cells

1. Position the mouse pointer in the first cell you want to select (see **Figure 9a**).
2. Press the mouse button down, and drag to highlight all the cells in the selection (see **Figure 9b**).

or

1. Click in the first cell of the range you want to select.
2. Hold down the Shift key, and click in the last cell of the range. (This technique is known as “Shift-Click.”)

or

1. Choose Go To from the Edit menu or press F5 or Control+G.
2. Enter the reference for the range of cells you want to select in the Reference edit box of the Go To dialog box (see **Figure 10**).
3. Click OK.

✔ Tips

- Although the active cell is always part of a selection of multiple cells, it is never highlighted like the rest of the selection. You should, however, see a dark border around it (see **Figures 8** and **9b**).
- Although you can select more than one cell at a time, only one cell—the one referenced in the formula bar—is active and can receive information you type in.
- To specify a reference for a range, enter the addresses of the first and last cells of the range with a colon (:) between them.

To select an entire column

Click on the column heading of the column you want to select (see **Figure 11**).

or

Press Control+Spacebar when the cell pointer is in any cell of the column you want to select.

Figure 11. *Click on a column heading to select that column.*

To select an entire row

Click on the row heading of the row you want to select (see **Figure 12**).

or

Press Shift+Spacebar when the cell pointer is in any cell of the row you want to select.

Figure 12. *Click on a row heading to select that row.*

To select multiple columns or rows

Position the mouse pointer on the first column or row heading, press the mouse button down, and drag along the headings until all the desired columns or rows are selected.

✔ Tip

■ When selecting multiple columns or rows, be careful to position the mouse pointer *on* the heading and not *between* two headings! If you drag the border of two columns, you will change a column's width rather than make a selection.

To select the entire worksheet

Press Control+A.

or

Click the Select All button at the upper left corner of the worksheet window (see **Figure 13**).

Figure 13. *The Select All button is in the corner of the worksheet where column and row headings meet.*

Sales	$ 1,000.00
Cost	400.00
Profit	$ 600.00

Owner	Percentage	Share
Nancy	50%	$ 300.00
Bess	20%	120.00
George	20%	120.00
Ned	10%	60.00
Totals	100%	$ 600.00

Figure 14a. *To select both ranges of cells, start by selecting this range…*

Sales	$ 1,000.00
Cost	400.00
Profit	$ 600.00

Owner	Percentage	Share
Nancy	50%	$ 300.00
Bess	20%	120.00
George	20%	120.00
Ned	10%	60.00
Totals	100%	$ 600.00

Figure 14b. *…then hold down the Control key and select this range.*

To select multiple ranges

1. Use any selection technique to select the first cell or range of cells (see **Figure 16a**).
2. Hold down the Control key and drag to select the second cell or range of cells (see **Figure 16b**).
3. While holding down the Control key, continue to select additional cells or ranges of cells until all ranges are selected.

✔ Tips

■ Selecting multiple ranges can be tricky and takes practice. Don't be frustrated if you can't do it on the first few tries!

■ To add ranges that are not visible in the worksheet window, be sure to use the scroll bars to view them. Using the keyboard to move to other cells while selecting multiple ranges will remove the selections you've made so far or add undesired selections.

■ Do not click in the worksheet window or use the movement keys while multiple ranges are selected unless you are finished working with them. Doing so will deselect all the cells.

To deselect cells

Click anywhere in the worksheet.

or

Press any arrow key, Tab, Page Up, Page Down, or Home.

✔ Tip

■ Remember, at least one cell must be selected at all times—that's the active cell.

Selecting Multiple Ranges

About Entering Values and Formulas

To enter a value or formula into a cell, you begin by making the cell active. As you type or click to enter information, the information appears in both the cell and in the formula bar just above the window's title bar. You complete the entry by pressing Enter or clicking the Enter button on the formula bar.

While you are entering information into a cell, the formula bar is *active*. You can tell that it's active because three buttons appear between the cell reference and cell contents areas (see **Figure 15**) and the word *Enter* appears in the status bar at the bottom of the screen.

There are two important things to remember when the formula bar is active:

- Anything you type or click on may be included in the active cell.

- Some Excel options and menu commands are unavailable (see **Figures 16a** and **16b**).

You deactivate the formula bar by accepting or cancelling the current entry. The three buttons disappear (see **Figures 17b** and **18b**).

✔ Tips

- To cancel an entry before it has been completed, press the Esc key or click the Cancel button on the formula bar. This restores the cell to the way it was before you began.

- If you include formatting notation like dollar signs, commas, and percent symbols when you enter numbers, you may apply formatting styles. I tell you more about formatting the contents of cells in Chapter 6.

Figure 15. *An active formula bar.*

Figure 16a. *The Edit menu when the formula bar is inactive…*

Figure 16b. *…and when the formula bar is active.*

About Values

As discussed at the beginning of this chapter, a value is any text, number, date, or time you enter into a cell. Values are constant—they don't change unless you change them.

To enter a value

1. Make the cell in which you want to enter the value the active cell.

2. Type in the value. As you type, the information appears in two places: the active cell and the formula bar, which becomes active (see **Figure 17a**).

3. To complete and accept the entry (see **Figure 17b**), press Enter.

   or

   Click the Enter button on the formula bar.

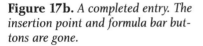

Figure 17a. *As data is entered into a cell, it appears in both the cell and the formula bar.*

Figure 17b. *A completed entry. The insertion point and formula bar buttons are gone.*

✔ Tips

- Pressing Enter to complete an entry accepts the entry and makes the next cell down the active cell. Clicking the Enter button accepts the entry without changing the active cell.

- Although you can often use the arrow keys or other movement keys to complete an entry by moving to another cell, it's a bad habit because it won't always work.

- Excel aligns text against the left side of the cell and aligns numbers against the right side of the cell. I tell you how to change alignment in Chapter 6.

- Don't worry if the data you put into a cell doesn't seem to fit. You can always change the column width to make it fit. I tell you how in Chapter 6.

Entering Values

About Formulas

Excel makes calculations based on formulas you enter into cells. When you complete the entry of a formula, Excel displays the results of the formula rather than the formula you entered.

■ If a formula uses cell references to refer to other cells and the contents of one or more of those cells changes, the result of the formula changes, too.

■ All formulas begin with an equal (=) sign. This is how Excel knows that a cell entry is a formula and not a value.

■ Formulas can contain any combination of values, references, operators (see **Table 2**), and functions. I tell you about using operators in formulas in this chapter and about using functions in Chapter 5.

■ Formulas are not case sensitive. This means that =A1+B10 is the same as =a1+b10. Excel automatically converts characters in cell references and functions to uppercase.

How Excel Calculates Complex Formulas

When calculating the results of expressions with a variety of operators, Excel makes calculations in the following order:

1. Negation.
2. Expressions in parentheses.
3. Percentages.
4. Exponentials.
5. Multiplication or division.
6. Addition or subtraction.

Table 3 shows some examples of formulas and their results to illustrate this. As you can see, the inclusion of parentheses can really make a difference when you write a formula!

Operator	Use	Example
+	Addition	=A1+B10
-	Subtraction	=A1-B10
-	Negation	=-A1
*	Multiplication	=A1*B10
/	Division	=A1/B10
^	Exponential	=A1^3
%	Percentage	=20%

Table 2. *Mathematical operators understood by Excel. Comparison and text operators are discussed in Chapter 5.*

Assumptions:		
A1=5		
B10=7		
C3=4		

Formula	Evaluation	Result
=A1+B10*C3	=5+7*4	33
=C3*B10+A1	=4*7+5	33
=(A1+B10)*C3	=(5+7)*4	48
=A1+10%	=5+10%	5.1
=(A1+10)%	=(5+10)%	0.15
=A1^2-B10/C3	=5^2-7/4	23.25
=(A1^2-B10)/C3	=(5^2-7)/4	4.5
=A1^(2-B10)/C3	=5^(2-7)/4	0.00008

Table 3. *Excel evaluates expressions based on operators, no matter what order the expressions appear in the formula. Adding parentheses can change the order of evaluation and the results.*

	A	B	C
1	Sales	1000	
2	Cost	400	
3	Profit	=b1-	

B3   ▼ ✗ ✓ *fx* =b1-

Figure 18a. *As a formula is entered into a cell, it appears in both the cell and the formula bar.*

	A	B	C
1	Sales	1000	
2	Cost	400	
3	Profit	600	

B3   ▼   =B1-B2

Figure 18b. *A completed formula entry. The cell shows the results of the formula rather than the formula. But you can still see and edit the formula in the formula bar.*

	A	B	
1	Sales	1000	
2	Cost	400	
3	Profit	600	— =1000-400
4			
5	Commission	90	— =600*15%

Figure 19a. *If any of the values change, the formulas will need to be rewritten!*

	A	B	
1	Sales	1000	
2	Cost	400	
3	Profit	600	— =B1-B2
4			
5	Rate	15%	
6			
7	Commission	90	— =B3*B5

Figure 19b. *But if the formulas reference cells containing the values, when the values change, the formulas will not need to be rewritten to show correct results.*

To enter a formula by typing

1. Make the cell in which you want to enter the formula the active cell.

2. Type in the formula. As you type, the formula appears in two places: the active cell and the formula bar, which becomes active (see **Figure 18a**).

3. To complete and accept the entry (see **Figure 18b**), press Enter.

   or

   Click the Enter button on the formula bar.

✔ Tips

- Pressing Enter to complete an entry accepts the entry and makes the next cell down the active cell. Clicking the Enter button accepts the entry without changing the active cell.

- Do not use the arrow keys or other movement keys to complete an entry by moving to another cell. Doing so may add cells to the formula!

- Use cell references for values rather than amounts or results of formulas whenever possible. This way, you don't have to rewrite formulas when amounts change. **Figures 19a** and **19b** illustrate this.

- To add a range of cells to a formula, type the first cell in the range followed by a colon (:) and then the last cell in the range. For example: *B1:B10* references the cells from *B1* straight down through *B10*.

Entering Formulas by Typing

To enter a formula by clicking

1. Make the cell in which you want to enter the formula the active cell.

2. Type an equal (=) sign to begin the formula (see **Figure 20a**).

3. To enter a constant value or operator, type it in (see **Figure 20c**).

   or

   To enter a cell reference, click on the cell you want to reference (see **Figures 20b** and **20d**).

4. Repeat step 3 until the entire formula appears in the formula bar.

5. Press Enter (see **Figure 20e**).

   or

   Click the Enter button on the formula bar.

✔ Tips

- If you click a cell reference without typing an operator, Excel assumes you want to add that reference to the formula.

- Be careful where you click when writing a formula! Each click you make will add a reference to the formula you're writing. If you add an incorrect reference, use the Delete key to delete it or click the Cancel button to start the entry from scratch. (I tell you more about editing a cell's contents in Chapter 3.)

- You can add a range of cells to a formula by dragging over the cells.

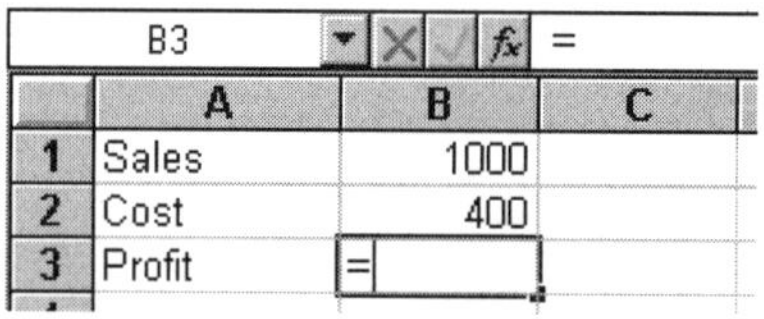

Figure 20a. *To enter the formula =B1–B2, begin by typing = to begin the formula...*

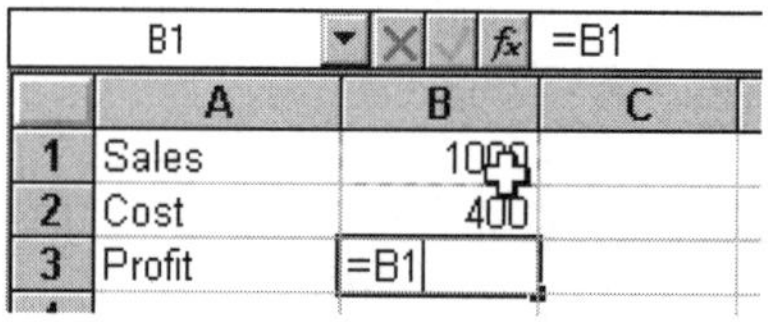

Figure 20b. *...click cell B1 to add its reference to the formula...*

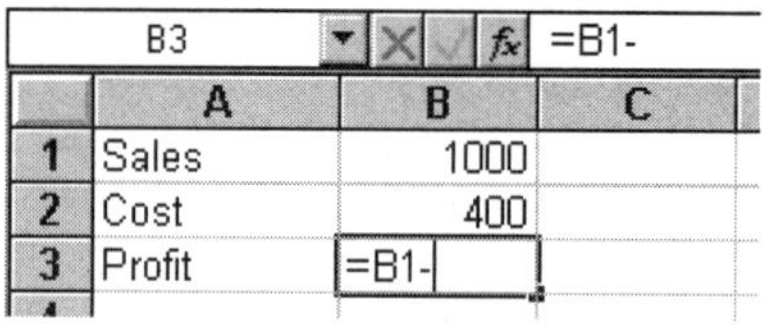

Figure 20c. *...type – to tell Excel to subtract...*

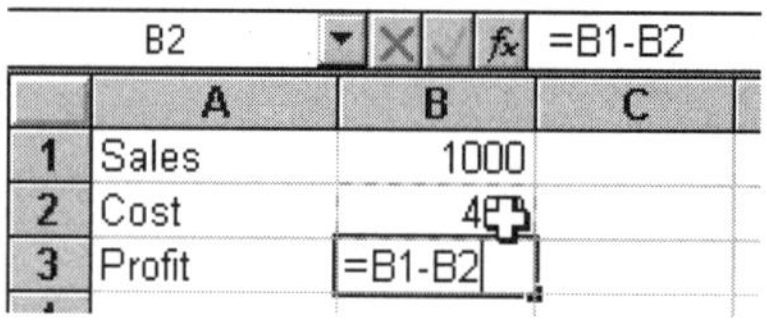

Figure 20d. *...click cell B2 to add its reference to the formula...*

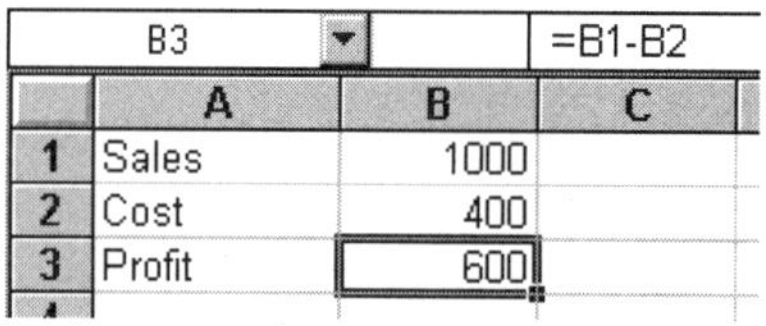

Figure 20e. *...and finally, click the Enter button or press Enter to complete the formula.*

Entering Formulas by Clicking

About Editing

You can easily make the following edits in an Excel worksheet:

- Change the contents of cells.
- Insert or delete cells, columns, and rows.
- Copy or move cells from one location to another.

This chapter covers all of these techniques as well as the Undo command, which can help you out of a jam when you make an editing mistake.

Figure 1a. *To edit a cell while it is being written, click to reposition the insertion point in the cell...*

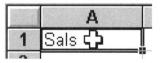

Figure 1b. *...or in the formula bar and make changes as necessary.*

To change an entry as you type it

Use the Backspace key to delete incorrect characters and type in new ones.

or

Use the mouse pointer (which turns into an I-beam pointer) to position the insertion point within the cell (see **Figure 1a**) or formula bar (see **Figure 1b**) and insert or delete characters.

To change a completed entry

Click the cell containing the incorrect entry, click in the formula bar to make it active, then insert or delete characters as necessary.

or

Double-click on the cell containing the incorrect entry (see **Figure 2**), then insert or delete characters as necessary right in the cell.

Figure 2. *You can edit a completed entry by making it active again.*

To clear cell contents

1. Select the cell(s) you want to clear.

2. Choose Contents from the Clear sub-menu under the Edit menu (see **Figure 3**).

   or

   Press the Del key.

✔ Tips

■ To clear the contents of only one cell, make the cell active, press Backspace, and then press Enter.

■ Do *not* use the Spacebar to clear a cell's contents! Doing so inserts a space character into the cell. Although the contents seem to disappear, they are just replaced by an invisible character.

■ Clearing a cell is very different from deleting a cell. When you clear a cell, the cell remains in the worksheet—only its contents are removed. When you delete a cell, the entire cell is removed from the worksheet and other cells shift to fill the gap. I tell you about inserting and deleting cells next.

■ The Contents command clears only the values or formulas entered into a cell. To clear everything, including formatting and notes, choose All from the Clear submenu under the Edit menu. To clear only formats or notes, choose Formats or Notes from the Clear submenu. I tell you about formatting cells and adding cell notes in Chapter 6.

Figure 3. *The Edit menu's Clear sub-menu offers four options to clear selected cells.*

Clearing Cells

About Inserting and Deleting Cells

Excel offers an Insert command and a Delete command to insert and delete columns, rows, or cells. When you use the Insert command, Excel shifts cells down or to the right to make room for the new cells. When you use the Delete command, Excel shifts cells up or to the left to fill the gap left by the missing cells.

Figures 4a, **4d**, and **5c** show examples of how inserting a column or deleting a row affects the references of the cells in a worksheet. Fortunately, Excel is smart enough to know how to adjust cell references in formulas so that the formulas you write remain correct.

	A	B	C	D
1		Jan	Feb	Mar
2	Nancy	443	419	841
3	Bess	493	277	45
4	George	301	492	179
5	Ned	67	856	842

Figure 4a. *A simple worksheet.*

	A	B	C	D
1		Jan	Feb	Mar
2	Nancy	443	419	841
3	Bess	493	277	45
4	George	301	492	179
5	Ned	67	856	842

Figure 4b. *To insert a column, begin by selecting the column where you want the new column to go…*

To insert a column or row

1. Select a column or row (see **Figure 4b**).
2. Choose Columns or Rows from the Insert menu (see **Figure 4c**).

   or

   Choose Cells from the Insert menu.

Figure 4c. *…then choose Columns from the Insert menu.*

✔ Tips

- To insert multiple columns or rows, select the number of columns or rows you want to insert. For example, if you want to insert three columns before column B, select columns B, C, and D.

- If a complete column or row is not selected when you choose Cells from the Insert menu, the Insert dialog box will appear (see **Figure 6b**). Just click the appropriate option button (Entire Row or Entire Column) for what you want to insert, then click OK.

	A	B	C	D	E
1			Jan	Feb	Mar
2	Nancy		443	419	841
3	Bess		493	277	45
4	George		301	492	179
5	Ned		67	856	842

Figure 4d. *Here's what you wind up with when you insert a column.*

Inserting Columns or Rows

To delete a column or row

1. Select a column or row (see **Figure 5a**).

2. Choose Delete from the Edit menu (see **Figure 5b**).

✔ Tips

■ To delete more than one column or row at a time, select all of the columns or rows you want to delete before choosing Delete from the Edit menu.

■ If a complete column or row is not selected when you choose Delete, the Delete dialog box will appear (see **Figure 6d**). Just click the appropriate option button (Entire Row or Entire Column) for what you want to delete, then click OK.

■ If you delete a column or row that contains referenced cells, the formulas that reference the cells may display a *#REF!* error message. This means that Excel can't find a referenced cell. If this happens, you'll have to rewrite any formulas in cells displaying the error.

	A	B	C	D
1		Jan	Feb	Mar
2	Nancy	443	419	841
3	Bess	493	277	45
4	George	301	492	179
5	Ned	67	856	842

Figure 5a. *To delete a row, begin by selecting the row you want to delete...*

Figure 5b. *...then choose Delete from the Edit menu.*

	A	B	C	D
1		Jan	Feb	Mar
2	Nancy	443	419	841
3	Bess	493	277	45
4	Ned	67	856	842

Figure 5c. *Here's what you wind up with when you delete a row.*

Deleting Columns or Rows

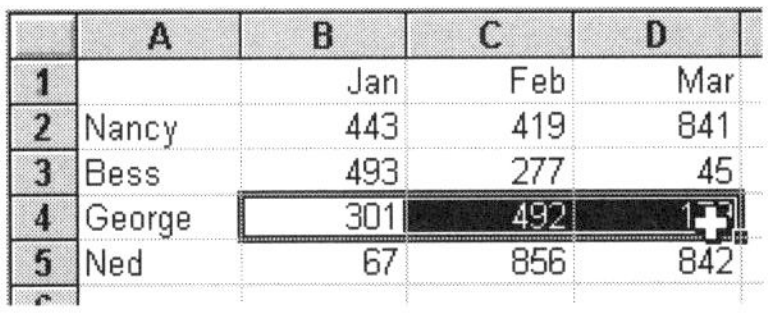

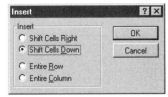

	A	B	C	D
1		Jan	Feb	Mar
2	Nancy	443	419	841
3	Bess	493	277	45
4	George	301	492	1
5	Ned	67	856	842

Figure 6a. *To insert or delete cells, begin by selecting cells.*

Figure 6b. *Use the Insert dialog box to tell Excel to shift existing cells to the right or down.*

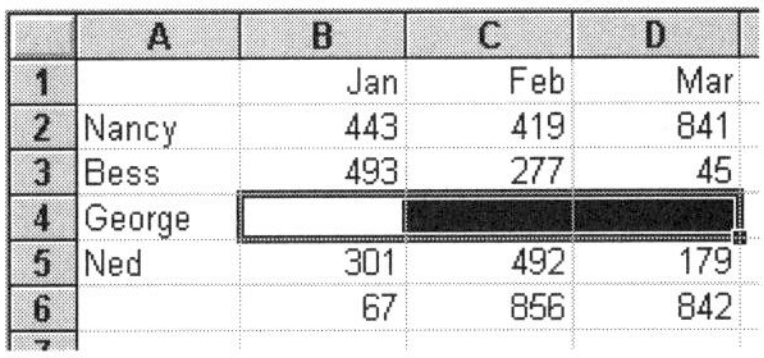

	A	B	C	D
1		Jan	Feb	Mar
2	Nancy	443	419	841
3	Bess	493	277	45
4	George			
5	Ned	301	492	179
6		67	856	842

Figure 6c. *Here's what you get if you shift cells down.*

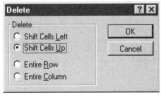

Figure 6d. *Use the Delete dialog box to tell Excel to shift cells around the deleted cells to the left or up.*

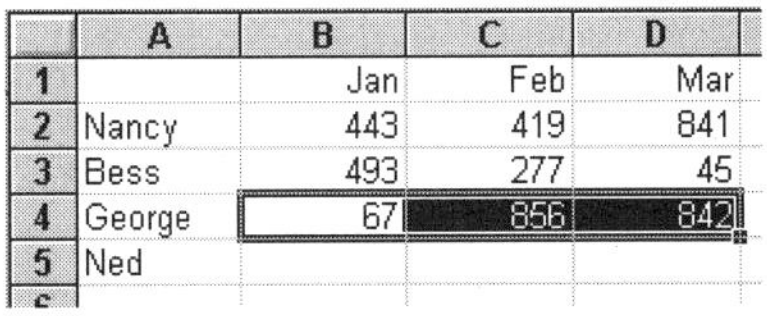

	A	B	C	D
1		Jan	Feb	Mar
2	Nancy	443	419	841
3	Bess	493	277	45
4	George	67	856	842
5	Ned			

Figure 6e. *Here's what you get if you shift cells up.*

To insert cells

1. Select a cell or range of cells (see **Figure 6a**).
2. Choose Cells from the Insert menu.
3. In the Insert dialog box that appears (see **Figure 6b**), choose the appropriate option button to tell Excel how to shift the cells—Shift Cells Right or Shift Cells Down.
4. Click OK to insert the cells (see **Figure 6c**).

✔ Tip

■ Excel always inserts the number of cells that is selected when you use the Insert command. You can see this in **Figures 6a** and **6c**.

To delete cells

1. Select a cell or range of cells to delete (see **Figure 6a**).
2. Choose Delete from the Edit menu.
3. In the Delete dialog box that appears (see **Figure 6d**), choose the appropriate option button to tell Excel how to shift the cells—Shift Cells Left or Shift Cells Up.
4. Click OK to delete the cells (see **Figure 6e**).

✔ Tip

■ If you delete a cell that is referenced in one or more formulas, the formulas that reference the deleted cells may display a *#REF!* error message. If this happens, you'll have to rewrite any formulas in cells displaying the error.

Inserting or Deleting Cells

About Copying Cells

Excel offers several ways to copy the contents of one cell to another: the Copy and Paste commands, the fill handle on the active cell or selected cells' border, and the Fill command.

How Excel copies depends not only on the method used, but on the contents of the cell(s) being copied.

- When you use the Copy and Paste commands to copy a cell containing a value, Excel makes an exact copy of the cell, including any formatting (see **Figure 7**). I tell you about formatting cells in Chapter 6.

- When you use the fill handle or Fill command to copy a cell containing a value, Excel either makes an exact copy of the cell, including any formatting, or creates a series based on the original cell's contents (see **Figure 8**).

- When you copy a cell containing a formula, Excel copies the formula, changing any relative references in the formula so they're relative to the destination cell(s) (see **Figure 9**).

✔ Tips

- Copy cells that contain formulas whenever possible to save time and ensure consistency.

- The Edit menu's Paste Special command offers additional options over the regular Paste command. For example, you can use it to paste only the formatting of a copied selection, convert formulas in the selection into values, or add the contents of the selection to the destination cells.

Figure 7. *The Copy and Paste commands make an exact copy.*

Figure 8. *Using the fill handle on a cell containing the word* Monday *generates a list of the days of the week.*

Figure 9. *Copying a formula that totals a column automatically writes correctly referenced formulas to total similar columns.*

Understanding Copying

Figure 10a. *Begin by selecting the cell(s) you want to copy...*

Figure 10b. *...choose Copy from the Edit menu...*

Figure 10c. *...a marquee appears around the selection...*

Figure 10d. *...select the destination cell...*

Figure 10e. *...and choose Paste from the Edit menu.*

To copy with Copy and Paste

1. Select the cell(s) you want to copy (see **Figure 10a**).

2. Choose Copy from the Edit menu (see **Figure 10b**).

   or

   Press Control+C.

   or

   Click the Copy button on the Standard toolbar.

   An animated marquee appears around the selection (see **Figure 10c**).

3. Select the cell(s) to which you want to paste the selection (see **Figure 10d**). If more than one cell has been copied, you can select the first cell of the destination range or the entire range.

4. Choose Paste from the Edit menu.

   or

   Press Control+V

   or

   Click the Paste button on the Standard toolbar.

   or

   Press Enter.

   The values are copied to the new location (see **Figure 10e**).

✔ Tips

■ If you use the Paste command, Control+V, or the Paste button, the marquee remains around the copied range, indicating that it may be pasted elsewhere. The marquee will disappear automatically as you work, but if you want to remove it manually, press Esc.

■ Be careful when you paste cells! If the destination cells contain information, Excel will overwrite them without warning you!

Copying with Copy and Paste

About the Fill Handle

The fill handle is a small black box in the lower right corner of the border around the active cell (see **Figure 11a**) or selected cells (see **Figure 11b**). You can use the fill handle to copy the contents of one or more cells to adjacent cells.

To copy with the fill handle

1. Select the cell(s) containing the information you want to copy.

2. Position the mouse pointer on the fill handle. The mouse pointer turns into a crosshairs (see **Figure 12a**).

3. Press the mouse button down and drag to the adjacent cells. A dark border surrounds the destination cells (see **Figure 12b**).

4. When all the destination cells are surrounded by the dark border, release the mouse button. The cells are filled. (see **Figure 12c**).

✔ Tips

■ You can use the fill handle to copy any number of cells. The destination cells, however, must be adjacent to the original cells.

■ When using the fill handle, you can only copy in one direction (up, down, left, or right) at a time.

■ Be careful when you use the fill handle to copy cells! If the destination cells contain information, Excel may overwrite them without warning you!

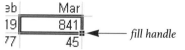

Figure 11a. *The fill handle on a single active cell.*

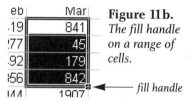

Figure 11b. *The fill handle on a range of cells.*

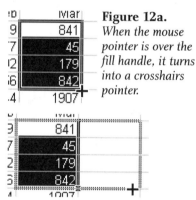

Figure 12a. *When the mouse pointer is over the fill handle, it turns into a crosshairs pointer.*

Figure 12b. *As you drag the fill handle, a dark border indicates the destination cells.*

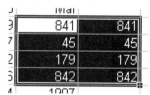

Figure 12c. *When you release the mouse button, the cells in the original selection are copied to the destination cells.*

Copying with the Fill Handle

About the Fill Command

The Fill command works a lot like the fill handle in that it copies information to adjacent cells. But rather than drag to copy, you select the source and destination cells at the same time, then use the Fill command to complete the copy. There are several options to copy:

■ Down copies the contents of the top cell(s) in the selection to the selected cells beneath it.

■ Right copies the contents of the left cell(s) in the selection to the selected cells to the right of it.

■ Up copies the contents of the bottom cell(s) in the selection to the selected cells above it.

■ Left copies the contents of the right cell(s) in the selection to the selected cells to the left of it.

To use the Fill command

1. Select the cell(s) you want to copy along with the adjacent destination cell(s) (see **Figure 13a**).

2. Choose the appropriate command from the Fill submenu under the Edit menu (see **Figure 13b**): Down, Right, Up, Left.

✔ Tip

■ You *must* select both the source and destination cells when using the Fill command. If you only select the destination cells, Excel won't copy the correct cells!

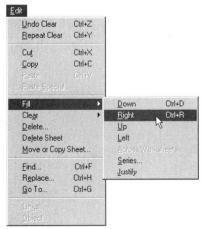

Figure 13a. *To use the Fill command, begin by selecting the source and destination cells…*

Figure 13b. *…then choose a command from the Fill submenu under the Edit menu.*

Copying with the Fill Command

About AutoFill

A *series* is a sequence of cells that form a logical progression. Excel's AutoFill feature can generate a series of numbers, months, days, dates, and quarters.

To create a series with the fill handle

1. Enter the first item of the series in a cell (see **Figure 14a**). Be sure to complete the entry by pressing Enter.

2. Position your mouse pointer on the fill handle and drag. All the cells that will be part of the series are surrounded by a dark border (see **Figure 14b**).

3. Release the mouse button to complete the series (see **Figure 14f**).

To create a series with the Series command

1. Enter the first item in the series in a cell (see **Figure 14a**).

2. Select all cells that will be part of the series, including the first cell (see **Figure 14c**).

3. Choose the Series from the Fill submenu under the Edit menu (see **Figure 14d**).

4. In the Series dialog box that appears (see **Figure 14e**), turn on the AutoFill option button.

5. Click OK to complete the series (see **Figure 14f**).

✔ Tip

■ To generate a series that skips values, enter the first two values of the series in adjoining cells, then use the fill handle or Fill command to create the series, including both cells as part of the source (see **Figures 15a** and **15b**).

Figure 14a. *Start by entering the first item of the series in a cell...*

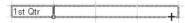

Figure 14b. *...then drag the fill handle to include all cells that will contain the series.*

Figure 14c. *...or select the cells that will contain the series...*

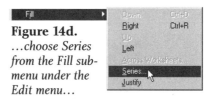

Figure 14d. *...choose Series from the Fill submenu under the Edit menu...*

Figure 14e. *...turn on the AutoFill option button in the Series dialog box, and click OK.*

Figure 14f. *The end result is the same: a series automatically built by Excel.*

Figures 15a and **15b.** *Enter the first two numbers in the series, select them, and then drag the fill handle to complete the series.*

About Copying Formulas

You copy a cell containing a formula the same way you copy any other cell in Excel: with the Copy and Paste commands, with the fill handle, or with the Fill command. These methods are discussed earlier in this chapter.

Generally speaking, Excel does not make an exact copy of a formula. Instead, it copies the formula based on the kinds of references used within it. Types of references are discussed in detail on the next page.

	A	B	C	D
1	Item	Price	Cost	Markup
2	Product A	24.95	16.73	=(B2-C2)/C2
3	Product B	15.95	5.69	
4	Product C	12.99	4.23	
5	Product D	99.99	62.84	

Figure 16a. *Here's a formula to calculate markup percentage. If the company has 534 products, would you want to write the same basic formula 533 more times?*

	A	B	C	D	
1	Item	Price	Cost	Markup	
2	Product A	24.95	16.73	49%	=(B2-C2)/C2
3	Product B	15.95	5.69	180%	=(B3-C3)/C3
4	Product C	12.99	4.23	207%	=(B4-C4)/C4
5	Product D	99.99	62.84	59%	=(B5-C5)/C5

Figure 16b. *Of course not! That's when copying formulas comes in handy. If the original formula is properly written, the results of the copied formulas should also be correct.*

✔ Tips

- You'll find it much quicker to copy formulas rather than to write each and every formula from scratch. You can see an example of this in **Figures 16a** and **16b**.

- Not all formulas can be copied with accurate results. For example, you can't copy a formula that sums up a column of numbers to a cell that should represent a sum of cells in a row (see **Figure 17**).

	A	B	C	D	E	F
1			January	February	March	
2		Sales	$ 1,000.00	$ 1,250.00	$ 1,485.00	
3		Cost	400.00	395.00	412.00	
4		Profit	$ 600.00	$ 855.00	$ 1,073.00	
5						
6	Owner	Pctg	Jan Share	Feb Share	Mar Share	Total
7	Nancy	50%	$ 300.00	$ 427.50	$ 536.50	0
8	Bess	20%	120.00	171.00	214.60	
9	George	20%	120.00	171.00	214.60	=SUM(F3:F6)
10	Ned	10%	60.00	85.50	107.30	
11	Totals	100%	$ 600.00	$ 855.00	$ 1,073.00	

=SUM(C7:C10)

Figure 17. *In this illustration, the formula in cell C11 was copied to cell F7. This doesn't work because the two cells don't add up similar ranges. The formula in cell F7 would have to be rewritten from scratch. It could then be copied to F8 through F10. (I tell you about the SUM function in Chapter 5.)*

Relative vs. Absolute Cell References

There are two main kinds of cell references:

- A *relative cell reference* is the address of a cell relative to the cell the reference is in. For example, a reference to cell *B1* in cell *B3*, tells Excel to look at the cell two cells above *B3*. Most of the references you use in Excel are relative references.

- An *absolute cell reference* is the exact location of a cell. To indicate an absolute reference, enter a dollar sign ($) in front of the column letter(s) and row number of the reference. An absolute reference to cell *B1*, for example, would be written *$B$1*.

As **Figures 18a** and **18b** illustrate, relative cell references change when you copy them to other cells. Although in many cases you might want the references to change, sometimes you don't. That's when you use absolute references (see **Figures 18c** and **18d**).

✔ Tips

- Here's a trick for remembering the meaning of the notation for absolute cell references: in your mind, replace the dollar sign with the word *always*. Then you'll read *$B$1* as *always B always 1—always B1!*

- If you're having trouble understanding how these two kinds of references work and differ, don't worry. This is one of the most difficult spreadsheet concepts you'll encounter. Try creating a worksheet like the one illustrated on this page and working your way through the figures one at a time. Pay close attention to how Excel copies the formulas you write!

Figure 18a. *This formula correctly calculates a partner's share of profit.*

Figure 18b. *But when the formula is copied for the other partners, the relative reference to cell C3 is changed, causing incorrect results and an error message!*

Figure 18c. *Rewrite the original formula with an absolute reference to cell C3, which all the formulas must reference.*

Figure 18d. *When the formula is copied for the other partners, only the relative reference (to the percentages) changes. The results are correct.*

Share

| 6 | =$C$3 |

Figure 19. *To write an absolute reference, include a dollar sign before the column and/or row references.*

To include an absolute reference in a formula

1. Enter the formula as discussed in Chapter 2.

2. Type a dollar sign before the column and row references for the cell reference you want to be absolute (see **Figure 19**).

3. Complete the entry by pressing Enter or clicking the Enter button on the formula bar.

✔ Tips

■ You can edit an existing formula to include absolute references by inserting dollar signs where needed. I tell you how to edit cell contents earlier in this chapter.

■ Do not use a dollar sign in a formula to indicate currency formatting. I tell you how to apply formatting to cell contents, including currency format, in Chapter 6.

About Mixed References

There's another kind of cell reference. In a *mixed cell reference*, either the column or row reference is absolute while the other reference remains relative. Thus, you can use cell references like *A$1* or *$A1*. Use this when a column reference must remain constant but a row reference changes or vice versa. **Figure 20** shows a good example.

	A	B	C	D	E
1			January	February	March
2		Sales	$ 1,000.00	$ 1,250.00	$ 1,485.00
3		Cost	400.00	395.00	412.00
4		Profit	$ 600.00	$ 855.00	$ 1,073.00
5					
6	Owner	Pctg	Jan Share	Feb Share	Mar Share
7	Nancy	50%	$ 300.00		
8	Bess	20%			
9	George	20%	=C$4*$B7		
10	Ned	10%			

Figure 20. *The formula in cell C7 includes two different kinds of mixed references. It can be copied to cells C8 through C10 and D7 through E10 for correct results in all cells. Try it!*

Using Absolute and Mixed References

About Moving Cells

Excel offers two ways to move the contents of one cell to another: the Cut and Paste commands and dragging the border of a selection. Either way, Excel moves the contents of the cell, including any formatting. I tell you about cell formatting in Chapter 6.

✔ Tip

■ When you move a cell, Excel searches the worksheet for any cells that contain references to it and changes the references to reflect the cell's new location (see **Figures 21a** and **21b**).

To move with Cut and Paste

1. Select the cell(s) you want to move (see **Figure 22a**).

2. Choose Cut from the Edit menu (see **Figure 22b**).

   or

   Press Control+X.

   or

   Click the Cut button on the Standard toolbar.

   An animated marquee appears around the selection (see **Figure 22c**).

3. Select the cell(s) to which you want to paste the selection (see **Figure 22d**).

4. Choose Paste from the Edit menu.

   or

   Press Control+V.

   or

   Click the Paste button on the Standard toolbar.

   or

   Press Enter.

   The cell contents are moved to the new location (see **Figure 22e**).

Figure 21a. *Note the formula in cell C6.*

Figure 21b. *See how it changes when one of the cells it references changes?*

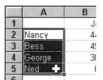

Figure 22a. *Begin by selecting the cell(s) you want to move...*

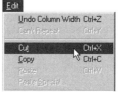

Figure 22b. *...choose Cut from the Edit menu...*

Figure 22c. *...a marquee appears around the selection but it does not disappear...*

Figure 22d. *...select the destination cell(s)...*

Figure 22e. *...and choose Paste from the Edit menu.*

Moving with Cut and Paste

To move with drag and drop

1. Select the cell(s) you want to move.

2. Position the mouse pointer on the border of the selection. When it is in the proper position, it turns into an arrow pointing up and to the left (see **Figure 23a**).

3. Press the mouse button down and drag toward the new location. As you move the mouse, a dark border the same shape as the selection moves along with it (see **Figure 23b**).

4. Release the mouse button. The selection moves to its new location.

✔ Tips

- If you try to drag a selection to cells already containing information, Excel warns you with a dialog box like the one in **Figure 24**. If you click OK to complete the move, the cells will be overwritten with the contents of the cells you are moving.

- To copy using drag and drop, hold down the Control key as you press the mouse button down. The mouse pointer turns into an arrow with a tiny plus sign (+) beside it (see **Figure 25**). When you release the mouse button, the selection is copied.

- To insert cells using drag and drop, hold down the Shift key as you press the mouse button down. As you drag, a dark bar moves along with the mouse pointer (see **Figure 26**), indicating where the cells will be inserted when you release the mouse button.

Figure 23a. *Position the mouse pointer on the border of the selection.*

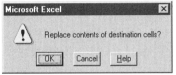

Figure 23b. *As you drag, a dark border with the same shape as the selection moves along with your mouse pointer.*

Figure 24. *Excel warns you when you try to drag a selection to occupied cells.*

Figure 25. *Holding the Control key down while dragging a border copies the selection.*

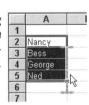

Figure 26. *Holding the Shift key down while dragging a border inserts the cells.*

Moving with Drag and Drop

About Undoing Commands

If you issue a command or change the contents of a cell by mistake, don't panic! Many Excel actions and commands can be reversed with the Undo command.

To undo a command

Choose Undo from the Edit menu (see **Figure 27**). When available, this is the first command on the Edit menu.

or

Press Control+Z.

or

Click the Undo button on the Standard toolbar.

About Repeating Commands

You can also repeat an action or command. This is especially useful if you've made changes to a cell and want to make the same changes to another cell or group of cells.

To repeat a command

Choose Repeat from the Edit menu (see **Figure 27**). When available, this is the second command on the Edit menu.

or

Press Control+Y.

or

Click the Repeat button on the Standard toolbar.

✔ Tip

■ If the last command or action was to undo the previous action, the Undo command changes to a Redo command (see **Figure 28**). This restores the document to the way it was before the Undo command was used.

Figure 27. *The Edit menu's Undo command will reverse the last action taken.*

Figure 28. *After undoing an action or command, the Undo command turns into a Redo command.*

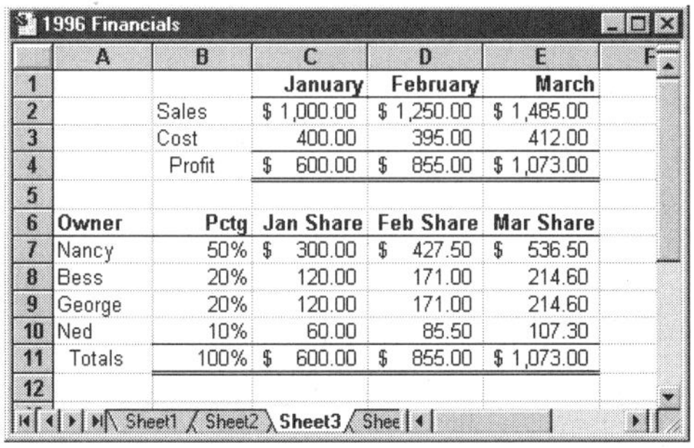

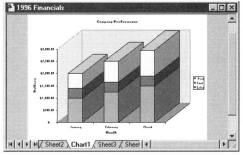

Figure 1a. *Here's a worksheet to calculate profit and each partner's share.*

Figure 1b. *In the same workbook, here's a sheet to show company sales, cost, and profit.*

Figure 1c. *Also in the same workbook, here's a Visual Basic macro to create formatted worksheet headings.*

About Workbook Files

In Excel, there's only one kind of file: a *workbook* file. A workbook file can include up to 255 *sheets*, which are like pages in the workbook. Each workbook, by default, includes 16 sheets named *Sheet 1* through *Sheet 16*.

Although there are five kinds of sheets, you'll work most often with only two or three:

- A *worksheet* is for entering information and performing calculations. **Figure 1a** shows an example. You can also embed charts in a worksheet.

- A *chart sheet* is for creating charts that aren't embedded in a worksheet (see **Figure 1b**).

- A *Visual Basic module* is for creating and editing macros with the Microsoft Excel Visual Basic language (see **Figure 1c**). This is an advanced feature of Excel.

The other two kinds of sheets are dialog sheets and Microsoft 4.0 macro sheets.

✔ Tip

- Use the multiple sheet capabilities of Excel workbooks to keep sheets for the same project together. This is an excellent way to organize related work.

Understanding Workbooks

To switch between sheets in a workbook

Click the sheet tab at the bottom of the workbook window (see **Figure 2**) for the sheet you want.

✔ Tips

- If the sheet tab for the sheet you want is not displayed, use the tab scrolling buttons (see **Figure 3**) to scroll through the sheet tabs. Remember, you must click on the tab for a sheet to see the sheet.

- To display more or less sheet tabs, drag the tab split box (see **Figure 4**) to increase or decrease the size of the sheet tab area. As you change the size of the sheet tab area, you'll also change the size of the bottom scroll bar for the workbook window.

To select multiple sheets

1. Click the sheet tab for the first sheet you want to select.

2. Hold down the Control key and click the sheet tab(s) for the other sheet(s) you want to select. The sheet tabs for each sheet you include in the selection turn white (see **Figure 5**).

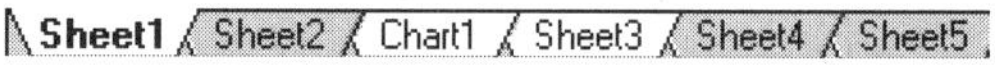

✔ Tips

- To select multiple adjacent sheets, click the sheet tab for the first sheet, then hold down the Shift key and click on the sheet tab for the last sheet you want to select. All sheet tabs in between also become selected.

- Selecting multiple sheets makes it quick and easy to print, delete, edit, format, or perform other tasks with more than one sheet at a time.

Figure 2. *Sheet tabs let you move from sheet to sheet within a workbook.*

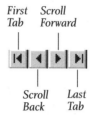

Figure 3. *Use the tab scrolling buttons to view sheet tabs that are not displayed.*

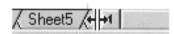

Figure 4. *Drag the tab split box to change the size of the sheet tab area and display more or less sheet tabs.*

Figure 5. *To select multiple sheets, hold down the Control key while clicking each sheet tab.*

- Although you can select more than one sheet at a time, there is only one active sheet. The active sheet's name appears in bold type on its sheet tab (see **Figure 5**).

Switching and Selecting Sheets

Figure 6a. *Begin by selecting the sheet you want the new sheet to be inserted before…*

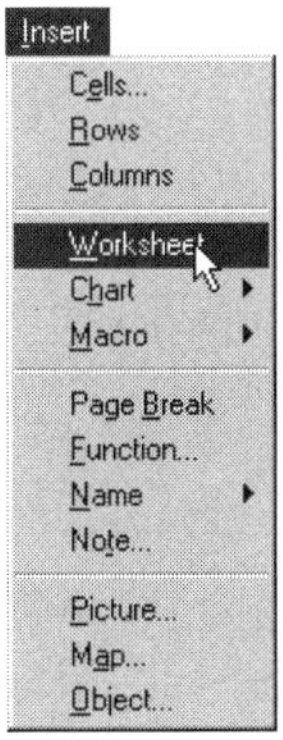

Figure 6b.
…then choose Worksheet from the Insert menu.

Figure 6c. *The new sheet is inserted.*

Figure 7.
Use the Chart submenu under the Insert menu to insert a chart sheet.

Figure 8.
Use the Macro submenu under the Insert menu to insert a Visual Basic module.

To insert a worksheet

1. Click the tab for the sheet you want to insert before (see **Figure 6a**).

2. Choose Worksheet from the Insert menu (see **Figure 6b**).

   A new worksheet is inserted before the one you originally selected (see **Figure 6c**).

✔ Tip

■ To insert more than one worksheet at a time, hold down the Shift key and click sheet tabs to select the number of worksheets you want to insert. When you choose Worksheet from the Insert menu (see **Figure 6b**), the number of worksheets you selected is inserted before the first selected sheet.

To insert a chart sheet

1. Click the tab for the sheet you want to insert before (see **Figure 6a**).

2. Choose As New Sheet from the Chart submenu under the Insert menu (see **Figure 7**).

The new sheet is inserted and the first dialog box of the ChartWizard appears. I tell you how to create charts with the ChartWizard in Chapter 8.

To insert a Visual Basic module

1. Click the tab for the sheet you want to insert before (see **Figure 6a**).

2. Choose Module from the Macro submenu under the Insert menu (see **Figure 8**).

The new sheet is inserted and the Visual Basic toolbar appears. I tell you a little more about macros and Visual Basic in Chapter 13.

Inserting Sheets

To delete a sheet

1. Click on the sheet tab for the sheet you want to delete to make it active.

2. Choose Delete Sheet from the Edit menu (see **Figure 9a**).

3. A warning dialog box appears (see **Figure 9b**). Click OK to confirm that you want to delete the sheet.

✔ Tips

■ As the dialog box warns, sheets are permanently deleted. That means even the Undo command won't get a deleted sheet back.

■ If another cell in the workbook contains a reference to a cell on the sheet you've deleted, that cell will display a #REF! error message. The formula in that cell will have to be rewritten.

To rename a sheet

1. Click on the sheet tab for the sheet you want to rename to make it active.

2. Choose Rename from the Sheet submenu under the Format menu (see **Figure 10a**).

   or

   Double-click the sheet tab.

3. In the Rename Sheet dialog box that appears (see **Figure 10b**), enter a new name for the sheet.

4. Click OK to accept the name.

The sheet tab for that sheet displays the new name you gave it (see **Figure 10c**).

✔ Tip

■ Sheet names can be up to 31 characters long and can contain any character you can type from your keyboard.

Figure 9a. *Choose Delete Sheet from the Edit menu...*

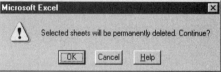

Figure 9b. *...then click OK to confirm that you really do want to delete the sheet.*

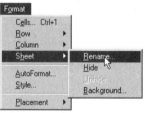

Figure 10a. *To rename a sheet, choose Rename from the Sheet submenu...*

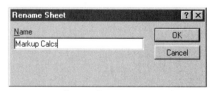

Figure 10b. *...then enter a new name for the sheet and click OK.*

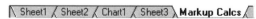

Figure 10c. *The name appears on the sheet tab.*

Figure 11. *Use the Hide command under the Sheet submenu to hide selected sheets.*

To hide a sheet

1. Select the sheet(s) you want to hide.

2. Choose Hide from the Sheet submenu under the Format menu (see **Figure 11**).

The sheet and its sheet tab disappear, just as if the sheet were deleted! But don't worry—the sheet still exists in the workbook file.

✔ Tips

- You cannot hide a sheet if it is the only sheet in a workbook.

- Don't confuse this command with the Hide command under the Window menu. These commands do two different things! I tell you about the Window menu's Hide command later in this chapter.

Figure 12a. *To unhide a sheet, choose Unhide from the Sheet submenu under the Format menu...*

To unhide a sheet

1. Choose Unhide from the Sheet submenu under the Format menu (see **Figure 12a**).

2. In the Unhide Sheet dialog box that appears, select the sheet you want to unhide (see **Figure 12b**).

3. Click OK.

The sheet and its sheet tab reappear.

✔ Tips

- You can only unhide one sheet at a time.

- If the Unhide command is gray, no sheets are hidden (see **Figure 11**).

- Don't confuse this command with the Unhide command under the Window menu. I tell you about the Window menu's Unhide command later in this chapter.

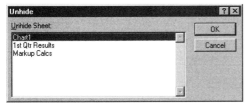

Figure 12b. *...then select the sheet you want to unhide from the Unhide dialog box and click OK.*

To move or copy a sheet

1. Select the sheet(s) you want to move or copy.

2. Choose Move or Copy Sheet from the Edit menu (see **Figure 13a**). The Move or Copy dialog box appears (see **Figure 13b**).

3. Use the To Book drop-down list (see **Figure 13c**) to choose the workbook you want to move or copy the sheet(s) to.

4. Use the Before Sheet list box to choose the sheet you want the sheet(s) to be copied before.

5. If you want to copy or duplicate the sheet rather than move it, turn on the Create a Copy check box.

6. Click OK.

✔ Tips

■ To move or copy sheets to another workbook, make sure that workbook is open (but not active) *before* you choose the Move or Copy Sheet command. Otherwise, it will not be listed in the To Book drop-down list (see **Figure 13c**).

■ If you choose (new book) from the To Book drop-down list (see **Figure 13c**), Excel creates a brand new, empty workbook file and places the selected sheet(s) into it.

■ You can use the Move or Copy Sheet command to change the order of sheets in a workbook. Just make sure the current workbook is selected in the To Book drop-down list (see **Figure 13c**). Then select the appropriate sheet from the Before Sheet list box or choose (move to end), which is the last option in the list.

Figure 13a. *The Move or Copy Sheet command lets you do just that.*

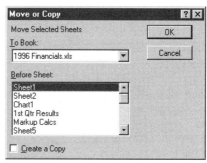

Figure 13b. *Use the Move or Copy dialog box to pick a destination for the sheet(s) and tell Excel that you want to copy them rather than move them.*

Figure 13c. *The To Book drop-down list displays the names of all the open workbooks.*

■ You can also move or copy a sheet within a workbook by dragging. To move the sheet, simply drag the sheet tab to the new position. To copy the sheet, hold down the Control key while dragging the sheet tab.

About Workbook Windows

Like most Windows programs, Excel lets you have more than one document open at a time. (I tell you how to create a new workbook and open an existing workbook in Chapter 2.) But Excel goes a step further by enabling you to open multiple windows for the same workbook. Then, by arranging the windows on screen, you can see and work with more than one of them.

To make another window active

Choose the name of the window you want to make active from the list of open windows at the bottom of the Window menu (see **Figure 14**).

or

Press Control+Tab to go to the next window.

or

Press Control+Shift+Tab to go to the previous window.

To create a new window

1. Make the workbook you want to create another window for the active window.

2. Choose New Window from the Window menu (see **Figure 14**).

A new window for that workbook appears. It has the same name as the workbook, but the name is followed by the window number, as shown in **Figure 15**. In addition, a separate item appears at the bottom of the Window menu for the new window (see **Figure 16**).

✔ Tip

- If more than one window is open for a workbook and you close one of them, the workbook does not close—just that window.

Figure 14. *The Window menu offers commands for working with workbook windows.*

Figure 15. *The title bar for a new window displays the workbook file name as well as the window number.*

Figure 16. *The new window is added to the Window menu.*

Making Windows Active

To arrange windows

1. Choose Arrange from the Window menu (see **Figure 14**).

2. In the Arrange Windows dialog box that appears (see **Figure 17a**), choose an arrange option. **Figures 17b** through **17e** illustrate all of them.

3. If you want to arrange only the windows of the active workbook, turn on the Windows of Active Workbook check box.

4. Click OK.

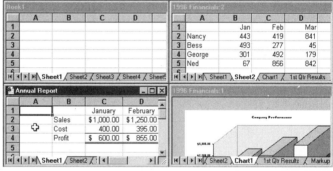

Figure 17a. *The Arrange Windows dialog box offers four arrangement options.*

✔ Tips

■ To work with one of the arranged windows, click in it to make it active.

■ The window with the buttons in its title bar is the active window.

■ To make one of the arranged windows full size again, click on it to make it active and then click the maximize button (see **Figure 18**). The window fills the screen while the other windows remain arranged behind it. Click the window's restore button to shrink it back down to its arranged size.

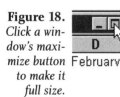

Figure 18. *Click a window's maximize button to make it full size.*

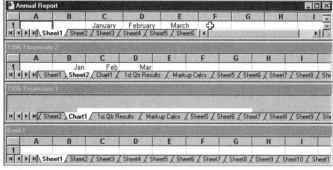

Figure 17b. *Tiled windows.*

Figure 17c. *Horizontally arranged windows.*

To hide a window

1. Make the window you want to hide the active window.

2. Choose Hide from the Window menu (see **Figure 14**).

✔ Tip

■ Hiding a window is not the same as closing it. A hidden window remains open, even though it is not listed at the bottom of the Window menu.

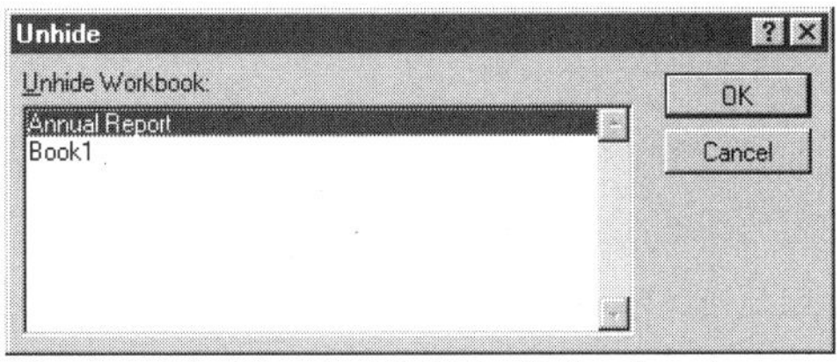

To unhide a window

1. Choose Unhide from the Window menu.

2. In the Unhide dialog box that appears (see **Figure 19**), choose the window you want to unhide.

3. Click OK.

✔ Tips

■ If the Unhide command is gray, no windows are hidden.

■ You can only unhide one window at a time.

Figure 19. *Use the Unhide dialog box to unhide hidden windows.*

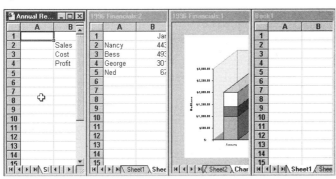

Figure 17d. *Vertically arranged windows.*

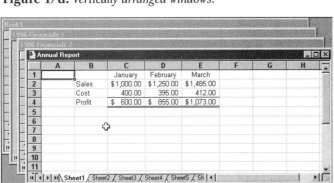

Figure 17e. *Cascading windows.*

To zoom a window's view

1. Choose Zoom from the View menu (see **Figure 20a**).

2. In the Zoom dialog box that appears (see **Figure 20b**), select the option button for the magnification you want.

3. Click OK.

or

1. Click the arrow beside the Zoom control on the Standard toolbar to display a drop-down list of magnifications (see **Figure 21**).

2. Choose the magnification you want from the list.

Figure 20a.
The Zoom command…

Figure 20b.
…displays the Zoom dialog box, which you can use to change the active window's magnification.

✔ Tips

- Zoom selected cells so they fill the window by selecting the Fit Selection option button in the Zoom dialog box (see **Figure 20b**) or the Selection option on the Zoom control (see **Figure 21**).

- Enter a custom magnification in the Zoom dialog box (see **Figure 20b**) by selecting the Custom option button and entering a value of your choice.

- Enter a custom magnification in the Zoom control on the Standard toolbar (see **Figure 21**) by clicking the value in the text box to select it, typing in a new value, and pressing Enter.

- Custom zoom percentages must be between 10% and 400%.

- Changing the magnification with the Zoom dialog box or Zoom control on the Standard toolbar does not affect the way a worksheet will print.

- When you save a workbook, the magnification settings of its sheets are saved. When you reopen the workbook, the saved magnifications are used.

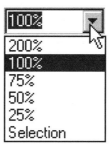

Figure 21.
Or use the Zoom control on the Standard toolbar to set the magnification.

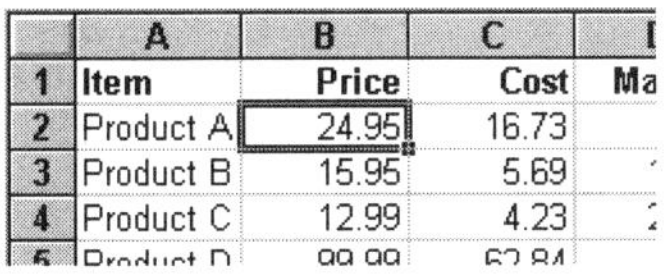

Figure 22a. *Activate the cell where you want the split to occur...*

Figure 22b. *...then choose Split from the Window menu.*

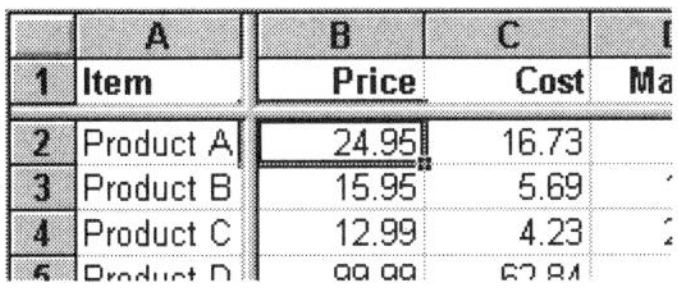

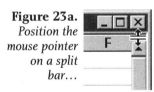

Figure 22c. *The window splits at the active cell.*

Figure 23a. *Position the mouse pointer on a split bar...*

Figure 23b. *...then press down the mouse button and drag to split the window.*

Figure 24. *When the window has a split in it, the Split command turns into a Remove Split command.*

About Splitting Windows

Splitting a window is useful when you need to see and work with two or more parts of a sheet at a time. When you split a window, you separate it into two or four *panes* (see **Figure 22c**). Each pane has its own scroll bars, so you can scroll the view in any pane until it shows exactly what you want it to.

To split a window

1. Activate the cell immediately below and to the right of where you want the split(s) to occur (see **Figure 22a**).

2. Choose Split from the Window menu (see **Figure 22b**).

or

1. Position the mouse pointer on the gray split bar at the top or right end of the scroll bar. The mouse pointer turns into a double line with arrows coming out of it (see **Figure 23a**).

2. Press the mouse button down and drag. A dark split bar moves along with the mouse pointer (see **Figure 23b**). When you release the mouse button, the window splits at the bar.

To adjust the size of panes

1. Position the mouse pointer on a split bar.

2. Press the mouse button down and drag until the split bar is in the desired position.

To remove a window split

Choose Remove Split from the Window menu (see **Figure 24**).

or

Double-click a split bar.

Splitting Windows

About Saving Workbooks

As you work with a file, everything you do is stored in only one place: *random access memory* or *RAM*. The contents of RAM are a lot like the light in a lightbulb—as soon as you turn it off or pull the plug, it's gone. Your hard disk or a floppy disk provides a much more permanent type of storage area. You use the Save command to copy the workbook file in RAM to disk.

To save a workbook file

1. Choose Save or Save As from the File menu (see **Figure 25a**).

   or

   Press Control+S.

   or

   Click the Save button on the Standard toolbar.

2. Use the Save As dialog box that appears (see **Figure 25b**) to select a directory in which to save the file.

3. Enter a name for the file in the Save As text box.

4. Click Save or press Enter.

Figure 25a. *Choose Save from the File menu.*

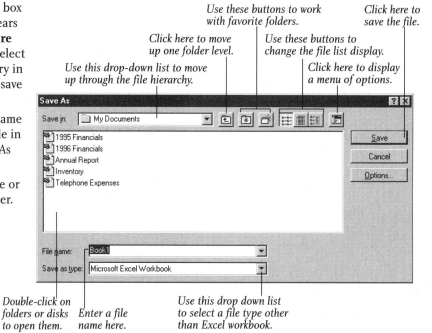

Use these buttons to work with favorite folders.

Click here to save the file.

Click here to move up one folder level.

Use these buttons to change the file list display.

Use this drop-down list to move up through the file hierarchy.

Click here to display a menu of options.

Double-click on folders or disks to open them.

Enter a file name here.

Use this drop down list to select a file type other than Excel workbook.

Figure 25b. *Use the Save As dialog box to save a workbook.*

Figure 26a.
Choose Properties from the File menu...

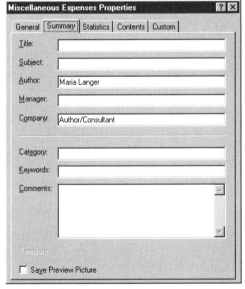

Figure 26b. *...to display and enter information into the Properties dialog box.*

☑ Prompt for File Properties

Figure 27. *This check box toggles the automatic appearance of the Properties dialog box on or off.*

About Properties

Excel's properties feature lets you specify information about a file that can help document it and make it easier to find.

To specify properties

1. Choose Properties from the File menu (see **Figure 26a**).

2. In the Properties dialog box that appears, click the Summary tab, if necessary to display its options (see **Figure 26b**).

3. Enter information in each text box of the dialog box. You may skip text boxes if you like. You may also change the contents of any text boxes automatically filled in by Excel, like the Author box.

4. If desired, click other tabs of the Properties dialog box to review automatically entered information or enter additional information about the file.

5. Click the close button to accept your entries and save them with the file.

✔ Tips

- To have the Properties dialog box appear automatically each time you save a file for the first time, choose Options from the Tools menu, click the General tab, and turn on the check box beside Prompt for File Properties (see **Figure 27**).

- Each Properties text box can accept up to 255 characters of information.

Specifying Properties

About File Formats

By default, Excel saves files in Microsoft Excel Workbook file format. This is the format that appears in the Save File As Type drop-down list in the Save As dialog box (see **Figures 25b** and **28**). If you display this list, you can see the other file types Excel can save. **Table 1** lists some of the more popular file types.

To save a file in another format

1. Choose Save As from the File menu (see **Figure 25a**).

2. Use the Save As dialog box (see **Figure 25b**) to select a directory in which to save the file.

3. Enter a name for the file in the Save As text box.

4. Choose a file format from the Save File As Type drop-down list (see **Figure 28**).

5. Click Save.

✔ Tips

- If the document has not yet been saved at all, in step 1 above you could also choose the Save command from the File menu, press Control+S, or click the Save button to display the Save As dialog box.

- If the format you chose in step 4 above saves only the active worksheet, a dialog box like the one in **Figure 29** will appear after you click Save. Click OK to complete the save.

- Text (Tab Delimited) is commonly used to save Excel information in a format that can be easily imported into files created with other applications, like Microsoft Word tables or Microsoft FoxPro databases.

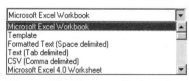

Figure 28. *Choose a file type from the Save File As Type drop-down list in the Save As dialog box to save a file in a different format.*

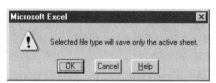

Figure 29. *Excel warns you when you're saving only a worksheet rather than an entire workbook.*

Template	Saves the worksheet in a special format that can be used to create similar Excel workbook files.
Text	Saves the active worksheet's contents as plain text, with tab characters between columns and return characters at the end of rows.
Microsoft Excel 4.0, 3.0, or 2.2 Worksheet	Saves the active worksheet in a format that can be read by an earlier version of Excel.
Microsoft Excel 4.0 Workbook	Saves the workbook in a format that can be read by Excel 4.0.
WKS, WK1, or WK3	Saves the active worksheet in a format that can be read by various versions of Lotus 1-2-3.

Table 1. *Here's a list of the more commonly used file formats Excel supports.*

Figure 30. *Once a file has been saved, you must use the Save As command to save it differently.*

Save vs. Save As

Once you've saved a file, using the Save command again automatically saves the file with the same name, in the same disk location. If you want to change the name, disk location, or file type of a file, you'll have to use the Save As command (see **Figure 30**). Doing so displays the Save As dialog box (see **Figure 25b**) so you can change the directory or file name or both.

✔ Tip

■ Save files often as you work to prevent losing work in the event of a system bomb or power outage. Remember the Control+S shortcut to access the Save command quickly without reaching for the mouse.

Figure 31a. *Click a window's close button to close the window or file.*

To close a file

Click the close button of the window for the file you want to close (see **Figure 31a**).

or

Choose Close from the File menu (see **Figure 31b**).

or

Press F4.

Figure 31b. *The Close command also lets you close the active window or file.*

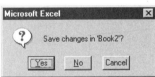

Figure 31c. *If you haven't saved changes, Excel warns you and lets you save them.*

✔ Tips

■ If the file you are closing has not been saved since changes were made to it, Excel displays a dialog box like the one in **Figure 31c**. Click Yes to save changes.

■ To close all open windows, hold down the Shift key and pull down the File menu. Choose Close All (see **Figure 32**). Excel offers to save unsaved documents before closing them all, one by one.

Figure 32. *Hold down the Shift key and pull down the File menu to see the Close All command.*

Save vs. Save As & Closing Files

About Finding Files

As seen in Chapter 2, the Open dialog box gives you access to Excel's powerful file searching feature. You can use this feature to search for any file on any disk that can be read by your computer, including disks accessible via network.

To find a file

1. Choose Open from the File menu.

2. Use any combination of the text boxes or drop-down lists at the bottom of the Open dialog box (see **Figure 33**) to specify search critera.

3. If desired, use the Look In drop-down list and file list box at the top of the dialog box to choose a specific disk location.

4. Click Find Now.

Figure 33. *The Open dialog box gives you access to Excel's powerful file finding feature.*

Excel displays the results of the search in the file list box at the top of the dialog box. You can open a found file by double-clicking it or you can use the options under the Commands and Settings button menu (see **Figure 34**) to perform other tasks on a selected file or the file list.

Figure 34. *You can use options under the Commands and Settings button menu to work with found files in the file list box.*

✔ Tips

■ Choose Search Subfolders from the Commands and Settings button menu (see **Figure 34**) to search subdirectories within the Look In folder or disk.

■ Excel's file finding feature has far more capabilities than I can cover in this book. Explore them on your own the next time you need to find a file. The Advanced Search button in the Open dialog box (see **Figure 33**) is a good place to start.

USING FUNCTIONS IN FORMULAS

About Functions

A *function* is a predefined formula for making a specific kind of calculation. Functions make it quicker and easier to write formulas.

For example, say you need to add up a column of numbers like the one in **Figure 1**. It's perfectly acceptable to write a formula using cell references separated by the addition operator (+) like this:

=C4+C5+C6+C7+C8+C9+C10+C11

But rather than enter a lengthy formula, you can use the SUM function to add up the same numbers like this:

=SUM(C4:C11)

The SUM function is only one of over 200 functions built into Excel.

Anatomy of a Function

As shown in **Figure 2**, each function has two main parts.

- The *function name* determines what the function does.

- The *arguments* determine what values or cell references the function should use in its calculation. Arguments are enclosed in parentheses and, if there's more than one, separated by commas.

✔ Tips

- If a function comes at the beginning of a formula, it *must* begin with an equal sign (=).

- Some arguments are optional. In the SUM function, for example, you can have only one argument, like the reference to a range of cells used in the example above.

	A	B	C
1	*Product Inventory*		
2			
3	Item Name	Item Number	Qty
4	Blank Tapes	T-00	62
5	Home with Fred	H-236	8
6	Franklin in Paris	F-734	54
7	Deuce Anaheim, Defe	D-154	108
8	Star Wreck	S-48	34
9	David Silvermeadow	D-183	69
10	Pulp Fractions	P-139	75
11	Woodland Gulch	W-87	87
12			

Figure 1. *Using the SUM function makes it easier to add up a column of numbers.*

function name   *arguments*

SUM(number1,number 2,...)

Figure 2. *The parts of a function.*

Understanding Functions

57

About Arguments

Arguments can consist of any of the following:

- *Numbers* (see **Figure 3**). Like any other formula, however, the result of a function that uses values for arguments will not change unless the formula is changed.

- *Text* (see **Figure 4**). Excel has a whole collection of functions just for text. I tell you about them later in this chapter.

- *Cell references* (see **Figures 4** through **8**). This is a practical way to write functions, since when you change cell contents, the results of functions that reference them change automatically.

- *Formulas* (see **Figures 6** and **7**). This lets you create complex formulas that perform a series of calculations at once.

- *Functions* (see **Figures 7** and **8**). When a function includes another function as one of its arguments, it's called *nesting*.

- *Error values* (see **Figure 8**). You may find this useful to "flag" errors or missing information in a worksheet.

- *Logical values.* Some functions' arguments require TRUE or FALSE values.

Figure 3. *This example uses numbers as arguments for the DATE function.*

Figure 4. *This example uses cell references, numbers, and text as arguments for the IF function to display a comment.*

Figure 5. *This example shows two different ways to use cell references as arguments for the SUM function to add numbers.*

Figure 6. *This example uses a formula as an argument for the ROUND function to round calculated commissions.*

=ROUND(IF(B8>400,B8*$B$4,B8*$B$5),2)

Figure 7. *This example uses the ROUND and IF functions to calculate commissions based on a rate that changes acccording to sales.*

Figure 8. *This example uses three functions (IF, COUNTBLANK, and SUM), cell references, and error values to either indicate missing information or add a column of numbers.*

Understanding Arguments

58

	A	B	C	D	E
1	Commissions Report				
2					
3		Sales	Rate	Calc. Amt	Amt. Paid
4	Nancy	443.16	15%	66.474	=ROUND(D4,2)
5	Bess	493.47	12%	59.2164	
6	George	410.18	12%	49.2216	
7	Ned	394.98	10%	39.498	
8		1,741.79			

Figure 9a. *You can type in a function just like you'd type in any other formula.*

	A	B	C	D	E
1	Commissions Report				
2					
3		Sales	Rate	Calc. Amt	Amt. Paid
4	Nancy	443.16	15%	66.474	66.47
5	Bess	493.47	12%	59.2164	
6	George	410.18	12%	49.2216	
7	Ned	394.98	10%	39.498	
8		1,741.79			

Figure 9b. *When you press Enter, the cell containing the function displays the result of the formula.*

Figure 10. *Excel usually displays an error message when the parentheses in a function don't match.*

About Entering Functions

Excel offers several ways to enter a function:

- by typing
- by typing and clicking
- by using the Function Wizard

There is no "best" way—use the methods that you like most.

To enter a function by typing

1. Begin the formula by typing an equal sign (=).
2. Type in the function name.
3. Type an open parenthesis character.
4. Type in the value or cell reference for the first argument.
5. If entering more than one argument, type each of them in with commas between them.
6. Type a closed parenthesis character (see **Figure 9a**).
7. Press Enter or click the Enter button on the formula bar.

The result of the function is displayed in the cell (see **Figure 9b**).

✔ Tips

- Function names are not case sensitive. *Sum* or *sum* is the same as *SUM*. Excel converts all function names to uppercase characters.
- Do *not* include spaces when writing formulas.
- When writing formulas with nested functions, it's vital that you properly match parentheses. Excel helps you by boldfacing parentheses as you type them. If parentheses don't match, Excel may display an error message (see **Figure 10**).

To enter a function by typing and clicking

1. Begin the formula by typing an equal sign (=).

2. Type in the function name.

3. Type an open parenthesis character.

4. Type in a value or click on the cell whose reference you want to include as the first argument (see **Figure 11a**).

5. If entering more than one argument, type a comma, then type in a value or click on the cell for the next reference (see **Figure 11b**). Repeat this step for each argument in the function.

6. Type a closed parenthesis character (see **Figure 11c**).

7. Press Enter or click the Enter button on the formula bar.

The result of the function is displayed in the cell (see **Figure 9b**).

✔ Tips

■ To include a range by clicking, in step 4 or 5 above, drag the mouse pointer over the cells you want to include (see **Figure 12**).

■ Be careful where you click or drag when entering a function or any formula. Each click or drag may add references to the formula! If you click on a cell by mistake, you can use the Backspace key to delete the incorrectly added reference or click the Cancel button on the formula bar to start over from scratch.

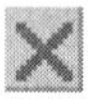

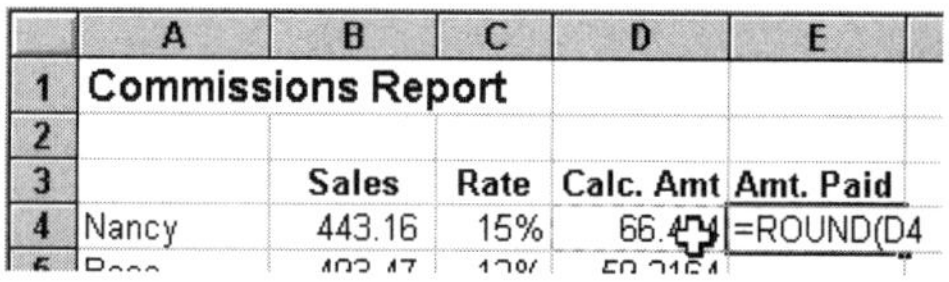

Entering Functions by Typing & Clicking

Figure 11a. *After typing the beginning of the function, you can click on cell references for arguments…*

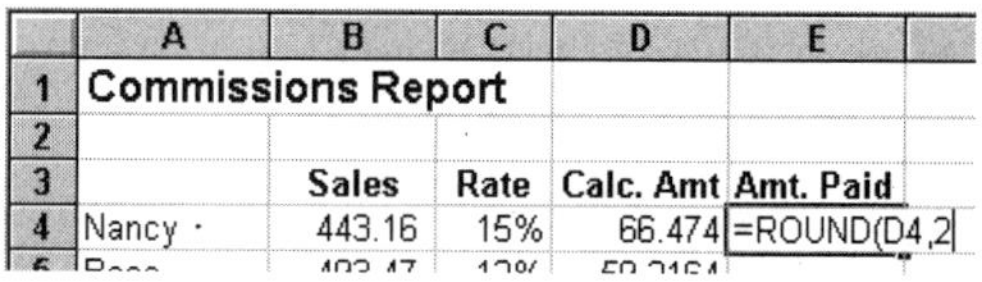

Figure 11b. *…and type in values for arguments…*

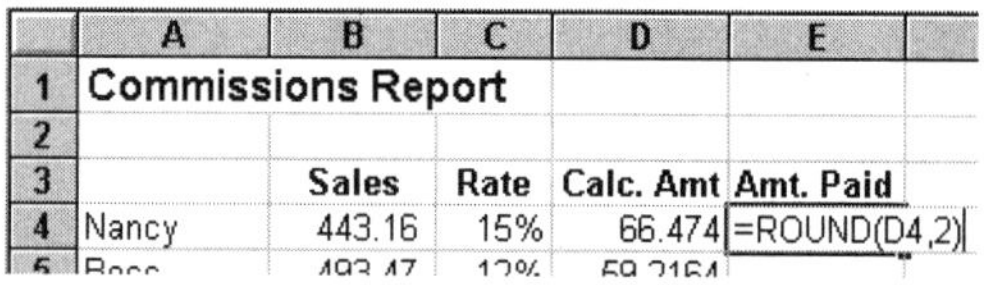

Figure 11c. *…until the function is complete.*

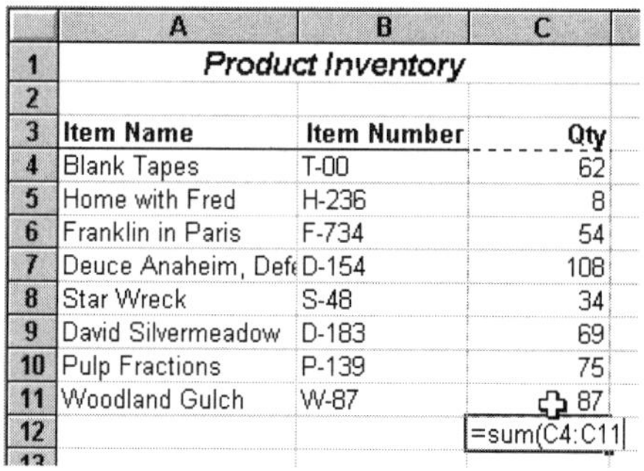

Figure 12. *You can enter a range in a formula by dragging, even when the range is an argument for a function.*

Figure 13a. *Choose Function from the Insert menu…*

Figure 13b. *…or click the Function button on the formula bar.*

To enter a function with the Function Wizard

1. Choose Function from the Insert menu (see **Figure 13a**).

    or

    Click the Function Wizard button on the Standard toolbar.

    or

    Click the formula bar to make it active, then click on the Function button (see **Figure 13b**).

2. In the Function Wizard – Step 1 dialog box that appears (see **Figure 13c**), choose a category from the Function Category list on the left side of the dialog box.

3. Choose a function from the Function Name list on the right side of the dialog box. You may have to use the scroll bar to locate the function name you want.

4. Click Next or press Enter.

5. In the Function Wizard – Step 2 dialog box (see **Figure 13d**), enter a value or cell reference for the first argument in its text box. The value of what you enter appears in the gray box to the right of the edit box.

6. Press Tab or click to move to the next argument's text box and enter a value or cell reference for it. Repeat this step for each argument. When you're finished, the result of the function appears in the gray Value box in the upper right corner of the Function Wizard window (see **Figure 13e**).

7. Click Finish or press Enter.

8. If you opened the Function Wizard by making the formula bar active and clicking the Function button, press Enter or click the Enter button to complete the formula.

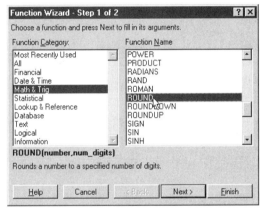

Figure 13c. *Choose a function category and name in Step 1 of the Function Wizard.*

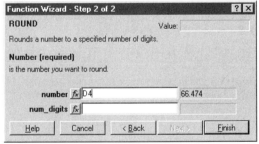

Figure 13d. *Fill in the values or cell references for arguments in Step 2.*

Figure 13e. *The result of the function appears in the Value box.*

Using the Function Wizard

✔ Tips

■ While in Step 1 of the Function Wizard dialog box, if you're not sure what category a function is in, choose All. The Function name scrolling list displays all the functions Excel has to offer.

■ While in Step 2 of the Function Wizard dialog box, you can click or drag in the worksheet window to enter a cell reference or range.

■ If the Function Wizard dialog box is blocking your view of the worksheet window, you can move it by dragging its title bar.

■ If an argument is not required, the Function Wizard tells you so when you click in the argument's edit box (see **Figure 14**).

■ You can nest a function as an argument by either typing it into the argument's edit box or using the function button beside the argument to bring up a Function Wizard [Nested] dialog box (see **Figure 15**).

■ The Back button available in Step 2 of the Function Wizard lets you go back to Step 1 to choose a different function.

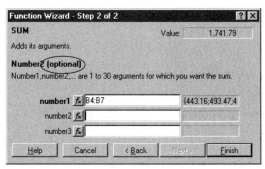

Figure 14. *If an argument is optional, the Function Wizard tells you.*

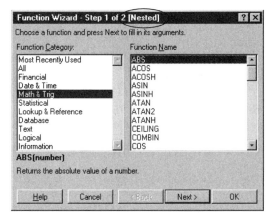

Figure 15. *The Function Wizard can help you write complex nested functions.*

Using the Function Wizard

About Math and Trigonometry Functions

Excel has over 50 math and trigonometry functions. On the next few pages, I tell you about the most commonly used ones, starting with one so popular it even has its own toolbar button: SUM.

About the SUM Function

The SUM function (see **Figure 16**) adds up numbers. It uses the following syntax:

SUM(number1,number2,...)

Although the SUM function can accept up to 30 arguments separated by commas, only one is required.

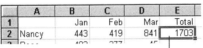

Figure 16. *Two ways to use the SUM function to add numbers.*
=SUM(B2:D2)   or
=SUM(B2,C2,D2)

To use the AutoSum button

1. Select the cell below the column or to the right of the row of numbers you want to add.

2. Click the AutoSum button on the Standard toolbar once.

   Excel examines the worksheet and makes a "guess" about which cells you want to add. It writes the corresponding formula and puts a marquee around the range cells it used (see **Figure 17**).

3. If the range in the formula is incorrect, type or select the correct range. Since the reference for the range of cells is selected in the formula, anything you type or select will automatically replace it.

4. When the formula is correct, press Enter, click the Enter button on the formula bar, or click the AutoSum button on the Standard toolbar a second time.

Figure 17. *Clicking the AutoSum button automatically writes a formula that adds up a column (or row) of numbers.*

SUM & Using the AutoSum Button

To use the AutoSum button on multiple cells

1. Select a range of cells adjacent to the columns or rows you want to add (see **Figure 18a**).

2. Click the AutoSum button once. Excel writes the formulas in the cells you selected (see **Figure 18b**).

   or

1. Select the cells containing the columns you want to add (see **Figure 19a**).

2. Click the AutoSum button once. Excel writes all the formulas in the row of cells immediately below the ones you selected (see **Figure 19b**).

   or

1. Select the cells containing the columns and rows you want to add, along with the empty row beneath them and the empty column to the right of them (see **Figure 20a**).

2. Click the AutoSum button once. Excel writes all the formulas in the bottom and rightmost cells (see **Figure 20b**).

✔ Tip

■ Be sure to check the formulas Excel writes when you use the AutoSum button. Excel is smart, but it's no mind-reader. The cells it includes may not be the ones you had in mind!

Figure 18a. *Select the cells adjacent to the columns (or rows) of cells you want to add...*

Figure 18b. *...then click the AutoSum button to write all the formulas at once.*

Figure 19a. *Select the cells containing the columns you want to add...*

Figure 19b. *...then click the AutoSum button to write all the formulas in the cells beneath the selection.*

Figure 20a. *Select the cells you want to add, as well as the cells in which you want the totals to appear...*

Figure 20b. *...then click the AutoSum button to add up the columns and rows all at once.*

	A	B	C	D	E
1	Item	Qty	Price	Rate	Value
2	T-00	62	3.98	80%	197.408
3	H-226	9	12.00	75%	

Figure 21. *Two ways to use the PRODUCT function to multiply numbers.*

=PRODUCT(B2:D2) **or**
=PRODUCT(B2,C2,D2)

	A	B	C	D	E	F
1	Item	Qty	Price	Rate	Value	Rounded
2	T-00	62	3.98	80%	197.408	197.41
3	H-226	9	12.00	75%		

Figure 22. *Use the ROUND function to round numbers to the number of decimal places you specify.*

=ROUND(E2,2)

	B	F	G
1		Total	Rounded
2	Sales	$3,735.00	$3,700.00
3	Cost	1,207.00	

Figure 23. *You can also use the ROUND function to round a number to the left of the decimal point.*

=ROUND(F2,-2)

	A	B	C	D	E
1	Item	Qty	Price	Rate	Value
2	T-00	62	3.98	80%	197.41
3	H-226	9	12.00	75%	

=ROUND(PRODUCT(B2:D2),2)

Figure 24. *You can also use the ROUND function to round the results of another formula or function.*

About the PRODUCT Function

The PRODUCT function (see **Figure 21**) multiplies its arguments much like the SUM function adds them. It uses the following syntax:

PRODUCT(number1,number2,...)

Although the PRODUCT function can accept up to 30 arguments separated by commas, only one is required.

About the ROUND Function

The ROUND function (see **Figure 22**) rounds a number to the number of decimal places you specify. It uses the following syntax:

ROUND(number,num_digits)

Both arguments are required. The *num_digits* argument specifies how many decimal places the number should be rounded to. If 0, the number is rounded to a whole number. If less than 0, the number is rounded on the left side of the decimal point (see **Figure 23**).

✔ Tips

- Rather than make a calculation in one cell and round it in another as shown in **Figures 22** and **23**, combine the two formulas in one cell (see **Figure 24**).

- The ROUNDUP function works like the ROUND function, but it always rounds up to the next higher number. The *num_digits* argument is not required; if omitted, the number is rounded to the next highest whole number.

- The ROUNDDOWN function works just like the ROUNDUP function, but it always rounds down.

PRODUCT & ROUND

About the EVEN and ODD Functions

The EVEN function (see **Figure 25**) rounds a number up to the next even number. It uses the following syntax:

EVEN(number)

The *number* argument, which is required, is the number you want to round.

The ODD function works exactly the same way, but rounds a number up to the next odd number.

	A	B	
1	Number	Converted	
2	159.487	160	—=EVEN(A2)
3	1647.1	1648	—=EVEN(A3)
4	-14.48	-16	—=EVEN(A4)

Figure 25. *Use the EVEN function to round a number up to the next even number.*

About the INT Function

The INT function (see **Figure 26**) rounds a number down to the nearest whole number or *integer*. It uses the following syntax:

INT(number)

The *number* argument, which is required, is the number you want to convert to an integer.

	A	B	
1	Number	Converted	
2	159.487	159	—=INT(A2)
3	1647.1	1647	—=INT(A3)
4	-14.48	-15	—=INT(A4)

Figure 26. *Use the INT function to round a number down to the next whole number.*

About the ABS Function

The ABS function (see **Figure 27**) returns the absolute value of a number—it leaves positive numbers alone but turns negative numbers into positive numbers. (Is that high school math coming back to you yet?) It uses the following syntax:

ABS(number)

The *number* argument, which is required, is the number you want to convert to an absolute value.

	A	B	
1	Number	Converted	
2	159.487	159.487	—=ABS(A2)
3	1647.1	1647.1	—=ABS(A3)
4	-14.48	14.48	—=ABS(A4)

Figure 27. *Use the ABS function to get the absolute value of a number.*

	A	B	
1	Number	Square Root	
2	36	6	— =SQRT(A2)
3	22	4.69041576	— =SQRT(A3)
4	-10	#NUM!	— =SQRT(A4)

Figure 28. *Use the SQRT function to find the square root of a number.*

	A	B	
1	Number	Square Root	
2	36	6	— =SQRT(ABS(A2))
3	22	4.69041576	— =SQRT(ABS(A3))
4	-10	3.16227766	— =SQRT(ABS(A4))

Figure 29. *Use the SQRT and ABS functions together to find the square root of a number.*

3.14159265358979 — =PI()

Figure 30. *The PI function calculates π up to 15 digits.*

Low	High	Random	
0	1	0.438411295	— =RAND()
0	547	408.215784	— =RAND()*547
36	42	37.27718254	— =RAND()*(42-36)+36
164	4835	2133.516157	

=RAND()*(4835-164)+164

Figure 31. *The RAND function can be used alone or as part of a formula to generate random numbers within a certain range.*

About the SQRT Function

The SQRT function (see **Figure 28**) calculates the square root of a number. It uses the following syntax:

SQRT(number)

The *number* argument, which is required, is the number you want to find the square root of.

✔ Tip

■ You'll get a *#NUM!* error message if you try to use the SQRT function to calculate the square root of a negative number (see **Figure 28**). Prevent the error by using the ABS function in the formula (see **Figure 29**).

About the PI Function

The PI function (see **Figure 30**) returns the value of π, accurate up to 15 digits. It uses the following syntax:

PI()

About the RAND Function

The RAND (see **Figure 31**) function generates a random number greater than or equal to 0 and less than 1 each time the worksheet is calculated. It uses the following syntax:

RAND()

✔ Tips

■ Although there is no argument in either the PI or RAND function, if you fail to include the parentheses characters, you'll get a *#NAME?* error.

■ To generate a random number between two numbers (*low* and *high*), write a formula like this:

=RAND()(high-low)+low*

See **Figure 31** for some examples.

About the RADIANS and DEGREES Functions

The RADIANS function (see **Figure 32**) converts degrees to radians. The DEGREES function converts radians to degrees. They use the following syntax:

RADIANS(angle)
DEGREES(angle)

The angle argument, which is required, is the angle you want converted. Use degrees in the RADIANS function and radians in the DEGREES function.

About the SIN Function

The SIN function (see **Figure 32**) calculates the sine of an angle. It uses the following syntax:

SIN(number)

The *number* argument, which is required, is the angle, in radians, for which you want the sine calculated.

About the COS Function

The COS function (see **Figure 32**) calculates the cosine of an angle. It uses the following syntax:

COS(number)

The *number* argument, which is required, is the angle, in radians, for which you want the cosine calculated.

About the TAN Function

The TAN function (see **Figure 32**) calculates the tangent of an angle. It uses the following syntax:

TAN(number)

The *number* argument, which is required, is the angle, in radians, for which you want the tangent calculated.

=RADIANS(B2)   =DEGREES(D1)

	A	B	C	D
1	Radians	0.785398163		1
2	Degrees	45		57.29577951
3	Sine	0.707106781	=SIN(B1)	0.841470985 =SIN(D1)
4	Arcsine	0.903339111	=ASIN(B1)	1.570796327 =ASIN(D1)
5	Cosine	0.707106781	=COS(B1)	0.540302306 =COS(D1)
6	Arccosine	0.667457216	=ACOS(B1)	0 =ACOS(D1)
7	Tangent	1	=TAN(B1)	1.557407725 =TAN(D1)
8	Arctangent	0.66577375	=ATAN(B1)	0.785398163 =ATAN(D1)

Figure 32. *This example shows several trigonometry functions in action.*

✔ Tips

■ To calculate the arcsine, arccosine, or arctangent of an angle, use the ASIN, ACOS, or ATAN function (see **Figure 32**). Each works in the same way as its counterpart.

■ Excel has far more trigonometry functions than those mentioned here. At the end of this chapter, I tell you how to get more information on other Excel functions you may need to use.

About Statistical Functions

Excel has over 70 statistical functions. On the next few pages, I tell you about a handful of the ones I think you'll use most.

About the AVERAGE Function

The AVERAGE function (see **Figure 33**) calculates the average or mean of its arguments. It uses the following syntax:

AVERAGE(number1,number2,...)

About the MEDIAN Function

The MEDIAN function (see **Figure 33**) calculates the median of its arguments. The median is the "halfway point" of the numbers—half the numbers have higher values and half have lower values. The MEDIAN function uses the following syntax:

MEDIAN(number1,number2,...)

About the MODE Function

The MODE function (see **Figure 33**) returns the mode of its arguments. The mode is the most common value. The MODE function uses the following syntax:

MODE(number1,number2,...)

If there are no repeated values, Excel returns a *#NUM!* error.

About the MIN and MAX Functions

The MIN function (see **Figure 33**) returns the minimum value of its arguments while the MAX function returns the maximum value of its arguments. They use the following syntax:

MIN(number1,number2,...)

MAX(number1,number2,...)

	A	B	C
1	Item	Qty	Price
2	T-00	62	3.98
3	H-236	8	12.99
4	F-734	54	15.99
5	D-154	108	9.99
6	S-48	34	14.99
7	D-183	69	19.99
8	P-139	75	24.99
9	W-87	87	12.99
10			
11	Average		14.489 — =AVERAGE(C2:C9)
12	Median		13.99 — =MEDIAN(C2:C9)
13	Mode		12.99 — =MODE(C2:C9)
14	Minimum		3.98 — =MIN(C2:C9)
15	Maximum		24.99 — =MAX(C2:C9)

Figure 33. *This example shows a few of Excel's statistical functions at work.*

✔ Tips

■ Excel's AVERAGE function does not include empty cells when calculating the average for a range of cells.

■ Although the AVERAGE, MEDIAN, MODE, MIN and MAX functions can each accept up to 30 arguments separated by commas, only one argument is required.

AVERAGE, MEDIAN, MODE, MIN, & MAX

About the COUNT and COUNTA Functions

The COUNT function counts how many *numbers* are referenced by its arguments. The COUNTA function counts how many *values* are referenced by its arguments. Although this may sound like the same thing, it isn't. See **Figure 34** for an example of both that clarifies the difference.

The COUNT and COUNTA functions use the following syntax:

COUNT(number1,number2,...)

COUNTA(number1,number2,...)

Although either function can accept up to 30 arguments separated by commas, only one is required.

About the STDEV and STDEVP Functions

Standard deviation is a statistical measurement of how much values vary from the average or mean for the group. The STDEV function calculates the standard deviation based on a random sample of the entire population. The STDEVP function calculates the standard deviation based on the entire population. **Figure 35** shows an example of both.

The STDEV and STDEVP functions use the following syntax:

STDEV(number1,number2,...)

STDEVP(number1,number2,...)

Although either function can accept up to 30 arguments separated by commas, only one is required.

✔ Tip

■ To get accurate results from the STDEVP function, the arguments must include data for the entire population.

	A	B
1	987	
2	154.69	
3	chocolate	
4		
5	-745.145	
6	4/5/96	
7	ice cream	
8	$75	
9		
10	Numbers:	5 — =COUNT(A1:A8)
11	Values:	7 — =COUNTA(A1:A8)

Figure 34. *This example of the COUNT and COUNTA functions illustrates that while the COUNT function counts only cells containing numbers (including dates and times), the COUNTA function counts all non-blank cells.*

	A	B	C
1	Item	Qty	Price
2	T-00	62	3.98
3	H-236	8	12.99
4	F-734	54	15.99
5	D-154	108	9.99
6	S-48	34	14.99
7	D-183	69	19.99
8	P-139	75	24.99
9	W-87	87	12.99
10			
11	Average		14.489
12	STDEV		6.3043 — =STDEV(C2:C9)
13	STDEVP		5.8971 — =STDEVP(C2:C9)

Figure 35. *In this example, the STDEV function assumes that the range is a random sample from a larger population of information. The STDEVP function assumes that the same data is the entire population. That's why the results differ.*

About Financial Functions

Excel has over 50 financial functions that you can use to calculate depreciation, evaluate investment opportunities, or calculate the monthly payments on a loan. On the next few pages, I tell you about a few of the functions I think you'll find useful.

About the SLN Function

The SLN function (**see Figure 36**) calculates straight line depreciation for an asset. It uses the following syntax:

SLN(cost,salvage,life)

Cost is the acquisition cost of the asset, *salvage* is the salvage or scrap value, and *life* is the useful life expressed in years or months. All three arguments are required.

About the DB Function

The DB function (see **Figure 36**) calculates declining balance depreciation for an asset. It uses the following syntax:

DB(cost,salvage,life,period,month)

The *cost*, *salvage*, and *life* arguments are the same as for the SLN function. *Period*, which must be expressed in the same units as life, is the period for which you want to calculate depreciation. These first four arguments are required. *Month* is the number of months in the first year of the asset's life. If omitted, 12 is assumed.

	A	B
1	Depreciation Comparison	
2		
3	Cost	1500
4	Salvage Value	150
5	Life (in years)	3
6		
7	Year	1
8	Straight Line	$450.00
9	Declining Balance	$804.00
10	Double Declining Balance	$1,000.00
11	Sum of Years' Digits	$675.00

=SLN(B3,B4,B5)
=DB(B3,B4,B5,B7)
=DDB(B3,B4,B5,B7)
=SYD(B3,B4,B5,B7)

Figure 36. *A simple worksheet lets you compare different methods of depreciation using the SLN, DB, DDB, and SYD functions.*

About the DDB Function

The DDB function calculates the double-declining balance depreciation for an asset. It uses the following syntax:

DDB(cost,salvage,life,period,factor)

The *cost*, *salvage*, *life*, and *period* arguments are the same as for the DB function and are required. *Factor* is the rate at which the balance declines. If omitted, 2 is assumed.

About the SYD Function

The SYD function calculates the sum-of-years' digits depreciation for an asset. It uses the following syntax:

SYD(cost,salvage,life,period)

The *cost*, *salvage*, *life*, and *period* arguments are the same as for the DB and DDB functions. All arguments are required.

About the PMT Function

The PMT function calculates the periodic payment for an annuity based on constant payments and interest rate. This function is commonly used for two purposes: to calculate the monthly payments on a loan and to calculate the monthly contribution necessary to reach a specific savings goal.

The PMT function uses the following syntax:

PMT(rate,nper,pv,fv,type)

Rate is the interest rate per period, *nper* is the total number of periods, and *pv* is the present value or current worth of the total payments. These three arguments are required. The *fv* argument is the future value or balance desired at the end of the payments. If omitted, 0 is assumed. *Type* indicates when payments are due: use 0 for payments at the end of the period and 1 for payments at the beginning of the period. If omitted, 0 is assumed.

To calculate loan payments

1. Enter the text and number values shown in **Figure 37a** in a worksheet. If desired, use your own amounts.

2. Enter the following formula in cell *B5*:

   =PMT(B2/12,B3,B1)

   This formula uses only the first three arguments of the PMT function. The rate argument is divided by 12 to arrive at a monthly interest rate since the number of periods is expressed in months and payments will be made monthly (all time units must match).

3. Press Enter or click the Enter button on the formula bar.

The result of the formula is expressed as a negative number (see **Figure 37b**) because it is an outgoing cash flow. (A minus sign or parentheses indicates a negative number.)

	A	B
1	Loan Amount	10000
2	Annual Interest Rate	9.50%
3	Loan Term (in Months)	48
4		
5	Monthly Payment	

Figure 37a. *A basic structure for a worksheet that calculates loan payments.*

	A	B
1	Loan Amount	10000
2	Annual Interest Rate	9.50%
3	Loan Term (in Months)	48
4		
5	Monthly Payment	($251.23)

=PMT(B2/12,B3,B1)

Figure 37b. *The PMT function calculates loan payments based on only three pieces of information.*

	A	B
1	Loan Amount	10000
2	Annual Interest Rate	9.50%
3	Loan Term (in Months)	36
4		
5	Monthly Payment	($320.33)

Figure 37c. *Playing "what-if." Change one of the constants and the result of the formula changes.*

✔ Tips

- If you prefer, you can use the Function Wizard to write the formula in step 2. Be sure to include the formula *B2/12* in the *rate* edit box. Leave the *fv* and *type* edit boxes blank.

- You can calculate loan payments without creating a whole worksheet—simply enter values rather than cell references as arguments for the PMT function. But using cell references makes it easy to play "what-if"—see how payments change when the loan amount, rate, and number of periods changes. **Figure 37c** shows an example.

	A	B	C	D
1	Loan Amount	10000		
2	Annual Interest Rate	9.50%		
3	Loan Term (in Months)	48		
4				
5	Monthly Payment	($251.23)		
6				
7	Payment Number	Beg. Balance	Interest	Principal
8	1			
9	2			
10	3			
11	4			
12	5			
13	6			
14	7			

Figure 38a. *Start with this simple worksheet to create an amortization table...*

	A	B	C	D
1	Loan Amount	10000		
2	Annual Interest Rate	9.50%		
3	Loan Term (in Months)	48		
4				
5	Monthly Payment	($251.23)		
6				
7	Payment Number	Beg. Balance	Interest	Principal
8	=B1	10000	79.17	$172.06
9	=B8-D8	$9,827.94		

=ROUND(B8*$B$2/12,2)

=-$B$5-C8

Figure 38b. *...add formulas to calculate interest, principal, and beginning balance...*

	A	B	C	D
1	Loan Amount	10000		
2	Annual Interest Rate	9.50%		
3	Loan Term (in Months)	48		
4				
5	Monthly Payment	($251.23)		
6				
7	Payment Number	Beg. Balance	Interest	Principal
8	1	10000	79.17	$172.06
9	2	$9,827.94	77.8	$173.43
10	3	$9,654.51	76.43	$174.80
11	4	$9,479.71	75.05	$176.18
12	5	$9,303.52	73.65	$177.58
13	6	$9,125.94	72.25	$178.98

Figure 38c. *...then copy the formulas down each column for all months of the loan term.*

	A	B	C	D
53	46	$741.91	5.87	$245.36
54	47	$496.55	3.93	$247.30
55	48	$249.25	1.97	$249.26
56	Totals		2059.09	10000.02
57				

=ROUND(SUM(C8:C55),2)

=ROUND(SUM(D8:D55),2)

Figure 38d. *If desired, add column totals to sum the interest and principal paid.*

To create an amortization table

1. Create a loan payment worksheet following the steps on the previous page.

2. Enter text and number values for headings as shown in **Figure 38a**. Make sure there is a row with a payment number for each month of the loan term in cell *B3*.

3. In cell *B8*, enter *=B1*.

4. In cell *C8*, enter the following formula:

   =ROUND(B8*$B$2/12,2)

   This formula calculates the interest for the period and rounds it to two decimal places.

5. In cell *D8*, enter the following formula:

   =-$B$5-C8

   This formula calculates the amount of principal paid for the current month.

6. In cell *B9*, enter the following formula:

   =B8-D8

   This formula calculates the current month's beginning balance.

   At this point, your worksheet should look like the one in **Figure 38b**.

7. Use the fill handle to copy the formula in cell *B9* down the column for each month.

8. Use the Fill handle to copy the formulas in cells *C8* and *D8* down the columns for each month.

Your amortization table is complete. It should look like the one in **Figure 38c**.

✔ Tip

- If desired, you can add column totals at the bottom of columns *C* and *D* (see **Figure 38d**) to total interest (you may be shocked) and principal (which should match cell *B1*).

Creating an Amortization Table

To calculate contributions to reach a savings goal

1. Enter the text and number values shown in **Figure 39a** in a worksheet. If desired, use your own amounts.

2. Enter the following formula in cell *B5*:

   =PMT(B2/12,B3,,B1)

   This formula uses the first *four* arguments of the PMT function, although the *pv* argument is left blank—that's why there are two commas after *B3*. The rate argument is divided by 12 to arrive at a monthly interest rate.

3. Press Enter or click the Enter button on the formula bar.

The result of the formula is expressed as a negative number (see **Figure 39b**) because it is an outgoing cash flow. (A minus sign or parentheses indicates a negative number.)

✔ Tips

■ If you prefer, you can use the Function Wizard to write the formula in step 2. Be sure to include the formula *B2/12* in the *rate* edit box. Leave the *pv* and *type* edit boxes blank.

■ You can calculate the amount of a monthly contribution to reach a savings goal without creating a whole worksheet—simply enter values rather than cell references as arguments for the PMT function. But using cell references makes it easy to play "what-if"— see how contributions change when the desired amount, rate, and number of periods changes. **Figure 39c** shows an example.

■ To force an outgoing cash flow to be expressed as a positive number, simply include a minus sign (-) right after the equal sign (=) at the beginning of the formula.

	A	B
1	Desired Amount	100000
2	Annual Interest Rate	7.50%
3	Months	240
4		
5	Monthly Contribution	

Figure 39a. *A basic structure for a worksheet to calculate contributions to reach a savings goal.*

	A	B
1	Desired Amount	100000
2	Annual Interest Rate	7.50%
3	Months	240
4		
5	Monthly Contribution	($180.59)

=PMT(B2/12,B3,,B1)

Figure 39b. *The PMT function calculates the monthly contribution.*

	A	B
1	Desired Amount	250000
2	Annual Interest Rate	7.50%
3	Months	240
4		
5	Monthly Contribution	($451.48)

Figure 39c. *Change one constant and the result of the formula changes.*

	A	B
1	Monthly Payment	150
2	Annual Interest Rate	8.50%
3	Number of Months	12
4		
5	Future Value	$1,871.81

=FV(B2/12,B3,-B1)

Figure 40. *Use the FV function to calculate the future value of constant cash flows, like those of periodic payroll savings deductions.*

	A	B
1	Initial Investment	-25000
2		
3	Monthly Cash In	200
4	Annual Interest Rate	9.00%
5	Number of Months	360
6		
7	Present Value	($24,856.37)

=PV(B4/12,B5,B3)

Figure 41. *This example uses the PV function to determine whether an investment is a good one. (It isn't good because the present value is less than the initial investment.)*

	A	B
1	Year 1	-500
2	Year 2	150
3	Year 3	100
4	Year 4	125
5	Year 5	135
6	Year 6	200
7		
8	Internal Rate of Return	12%

=IRR(B1:B6)

Figure 42. *This worksheet calculates the internal rate of return of an initial $500 investment that pays out cash over the next few years.*

About the FV Function

The FV function (see **Figure 40**) calculates the future value of an investment with constant cash flows and a constant interest rate. It uses the following syntax:

FV(rate,nper,pmt,pv,type)

Rate is the interest rate per period, *nper* is the total number of periods, and *pmt* is the amount of the periodic payments. These three arguments are required. The *pv* argument is the present value of the payments. *Type* indicates when payments are due: use 0 for payments at the end of the period and 1 for payments at the beginning of the period. If either optional argument is omitted, 0 is assumed.

About the PV Function

The PV function (see **Figure 41**) calculates the total amount that a series of payments in the future is worth now. It uses the following syntax:

PV(rate,nper,pmt,fv,type)

The *rate*, *nper*, *pmt*, and *type* arguments are the same in the FV function. Only the first three are required. The *fv* argument is the amount left after the payments have been made. If omitted, 0 is assumed.

About the IRR Function

The IRR Function (see **Figure 42**) calculates the internal rate of return for a series of periodic cash flows. It uses the following syntax:

IRR(values,guess)

The *values* argument, which is required, is a range of cells containing the cash flows. The *guess* argument, which is optional, is for your guess of what the result could be. Although seldom necessary, *guess* could help Excel come up with an answer when performing complex calculations.

FV, PV, & IRR

About Logical Functions

Excel has 6 logical functions you can use to evaluate conditions and act accordingly. I tell you about the most useful one: IF.

About the IF Function

The IF function (see **Figure 43b**) evaluates a condition and returns one of two different values depending on whether the condition is met (true) or not met (false). It uses the following syntax:

IF(logical_test,value_if_true,value_if_false)

The *logical_test* argument is the condition you want to meet. This argument is required. The *value_if_true* and *value_if_false* arguments are the values to return if the condition is met or not met. If omitted, the values *TRUE* and *FALSE* are returned.

To use the IF function

This example uses the IF function to calculate commissions based on two different commission rates.

1. Create a worksheet with text and number values as shown in **Figure 43a**.

2. In cell C6, enter the following formula:

   =IF(B6>400,$B$2*B6,$B$3*B6)

   This formula begins by evaluating the sales amount to see if it's over $400. If it is, it moves to the *value_if_true* argument and multiplies the higher commission rate by the sales amount. If it isn't, it moves on to the *value_if_false* argument and multiplies the lower commission rate by the sales amount.

3. Press Enter or click the Enter button on the formula bar (see **Figure 43b**).

4. Use the fill handle to copy the formula down the column for the rest of the salespeople (see **Figure 43c**).

	A	B	C
1		Rates	
2	Over $400	15%	
3	Up to $400	10%	
4			
5		Sales	Amt. Due
6	Nancy	443.16	
7	Bess	493.47	
8	George	410.18	
9	Ned	394.98	

Figure 43a. *To try the IF function for yourself, start with a basic worksheet…*

	A	B	C
1		Rates	
2	Over $400	15%	
3	Up to $400	10%	
4			
5		Sales	Amt. Due
6	Nancy	443.16	66.474
7	Bess	493.47	
8	George	410.18	
9	Ned	394.98	

=IF(B6>400,$B$2*B6,$B$3*B6)

Figure 43b. *…enter the IF function formula shown here…*

	A	B	C
1		Rates	
2	Over $400	15%	
3	Up to $400	10%	
4			
5		Sales	Amt. Due
6	Nancy	443.16	66.474
7	Bess	493.47	74.0205
8	George	410.18	61.527
9	Ned	394.98	39.498

Figure 43c. *…then use the fill handle to copy the formula to other cells.*

About Lookup and Reference Functions

Excel has over a dozen lookup and reference functions. These functions return values based on information stored elsewhere in the workbook or in a linked worksheet.

About the VLOOKUP and HLOOKUP Functions

The VLOOKUP (see **Figures 44a** and **44b**) and HLOOKUP functions return information based on data stored in a *lookup table*. The function attempts to match a value in one of its arguments to values in the first column (VLOOKUP) or first row (HLOOKUP) of the lookup table. If it finds a match, it returns the associated value.

The VLOOKUP and HLOOKUP functions use the following syntax:

VLOOKUP(lookup_value,table_array,
col_index_num,range_lookup)

HLOOKUP(lookup_value,table_array,
row_index_num,range_lookup)

Lookup_value is the value you want to match in the table. *Table_array* is the cell reference for the lookup table. *Col_index_num* or *row_index_number* is the number of the column or row, relative to the table, that contains the values you want returned. These three arguments are required. *Range_lookup*, which is not required, tells Excel what it should do if it can't match the *lookup_value*. TRUE tells Excel to return the value associated with the next lowest value; FALSE tells Excel to return the #N/A error value. If omitted, TRUE is assumed.

=VLOOKUP(B1,A5:D12,4,FALSE)

	A	B	C	D
1	Item #:	S-48		
2	Price:	14.99		
3				
4	Item #	Item Name	Qty	Price
5	D-154	Deuce Anaheim	108	9.99
6	D-183	David Silvermeadow	69	19.99
7	F-734	Franklin in Paris	54	15.99
8	H-236	Home with Fred	8	12.99
9	P-139	Pulp Fractions	75	24.99
10	S-48	Star Wreck	34	14.99
11	T-00	Blank Tapes	62	3.98
12	W-87	Woodland Gulch	87	12.99

Figure 44a. *This example illustrates the VLOOKUP function. When you enter an item number in cell* B1, *the formula in* B2 *attempts to match it to a value in the first column of the lookup table below it* (A5:D12). *If it finds a match, it returns the value in the fourth column of the same row as the match.*

	A	B	C	D
1	Item #:	K-123		
2	Price:	#N/A		
3				
4	Item #	Item Name	Qty	Price
5	D-154	Deuce Anaheim	108	9.99
6	D-183	David Silvermeadow	69	19.99
7	F-734	Franklin in Paris	54	15.99
8	H-236	Home with Fred	8	12.99
9	P-139	Pulp Fractions	75	24.99
10	S-48	Star Wreck	34	14.99
11	T-00	Blank Tapes	62	3.98
12	W-87	Woodland Gulch	87	12.99

Figure 44b. *If the formula in* B2 *doesn't find a match, it returns the #N/A error value, since the optional* range_lookup *argument is set to FALSE.*

✔ Tip

■ The first column or row of the lookup table must be sorted in ascending order for the VLOOKUP or HLOOKUP function to work properly.

VLOOKUP & HLOOKUP

To use the VLOOKUP function

This example is similar to the one for the IF function in that it calculates commissions based on a sales-driven commission rate. But in this example, there are six rates, all included in a lookup table.

1. Enter text and number values to create a worksheet like the one in **Figure 45a**.

2. In cell *C2*, enter the following formula:

   =VLOOKUP(B2,$A$9:$B$14,2)*B2

   This formula tells Excel to match the sales amount to an amount in the first column of the commission rates table in *A9:B14*. If it finds a match, multiply the corresponding commission rate by the sales amount. It it doesn't find a match, use the rate corresponding to the next lowest value in the first column of the commission rates table.

3. Press Enter or click the Enter button on the formula bar (see **Figure 45b**).

4. Use the fill handle to copy the formula in cell *C2* down the column for the other salespeople (see **Figure 45c**).

✔ Tips

- The lookup table can be on any sheet of the workbook or on a linked worksheet. I tell you about 3D references in Chapter 12.

- Any changes you make to the lookup table are instantly reflected in the results of any formula that reference the table.

- When copying a formula containing a VLOOKUP or HLOOKUP function, be sure to use absolute references if necessary (see **Figure 45b**) in the formula you copy. Otherwise, the references to the table might change.

	A	B	C
1		Sales	Amt. Due
2	Nancy	530.16	
3	Bess	175.84	
4	George	317.95	
5	Ned	200.00	
6			
7	Commission Rates		
8	Sales	Rate	
9	0	5%	
10	100	10%	
11	200	15%	
12	300	20%	
13	400	25%	
14	500	30%	

Figure 45a.
To try the VLOOKUP function, begin with a simple worksheet like this...

	A	B	C
1		Sales	Amt. Due
2	Nancy	530.16	159.048
3	Bess	175.84	
4	George	317.95	
5	Ned	200.00	

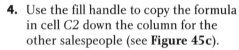

=VLOOKUP(B2,$A$9:$B$14,2)*B2

Figure 45b.
...enter the LOOKUP function formula...

	A	B	C
1		Sales	Amt. Due
2	Nancy	530.16	159.048
3	Bess	175.84	17.584
4	George	317.95	63.59
5	Ned	200.00	30

Figure 45c.
...then use the fill handle to copy the formula to other cells.

About Information Functions

Excel has over a dozen information functions. These functions return information about other cells.

	A	B	C	D	E
1	Test Values	673.24	anchovy		#N/A
2	Blank Cell	FALSE	FALSE	TRUE	FALSE
3	Error other than #N/A	FALSE	FALSE	FALSE	FALSE
4	Any error	FALSE	FALSE	FALSE	TRUE
5	Logical Value	FALSE	FALSE	FALSE	FALSE
6	#N/A Error	FALSE	FALSE	FALSE	TRUE
7	Not text	TRUE	FALSE	TRUE	TRUE
8	Number	TRUE	FALSE	FALSE	FALSE
9	Cell Reference	TRUE	TRUE	TRUE	TRUE
10	Text	FALSE	TRUE	FALSE	FALSE

Figure 46. *In this example, the nine built-in IS functions were used to evaluate the contents of the cells in row 1 of the worksheet. The results of each function appear below the value.*

	A	B
1	**Name:**	
2		
3	**Message:**	You did not enter your name.

=IF(ISTEXT(B1),"Hello "&B1,"You did not enter your name.")

	A	B
1	**Name:**	Maria
2		
3	**Message:**	Hello Maria

Figure 47a&b. *In this silly little example, a formula in cell B3, which utilizes the IF and ISTEXT functions, scolds the user for not entering a name, then greets her by name when she does enter it.*

	A	B	C
1	34		384.48
2	98		0
3		adios	384.48
4	65	goodbye	
5		hello	total
6			
7	Blank Cells:		5

=COUNTBLANK(A1:C5)

Figure 48. *The COUNTBLANK function counts blank cells in a range.*

About the IS Functions

Excel has nine built-in IS functions (see **Figure 46**), each with the following syntax:

ISBLANK(value)
ISERR(value)
ISERROR(value)
ISLOGICAL(value)
ISNA(value)
ISNONTEXT(value)
ISNUMBER(value)
ISREF(value)
ISTEXT(value)

In each case, Excel tests for a different thing. The value argument is the value or cell reference to be tested.

✔ Tip

■ Use an IS function in conjunction with the IF function to return a value based on the condition of a cell (see **Figures 47a&b**).

About the COUNTBLANK Function

The COUNTBLANK function (see **Figure 48**) counts the blank cells in a range. It uses the following syntax:

COUNTBLANK(range)

The *range* argument, which is required, is the range for which you want Excel to count the blank cells.

✔ Tip

■ If a cell contains a space character, it will not be counted as blank.

IS Functions & COUNTBLANK

About Date and Time Functions

Excel has over a dozen functions you can use for working with dates and times. I tell you about the most useful ones here.

✔ Tips

- Excel treats dates and times as *serial numbers*. This means that although you may enter information as a date or time—like 10/15/96 or 2:45 PM—Excel converts what you type into a number for its own internal use (see **Table 1**). A date is the number of days since January 1, 1900. A time is the portion of a day since midnight. Excel's formatting makes the number look like a date or time. I tell you about cell formatting in Chapter 6.

- You can change Excel's date system from the Windows 1900 system to the Macintosh 1904 system. Choose Options from the Tools menu, click the Calculation tab, and turn on the 1904 Date System check box (see **Figure 49**). This will change the serial numbers for dates for all worksheets in the current workbook.

You Enter	Excel "Sees"
10/15/96	35353
6/30/61	22462
2:45 PM	0.61458333
10:02:56 AM	0.4187037
1/1/1900	1
12:00 AM	0

Table 1. *How Excel interprets dates and times.*

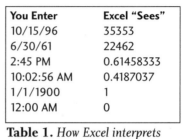

Figure 49. *The Options dialog box lets you switch between the Windows 1900 date system and the Macintosh 1904 date system.*

About the DATE Function

The DATE function (see **Figure 50**) returns the serial number for a date. It uses the following syntax:

=DATE(year,month,day)

The *year* argument is the year number, the *month* argument is the month number, and the *day* argument is the day number. All arguments are required.

—=DATE(96,10,15)

Figure 50. *The DATE function returns the serial number for a date, which Excel formats as a date.*

	A	B
1	First Date	8-May-96
2	Second Date	15-Oct-96
3	Days Between	160

=B2-B1

Figure 51. *Calculating the number of days between two dates is as simple as subtracting the contents of two cells.*

To calculate the number of days between two dates

Enter the two dates into separate cells of a worksheet, then write a formula using the subtraction operator (-) to subtract the earlier date from the later date (see **Figure 51**).

or

In a worksheet cell, write a formula using the date function, like this:

=DATE(96,10,15)-DATE(96,5,8)

11/29/95 11:38 — =NOW()

11/29/95 — =TODAY()

Figure 52. *The NOW function returns the current date and time while the TODAY function returns just the current date.*

About the NOW and TODAY Functions

The NOW and TODAY functions (see **Figure 52**) return the serial number for the current date and time (NOW) or current date (TODAY). Results are automatically formatted and will change each time the worksheet is recalculated or opened. They use the following syntax:

NOW()

TODAY()

Although there are no arguments, the parentheses characters must be included.

	A	B
1		15-Apr-96
2	Day	15
3	Weekday	2
4	Month	4
5	Year	1996

=DAY(B1)
=WEEKDAY(B1)
=MONTH(B1)
=YEAR(B1)

Figure 53. *The DAY, WEEKDAY, MONTH, and YEAR functions extract portions of a date.*

About the DAY, WEEKDAY, MONTH, and YEAR Functions

The DAY, WEEKDAY, MONTH, and YEAR functions (see **Figure 53**) return the day of the month, the day of the week, the month number, or the year number for a serial number. They use the following syntax:

DAY(serial_number)
WEEKDAY(serial_number)
MONTH(serial_number)
YEAR(serial_number)

The serial_number argument can be a cell reference, number, or date written as text, like "10/15/96" or "15-April-96."

NOW, TODAY, DAY, WEEKDAY, MONTH, & YEAR

About Text Functions

Excel includes over 20 text functions you can use to extract, convert, concatenate, and get information about text. I tell you about a few of the more commonly used ones here.

About the LOWER, UPPER, and PROPER Functions

The LOWER, UPPER, and PROPER functions (see **Figure 54**) convert text to lowercase, uppercase, and title case. They use the following syntax:

LOWER(text)
UPPER(text)
PROPER(text)

The *text* argument, which is required, is the text you want converted.

	A	B	
1	Original	This IS an eXample	
2	Lowercase	this is an example	*—=LOWER(B1)*
3	Uppercase	THIS IS AN EXAMPLE	*—=UPPER(B1)*
4	Title Case	This Is An Example	*—=PROPER(B1)*

Figure 54. *Use the LOWER, UPPER, and PROPER functions to change the case of text.*

About the LEFT, RIGHT, and MID Functions

The LEFT, RIGHT, and MID functions (see **Figure 55**) return the leftmost, rightmost, or middle characters of a text string. They use the following syntax:

LEFT(text,num_chars)
RIGHT(text,num_chars)
MID(text,start_num,num_chars)

The *text* argument, which is required, is the text characters extracted from. The *num_chars* argument is the number of characters you want extracted. If omitted from the LEFT or RIGHT function, 1 is assumed. The MID function has an additional argument, *start_num*, which is the number of the first character from which you want to extract text. The MID function requires all arguments.

	A	B	
1	Original Text	sassafras	
2	First 4 Characters	sass	*—=LEFT(B1,4)*
3	Last 4 Characters	fras	*—=RIGHT(B1,4)*
4	4 Chars Starting w/3rd	ssaf	*—=MID(B1,3,4)*

Figure 55. *Use the LEFT, RIGHT, and MID functions to extract characters from text.*

LOWER, UPPER, PROPER, LEFT, RIGHT, & MID

	A	B	C
1	Last Name	First Name	Full Name
2	Twain	Mark	Mark Twain

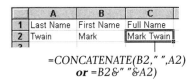

=*CONCATENATE(B2," ",A2)*
or =*B2&" "&A2)*

Figure 56. *Use the CONCATENATE function or operator to join strings of text.*

	A	B	C	D	E
1	Amount	$124.90			
2	Purchase Date	10/15/96			
3					
4	The total amount due is $124.90. Please pay by 11/14/96.				

="The total amount due is "&DOLLAR(B1)&". Please pay by "&TEXT(B2+30,"mm/dd/yy")&"."

Figure 57. *This formula writes a sentence using the contents of two cells, the contatenate operator, and two text functions.*

About the CONCATENATE Function and Operator

The CONCATENATE function (see **Figure 56**) joins or concatenates two or more strings of text. It uses the following syntax:

CONCATENATE(text1,text2,...)

Each text argument can include single cell references, text, or numbers you want to join. The CONCATENATE function can accept up to 30 arguments, but only two are required.

✔ Tips

- Excel recognizes the ampersand character (&) as a concatenation operator in formulas. You can concatenate text by including an ampersand between cells or text strings in a formula, like this:

  =B2&" "&A2

- If you want spaces between the strings, be sure to include the space character, between double quote characters, as an argument (see **Figure 56**).
- Creative use of the CONCATENATE function or operator makes it possible to give documents a personal touch. **Figure 57** shows an example.

To get more information about a function

1. Double-click the Help button on the Standard toolbar.

2. In the Help Topics window that appears, click the Index tab to display an alphabetical list of topics.

3. Type in the name of the function for which you want more information (see **Figure 58a**).

4. Double-click the function name in the list box.

Excel displays a help window for the function (see **Figure 58b**). It completely describes the function and its arguments, provides examples, and lets you quickly move to other help windows for related functions. I tell you more about Microsoft Excel Help in Chapter 1.

✔ Tips

■ You can write formulas that reference cells in other worksheets or other workbook files. I tell you how in Chapter 12.

■ Naming cells or ranges of cells makes cell references easier to remember and use. I tell you how to use names in Chapter 12.

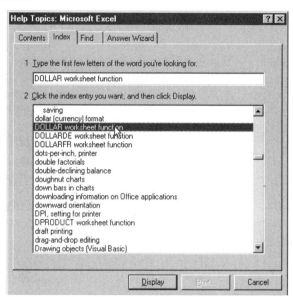

Figure 58a. *Use the Help Topics Index to locate a function for which you want more information.*

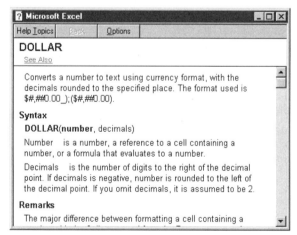

Figure 58b. *The Help window displays complete information about functions.*

FORMATTING WORKSHEET CELLS 6

ND Industries
First Quarter Sales Results

	Jan	Feb	Mar	Total
Nancy	443	419	841	1703
Bess	493	277	45	815
George	301	492	179	972
Ned	67	856	842	1765
Total	1304	2044	1907	5255

Figure 1a. *While content should be more important than appearance, you can bet that this worksheet won't get as much attention…*

ND Industries
First Quarter Sales Results

	Jan	Feb	Mar	Total
Nancy	443	419	841	1703
Bess	493	277	45	815
George	301	492	179	972
Ned	67	856	842	1765
Total	1304	2044	1907	5255

Figure 1b. *…as this one!*

About Formatting

To paraphrase an old Excel mentor of mine, formatting a worksheet is like putting on its makeup. The worksheet's contents may be perfectly correct, but by applying formatting, you can increase its impact to make an impression on the people who see it (see **Figures 1a** and **1b**).

Excel offers a wide range of formatting options you can use to beautify your worksheets:

- *Number formatting* lets you change the appearance of numbers, dates, and times.

- *Alignment* lets you change the way cell contents are aligned within the cell.

- *Font formatting* lets you change the appearance of text and number characters.

- *Borders* let you add lines around cells.

- *Patterns* let you add color, shading, and patterns to cells.

- *Column and row formatting* let you change column width and row height.

You can apply formatting to cells using a variety of techniques: with toolbar buttons, shortcut keys, menu commands, or the AutoFormat feature.

✔ Tip

- Excel may automatically apply formatting to cells, depending on what you enter. For example, if you use a date function, Excel formats the results of the function as a date. You can change Excel's formatting at any time to best meet your needs.

About Number Formatting

By default, Excel applies the General format to all cells on a worksheet. This format displays numbers just as they're entered. If the integer part of the number is longer than the width of the cell or 11 digits, it displays them in scientific notation. **Figure 2** shows some examples.

Change number formatting with toolbar buttons or the Format Cells dialog box.

1548.36
12458
14.2
-354.85
116.028
0.2
1.23457E+15

Figure 2. *General formatting displays the numbers just as they're typed in and uses scientific notation when they're very big.*

✔ Tips

- Number formatting changes only the *appearance* of a number. Although formatting may remove decimal places from displayed numbers, it does not round numbers. **Figure 3** illustrates this. Use the ROUND function, which I discuss in Chapter 5, to round numbers in formulas.

- If you include characters like dollar signs or percent symbols with a number you enter, Excel automatically assigns an appropriate built-in format to the cell.

Number 1	1.505	$	1.51
Number 2	3.50444	$	3.50
Total	5.00944	$	5.01

Figure 3. *The two columns contain identical values, but the column on the right has been formatted with the Currency Style. Because Excel performs calculations with the numbers underlying any formatting, the total on the right appears incorrect!*

To format numbers with toolbar buttons

1. Select the cell(s) containing the number(s) you want to format.

2. Click the Formatting toolbar button for the number format you want to apply (see **Figure 4**):

General	0.15	163.2	-12.785
Currency	$ 0.15	$ 163.20	$ (12.79)
Percent	15%	16320%	-1279%
Comma	0.15	163.20	(12.79)
Increase Decimal	0.150	163.200	-12.785
Decrease Decimal	0.2	163.2	-12.8

Figure 4. *This example shows three different numbers with each of the Formatting toolbar's number formatting options applied.*

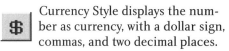 Currency Style displays the number as currency, with a dollar sign, commas, and two decimal places.

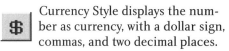 Percent Style displays a decimal number as a percentage with a percent symbol.

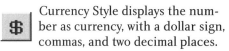 Comma Style displays the number with commas and two decimal places.

 Increase Decimal displays an additional digit after the decimal point.

 Decrease Decimal displays one less digit after the decimal point.

Figure 5a. *Choose Cells from the Format menu...*

To format numbers with the Format Cells dialog box

1. Select the cell(s) containing the number(s) you want to format.

2. Choose Cells from the Format menu (see **Figure 5a**).

   or

   Press Control+1.

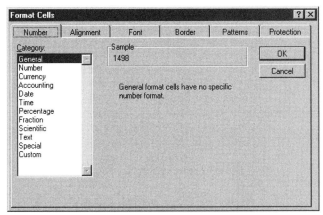

Figure 5b. *...to display the Format Cells dialog box.*

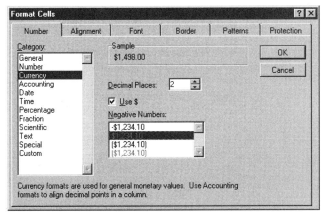

Figure 5c. *When you select formatting options, the number in the active cell appears in the Sample area with the format applied.*

3. The Format Cells Dialog box appears. If necessary, click the Number tab to display number formatting options (see **Figure 5b**).

4. Choose a category from the Category list box.

5. Select from among various options relating to that category. Options will vary depending on the category you chose in Step 4. For example, when you choose Currency (see **Figure 5c**), you can specify the number of decimal places, whether to use a dollar sign ($), and how the negative numbers should appear. A sample of the number in the active cell appears near the bottom of the dialog box with the format applied.

6. Click OK to accept the formatting.

✔ Tip

■ Take advantage of the sample area at the bottom of the dialog box to preview formatting options as you select them. This way, you can choose the perfect code on the first try.

Applying Number Formatting

About Custom Number Formatting

Excel also enables you to create custom number formats by entering number format codes that provide Excel with formatting instructions. These codes use symbols to tell Excel how to treat a number's digits and where to place other characters like spaces, commas, and dollar signs. **Table 1** lists most of the symbols that can be included in a number format code.

The symbols in number format codes are organized in up to four sections separated by semicolons (;):

1. Format for positive numbers.
2. Format for negative numbers.
3. Format for zeros.
4. Format for text.

✔ Tip

■ To create a custom number format, begin by selecting Custom from the Category list box in the Number tab of the Format Cells dialog box (see **Figure 6**). Then enter the appropriate symbols in the Type text box. When you click OK, the code you create is saved for future use in that workbook and applied to selected cells.

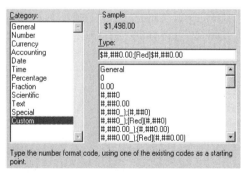

Figure 6. *Select Custom from the Category list box to create and apply a custom number format.*

Symbol	Purpose
#	Optional digit placeholder
0	Required digit placeholder
?	Required digit placeholder for aligning decimal places and fraction bars
.	Decimal point
,	Thousands separator
%	Percentage; Excel multiplies by 100 and appends the % character
$	Displays the character
-	Displays the character
+	Displays the character
/	Displays the character
(&)	Displays the character
:	Displays the character
space	Displays the character
*	Repeats the next character to fill cell
_	Skips the width of the next character
"text"	Displays the text inside the quotes
@	Text placeholder for text in cell
m	Month number without leading 0
mm	Month number with leading 0
mmm	Abbreviated month name
mmmm	Spelled out month name
d	Day number without leading 0
dd	Day number with leading 0
ddd	Abbreviated day name
dddd	Spelled out day name
yy	Two-digit year number
yyyy	Four-digit year number
h	Hour without leading 0
hh	Hour with leading 0
m	Minute without leading 0; must follow h or hh symbol
mm	Minute with leading 0; must follow h or hh symbol
s	Second without leading 0
ss	Second with leading 0
AM/PM	Displays AM or PM after time; uses 12-hour clock
[*color*]	Displays characters in *color*. Options are BLACK, BLUE, CYAN, GREEN, MAGENTA, RED, WHITE, YELLOW

Table 1. *Symbols used in Excel's number format codes.*

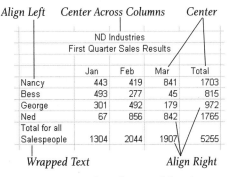

Figure 7. *Examples of some of the alignment options Excel offers.*

Figures 8a&b. *Which looks better: centered or right aligned headings?*

About Alignment

By default, within each cell, Excel left aligns text and right aligns numbers. This is called General alignment. You can change alignment to position cell contents exactly the way you want. **Figure 7** shows some examples.

You change alignment with toolbar buttons or the Format Cells dialog box.

✔ Tips

■ Although it's common to center headings over columns containing numbers, the worksheet may actually look better with headings right aligned. **Figures 8a&b** show an example.

■ Alignment is applied to cells, not cell contents. If you use the Clear Contents command or Del key to clear a cell, the formatting remains and will be applied to whatever data is next entered into it.

To align cell contents with toolbar buttons

1. Select the cell(s) whose contents you want to align (see **Figure 9a**).

Figure 9a. *Begin by selecting the cells whose alignment you want to change…*

Figure 9b. *…then click the appropriate alignment toolbar button.*

2. Click the Formatting toolbar button for the alignment you want to apply (see **Figure 9b**):

 The Align Left button aligns cell contents against the left side of the cell.

 The Center button centers cell contents between the left and right sides of the cell.

 The Align Right button aligns cell contents against the right side of the cell.

The cell contents shift accordingly (see **Figure 9c**).

Figure 9c. *The alignment you chose is applied.*

Aligning Cell Contents

To align cell contents with the Format Cells dialog box

1. Select the cell(s) whose contents you want to align (see **Figure 9a**).

2. Choose Cells from the Format menu (see **Figure 5a**).

    or

    Press Control+1.

3. The Format Cells dialog box appears. If necessary, click the Alignment tab to display the alignment options (see **Figure 10**).

4. Choose an option button for the kind of alignment you want.

5. Click OK.

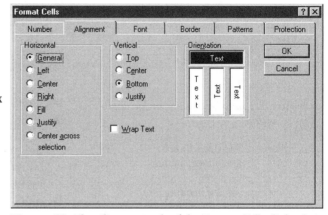

Figure 10. *The Alignment tab of the Format Cells dialog box offers many alignment options.*

To center cells across columns

1. Select the cell(s) whose contents you want to center, along with the cells of the columns to the right that you want to center across (see **Figure 11a**).

2. Click the Center Across Columns button on the Formatting toolbar (see **Figure 11b**).

    or

    Follow steps 2 and 3 above to display the Alignment tab of the Format Cells dialog box, select the Center Across Selection option button (see **Figure 11c**), and click OK.

The cell contents shift so they're centered between the left and right sides of the selected area (see **Figure 11d**).

Figure 11a. *Select the cells whose contents you want to center, as well as the cells you want to center across...*

Figure 11b. *...then click the Center Across Columns button.*

Figure 11c. *...or select the Center Across Selection option button.*

	ND Industries			
	First Quarter Sales Results			
	Jan	Feb	Mar	Total
Nancy	443	419	841	1703

Figure 11d. *The cells on the far left of the selection are centered across the entire selection.*

Figure 12a. *Select the cell whose contents you want to word wrap…*

Figure 12b. *…then turn on the Wrap Text check box.*

Figure 12c. *The text wraps within the cell.*

Figure 13a. *Select the cell whose orientation you want to change…*

Figure 13b. *…then choose the orientation option you want.*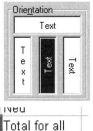

Figure 13c. *The cell's orientation shifts.*

To word wrap cell contents

1. Select the cell(s) whose contents you want to word wrap (see **Figure 12a**).

2. Choose Cells from the Format menu or press Control+1.

3. The Format Cells dialog box appears. If necessary, click the Alignment tab (see **Figure 10**).

4. Turn on the check box beside Wrap Text (see **Figure 12b**).

5. Click OK.

   The cell's contents word wrap within the cell (see **Figure 12c**). The entire row's height changes to accommodate the additional lines of text within it.

✔ Tip

■ In order for word wrap to occur, the text within the cell must be too wide to fit into the cell. I tell you how to change column widths and row heights later in this chapter.

To change the orientation of cell contents

1. Select the cell(s) whose orientation you want to change (see **Figure 13a**).

2. Choose Cells from the Format menu or press Control+1.

3. The Format Cells dialog box appears. If necessary, click the Alignment tab (see **Figure 10**).

4. Choose an orientation option by clicking it (see **Figure 13b**).

5. Click OK.

   The cell's contents change orientation (see **Figure 13c**). If necessary, the entire row's height changes to accommodate the shifted characters.

Wrapping Text & Changing Orientation

About Font Formatting

Excel uses 10 point Arial as the default font or typeface for worksheets. You can change the font applied to text, number, or symbol characters, as well as its size and its style using toolbar buttons, shortcut keys, and the Format Cells dialog box.

✔ Tip

■ You can change the formatting of individual characters within a cell (see **Figure 14b**) by double-clicking the cell to make it active, selecting the characters you want to change (see **Figure 14a**), and then using the appropriate font formatting technique to change the characters.

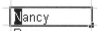

Figure 14a. *Double-click the cell and select the character(s) you want to format.*

Figure 14b. *When you make the change, only the selected character(s) are affected.*

To change a font with the Formatting toolbar

1. Select the cell(s) or character(s) whose font you want to change.

2. Click on the arrow beside the Font box on the Formatting toolbar to display a list of all available (see **Figure 15**) and choose the font you want to apply.

   or

   Click on the Font box to select its contents (see **Figure 16a**), type in the name of the font you want to apply (see **Figure 16b**), and press Enter.

   The font you chose is applied to the selected cell(s).

Figure 15. *The Font drop-down list on the Formatting toolbar lets you choose from all available fonts.*

✔ Tip

■ The font drop-down list on your computer may not look exactly like the one illustrated here. The fonts that appear in the list are those installed on your computer.

Figure 16a. *Click in the font box to select its contents…*

Figure 16b. *…then type in the name of a font installed in Windows and press Enter.*

To change font size with the Formatting toolbar

1. Select the cell(s) or character(s) whose font size you want to change.

2. Click on the arrow beside the Font Size box on the Formatting toolbar to display a menu of sizes (see **Figure 17**) and choose the size you want to apply.

   or

   Click on the Font Size box to select its contents, type in a size to apply (see **Figure 18**), and press Enter.

   The font size you chose is applied to the selected cell(s).

✔ Tips

- Font size is expressed in *points*. 72 points equals 1 inch.

- Font size must be between 1 and 409 points in half-point increments.

To change font style with the Formatting toolbar or shortcut keys

1. Select the cell(s) whose font style you want to change.

2. Click the Formatting toolbar button for the style you want to apply (see **Figure 19**):

Figure 17. *The Font Size drop-down list on the Formatting toolbar lets you change the size of characters in selected cells.*

Figure 18. *You can type almost any size you like into the Font Size box.*

Italic   *Bold and Underline*

Figure 19. *Examples of style options that can be applied with Formatting toolbar buttons.*

The Bold button or Control+B makes characters in the selected cell(s) appear in a bold style.

The Italic button or Control+I makes characters in the selected cell(s) appear in an italic style.

The Underline button or Control+U puts a single underline under characters in the selected cell(s).

✔ Tip

- Use border formatting or accounting underlines rather than the Underline button to put lines at the bottom of columns being totalled. I tell you about border formatting and accounting underlines later in this chapter.

Formatting Characters

To change font formatting with the Format Cells dialog box

1. Select the cell(s) or character(s) whose font you want to change.

2. Choose Cells from the Format menu or press Control+1.

3. The Format Cells dialog box appears. If necessary, click the Font tab to display the font formatting options (see **Figure 20a**).

4. Select a font from the Font list box or type a font name into the text box above it.

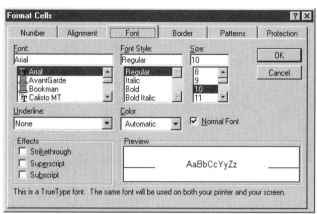

Figure 20a. *The Font tab of the Format Cells dialog box offers all kinds of font formatting options.*

5. Select a font style from the Font Style list box or type a style name into the text box above it.

6. Select a font size from the Size list box or type a size into the text box above it.

7. Choose an underline style from the Underline drop-down list (see **Figure 20b**). Accounting underlines stretch almost the entire width of the cell.

8. Choose a color from the Color drop-down list (see **Figure 20c**). Automatic color is determined by formatting options on the Number tab. I tell you about them earlier in this chapter.

9. Use the Effects check boxes to turn different character effects on or off.

10. When the sample in the Preview area looks just the way you want, click OK.

✔ Tips

■ The Font Color button/menu on the Formatting toolbar works the same way as the Color menu in the Format cells dialog box (see **Figure 20c**).

Figure 20b.
The Underline drop-down list offers five options.

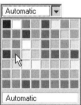

Figure 20c.
Use the color drop-down list to choose a color for the characters of selected cells.

■ To return a selection to the default font, turn on the Normal Font check box.

ND Industries
First Quarter Sales Results

	Jan	Feb	Mar	Total
Nancy	$ 443	$ 419	$ 841	$ 1,703
Bess	493	277	45	815
George	301	492	179	972
Ned	67	856	842	1,765
Total for all Salespeople	$1,304	$2,044	$ 1,907	$ 5,255

Figure 21. *Use borders to place rules below headings and above and below column totals.*

Figure 22a. *Click the Borders button to apply the currently displayed border style...*

Figure 22b. *...or click the triangle to display a menu of border styles and choose one.*

About Borders

Excel offers a number of different border styles that you can apply to separate cells or a selection of cells (see **Figure 21**). Use the Formatting toolbar or the Format Cells dialog box to add borders.

To add borders with the Borders button

1. Select the cell(s) to which you want to add borders.

2. Click on the picture part of the Borders button (see **Figure 22a**) to apply the border style illustrated on the button.

   or

   Click on the triangle on the right side of the Borders button to pull down a menu of border styles (see **Figure 22b**) and choose the style you want.

✔ Tips

■ All of the border styles on the Borders menu except the last two apply borders to each cell in the selection. The last two choices apply borders around the outside of the entire selection.

■ The last border selection you made from the Borders menu is the one that is illustrated on the button. This makes it quick and easy to apply the same border formatting again.

■ To remove borders from a selection, choose the first (top left) border style. If the border does not disappear, it may be applied to a cell adjoining the one you selected.

■ The accounting underlines available from the Underline drop-down list in the Format Cells dialog box are *not* the same as borders. They do not stretch the entire width of the cell and they only appear when the cell is not blank.

To add borders with the Format Cells dialog box

1. Select the cell(s) to which you want to add borders.

2. Choose Cells from the Format menu or press Control+1.

3. The Format Cells dialog box appears. If necessary, click the Border tab to display the border options (see **Figure 23**).

4. Select a line style from the Style section.

5. If desired, select a color from the Color drop-down list. This list looks and works exactly like the one on the Font tab (see **Figure 20c**).

6. Click on a border position option in the Border section. This places the line style you chose in that position for each of the selected cells. If you choose Outline, the line is placed around the selection.

7. Repeat steps 4, 5, and 6 until all the line styles, colors, and positions for the selected cells are set.

8. Click OK.

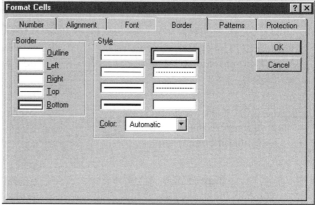

Figure 23. *You can add borders to selected cells with options from the Borders tab of the Format Cells dialog box.*

✔ Tip

■ To get the borders in your worksheet to look just the way you want, be prepared to make several selections and trips to either the Borders button on the Formatting toolbar or the Borders tab of the Format Cells dialog box.

Adding Borders

ND INDUSTRIES				
FIRST QUARTER SALES RESULTS				
	Jan	Feb	Mar	Total
Nancy	$ 443	$ 419	$ 841	$ 1,703
Bess	493	277	45	815
George	301	492	179	972
Ned	67	856	842	1,765
Total for all Salespeople	$1,304	$2,044	$ 1,907	$ 5,255

Figure 24. *Use Excel's pattern feature to add color, patterns, and shading to cells.*

About Colors, Patterns, and Shading

Excel's pattern feature lets you add color to cells (see **Figure 24**), either with or without patterns. Although the Color button/menu on the Formatting toolbar lets you add color to cells, the Format Cells dialog box offers far more flexibility.

✔ Tip

■ By combining two colors with a pattern, you can create various colors and levels of shading.

To add color with the Color button

1. Select the cell(s) to which you want to add color.

Figure 25a. *Click the Color button to apply the currently displayed color...*

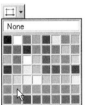

Figure 25b. *...or click the triangle to display a menu of colors and choose one.*

2. Click on the picture part of the Color button (see **Figure 25a**) to apply the color illustrated on the button.

   or

   Click on the triangle on the right side of the Color button to pull down a menu of colors (see **Figure 25b**) and choose the color you want.

✔ Tips

■ The last color selection you made from the Color menu is the one that is illustrated on the button. This makes it easy to apply the same color again and again.

■ To remove colors from a selection, choose None from the Color menu.

Adding Color

To add color, pattern, and shading with the Format Cells dialog box

1. Select the cell(s) to which you want to add colors, patterns, or shading.

2. Choose Cells from the Format menu or press Control+1.

3. The Format Cells dialog box appears. If necessary, click the Patterns tab to display the color and pattern options (see **Figure 26a**).

4. Select a color from the Color palette in the Cell Shading area of the dialog box. This is the foreground color.

5. If desired, choose a background color and pattern from the Pattern drop-down list (see **Figure 26b**).

6. When the Sample area of the dialog box looks just the way you want your selection to look, click OK.

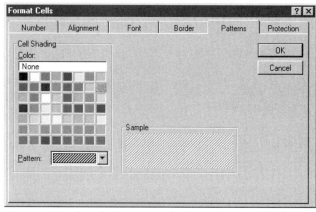

Figure 26a. *Use the Patterns tab of the Format Cells dialog box to add color, patterns, and shading to selected cells.*

✔ Tips

■ Be careful when adding colors to cells! If the color is too dark, cell contents may not be legible.

■ To improve the legibility of cell contents in colored cells, try making the characters bold.

■ For a different look, use a dark color for the cell and make its characters white.

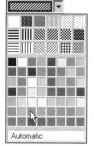

Figure 26b. *Choose a pattern from the top of the Pattern drop-down list and a background color from the bottom.*

Adding Color, Pattern, & Shading

About the Format Painter

The Format Painter button lets you copy cell formatting and apply it to other cells. This can help you format worksheets quickly and consistently.

To copy formatting with the Format Painter

1. Select a cell with the formatting you want to copy.

2. Click the Format Painter button  on the Standard toolbar (see **Figure 27a**). The mouse pointer turns into a little plus sign with a paintbrush beside it and a marquee appears around the original selection (see **Figure 27b**).

3. Use the Format Painter pointer to select the cells you want to apply the formatting to (see **Figure 27c**). When you release the mouse button, the formatting is applied (see **Figure 27d**).

Figure 27a. *Click the Format Painter button on the Standard toolbar.*

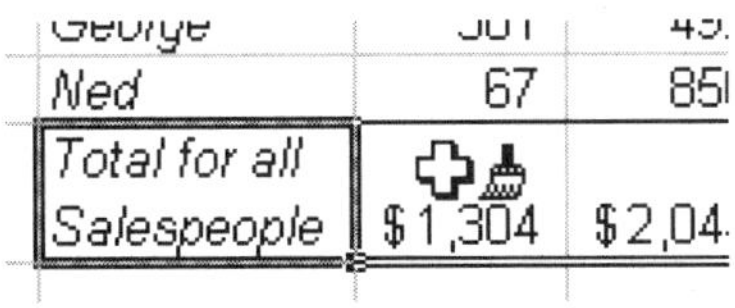

Figure 27b. *The mouse pointer changes and a marquee appears.*

Figure 27c. *Drag the mouse over the cells you want to apply formatting to.*

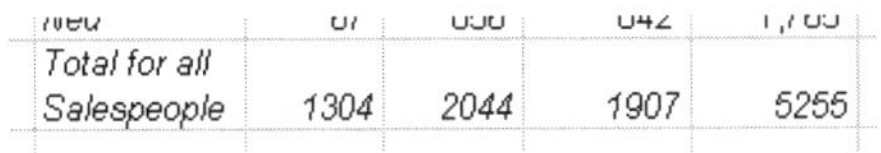

Figure 27d. *When you release the mouse button, the formatting of the cells changes to match the originally selected cell.*

✔ Tips

- Double-click the Format Painter button in step 1 above to keep applying a copied format throughout the worksheet. Press Esc or click the Format Painter button again to stop applying the format and return the mouse pointer to normal.

- If you copy a format that doesn't include number formatting to cells containing numbers, you'll have to apply (or reapply) appropriate number formatting. You can see an example of this in **Figures 27c** and **27d**.

- You can also use the Paste Special dialog box (which is discussed on the next page) to paste copied formats.

Copying Formatting

To copy formatting with the Copy and Paste Special commands

1. Select a cell with the formatting you want to copy.

2. Choose Copy from the Edit menu, press Control+C, or click the Copy button on the Standard toolbar.

3. Switch to the other worksheet and select the cell(s) to which you want to paste formatting.

4. Choose Paste Special from the Edit menu (see **Figure 28a**).

5. In the Paste Special dialog box that appears (see **Figure 28b**), select the Formats option button.

6. Click OK.

To remove formatting from cells

1. Select the cell(s) from which you want to remove just the formatting.

2. Choose Formats from the Clear submenu under the Edit menu (see **Figure 29**).

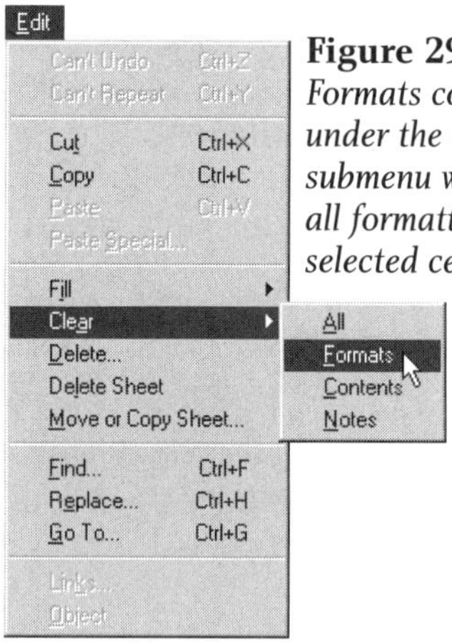

✔ Tip

- When you remove formats from a cell, you return font formatting to the normal font and number formatting to the General format. You also remove borders or colors added to the cell.

About Styles

Once you get the hang of using Excel's formatting options, check out its Style feature. This feature, which you access by choosing Styles from the Format menu, lets you combine formats into named styles that you can apply to any cell in the workbook. This can save time and ensure consistency.

Figure 28a. *To paste only formats from a copied cell, choose Paste Special from the Edit menu...*

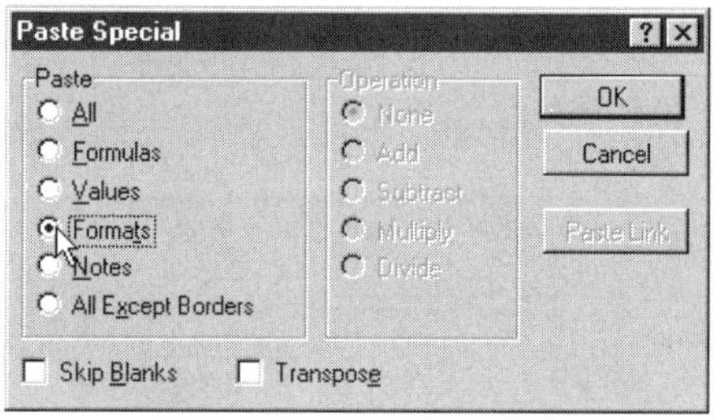

Figure 28b. *...then select the Formats option button in the Paste Special dialog box and click OK.*

Figure 29. *The Formats command under the Clear submenu will clear all formatting from selected cells.*

Copying & Clearing Formatting

About Column Width and Row Height

If the data you enter into a cell doesn't fit, you can make the column wider to accommodate all the characters. You can also make columns narrower to use worksheet space more efficiently. And although Excel automatically adjusts row height when you increase the font size of cells within the row, you can increase or decrease row height as desired.

Excel offers two ways to change column width and row height: with the mouse and with Format menu commands.

✔ Tips

- If text typed into a cell does not fit, it appears to overlap into the cell to its right (see **Figure 30a**). Even though the text may appear to be in more than one cell, all of the text is really in the cell in which you typed it. (You can see for yourself by clicking in the cell to the right and looking at the formula bar—it will not contain any part of the text!) If the cell to the right of the text is not blank, the text appears truncated (see **Figure 30b**). Don't let appearances fool you. The text is still all there. The missing part is just hidden by the contents of the cell beside it.

- If a number doesn't fit in a cell, the cell fills up with pound signs (#) (see **Figure 31a**). To display the number, make the column wider (see **Figure 31b**) or change the number formatting to omit symbols and decimal places (see **Figure 31c**). I tell you how to change number formatting earlier in this chapter.

- Setting column width or row height to 0 (zero) hides the column or row.

Figure 30a. *When text doesn't fit in a cell, it appears to overlap into the cell beside it...*

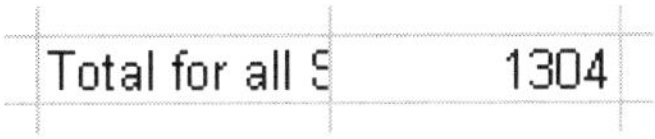

| Total for all S | | 1304 |

Figure 30b. *...unless the cell beside it isn't blank.*

Figure 31a. *When a number doesn't fit, the cell fills with # signs.*

| ######## |

Figure 31b. *Make the number fit by making the cell wider...*

| $1,234.56 |

Figure 31c. *...or changing the number formatting.*

To change column width or row height with the mouse

1. Position the mouse pointer on the line right after the column heading (see **Figure 32a**) or right below the row number (see **Figure 32b**) of the column or row you want to change. The mouse pointer turns into a line with two arrows coming out of it.

2. Press the mouse button down and drag.

   ☞ To make a column narrower, drag to the left.

   ☞ To make a column wider, drag to the right.

   ☞ To make a row taller, drag down.

   ☞ To make a row shorter, drag up.

   As you drag, a dotted line moves along with the mouse pointer (see **Figure 32c**). The width of the row or height of the column appears in the name box on the left end of the formula bar (see **Figure 32d**).

3. Release the mouse button. The column width or row height changes.

✔ Tips

■ When you change column width or row height, you change the width or height for the entire column or row, not just selected cells.

■ To change column width or row height for more than one column or row at a time, select multiple columns or rows and drag the border of one of them. I tell you how to select multiple columns or rows in Chapter 2.

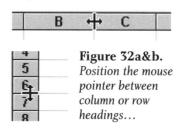

Figure 32a&b.
Position the mouse pointer between column or row headings...

Figure 32c.
...and drag.

Figure 32d. *As you drag, the column width or row height measurement appears in the name box.*

■ If you drag a column or row border all the way to the left or all the way up, you set the column width or row height to 0. The column or row disappears from view. I tell you more about hiding columns and rows on the next page.

■ To quickly set the width or height of a column or row to fit its contents, double-click the column or row border. I tell you more about the AutoFit feature later in this chapter.

Figure 33a. *Options under the Column submenu let you change column formatting.*

Figure 33b. *Options under the Row submenu let you change row formatting.*

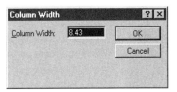

Figure 33c&d. *You're not seeing double. These two dialog boxes let you change column width and row height.*

Figure 34. *When you hide columns or rows, the data is still in the worksheet.*

To change column width or row height with menu commands

1. Select the column(s) or row(s) whose width or height you want to change.

2. Choose Width from the Column submenu under the Format menu (see **Figure 33a**) or choose Height from the Row submenu under the Format menu (see **Figure 33b**).

3. In the Column Width dialog box (see **Figure 33c**) or Row Height dialog box (see **Figure 33d**), enter a new value. Column width is expressed in standard font characters while row height is expressed in points.

4. Click OK.

To hide columns or rows

1. Select the column(s) or row(s) you want to hide.

2. Choose Hide from the Column submenu (see **Figure 33a**) or the Row submenu (see **Figure 33b**) under the Format menu.

   The selected columns or rows disappear (see **Figure 34**).

✔ Tip

■ Hiding a column or row is not the same as deleting it. Data in a hidden column or row still exists in the worksheet and can be referenced by formulas.

To unhide columns or rows

1. Drag to select the columns or rows on both sides of the hidden column(s) or row(s).

2. Choose Unhide from the Column submenu (see **Figure 33a**) or the Row submenu (see **Figure 33b**) under the Format menu.

Changing Column Width or Row Height

About AutoFit

Excel's AutoFit feature automatically adjusts a column's width or a row's height so it's only as wide or as high as it needs to be to display the information within it (see **Figure 35c**). This is a great way to adjust columns and rows to use worksheet space more efficiently.

To use AutoFit

1. Select the column(s) or row(s) for which you want to change the width or height (see **Figure 35a**).

2. Choose AutoFit Selection from the Column submenu or AutoFit from the Row menu under the Format menu (see **Figures 33a** and **33b**).

    or

    Double-click on the border to the right of the column heading or below the row heading (see **Figure 35b**).

✔ Tips

■   To adjust a column without taking every cell into consideration—for example, to exclude a cell containing a lot of text—select only the cells for which you want to adjust the column (see **Figure 36a**). When you choose AutoFit Selection from the Column submenu under the Format menu, only the cells you selected are measured for the AutoFit adjustment (see **Figure 36b**).

■   By using the Wrap Text feature in conjunction with AutoFit, you can keep your columns narrow. I tell you about Wrap Text earlier in this chapter.

Figure 35a. *Select the columns or rows for which you want to change the width or height and use the AutoFit command...*

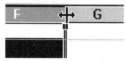

Figure 35b. *....or double-click the border between column or row headings.*

Figure 35c. *The width or height is changed so it's just wide or tall enough to fit cell contents.*

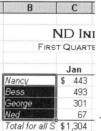

Figure 36a. *To use AutoFit without taking every cell in the column into consideration, select only the cells for which you want the column adjusted.*

Figure 36b. *Using AutoFit Selection makes it possible to keep columns narrow when some column cells contain a lot of text.*

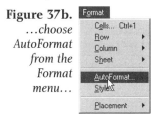

Figure 37a. *Select the portion of the worksheet you want to format…*

Figure 37b. *…choose AutoFormat from the Format menu…*

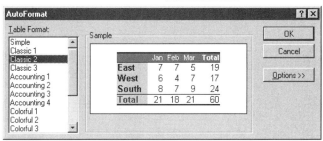

Figure 37c. *…then choose the predefined format you like best.*

Figure 37d. *Excel applies all kinds of formatting all at once.*

About AutoFormat

Excel's AutoFormat feature offers a quick way to dress up tabular data in worksheets by applying predefined formats. If you're like me and like to leave design for designers, you'll welcome this feature.

To use AutoFormat

1. Select the portion of the worksheet you want to format (see **Figure 37a**).

2. Choose AutoFormat from the Format menu (see **Figure 37b**).

3. In the AutoFormat dialog box that appears (see **Figure 37c**), choose a format from the Table Format list box. A preview of the format appears in the Sample area so you can decide whether you like it before you apply it.

4. When you're satisfied with your selection, click OK. Your worksheet is formatted instantly (see **Figure 37d**).

✔ Tip

■ To pick and choose among the different kinds of formatting automatically applied, click the Options button in the AutoFormat dialog box. The box expands to display check boxes for each type of formatting (see **Figure 38**). To exclude a type of change from the AutoFormat process, turn off its check box.

Figure 38. *Clicking the Options button expands the AutoFormat dialog box to display check boxes for the different kinds of formatting that can be applied.*

Using AutoFormat

About Cell Notes

Excel lets you add notes to any cell. You can use notes to annotate your worksheets, providing background information for complex or important calculations.

To add a Cell Note

1. Select the cell to which you want to add a note.

2. Choose Note from the Insert menu (see **Figure 39a**).

3. In the Cell Note dialog box (see **Figure 39b**), enter the text for the note in the Text Note scrolling text box.

4. Click the Add button.

5. Click OK.

   A tiny red mark appears in the upper right corner of the cell (see **Figure 39c**) to indicate that it has a note. This mark does not print.

Figure 39a.
Choose Note from the Insert menu...

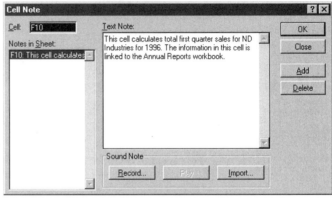

Figure 39b. *...then type your note into the Text Note edit box.*

✔ Tips

■ To add multiple notes, after you click Add for the first note, enter a new cell address in the Cell edit box and repeat steps 3 and 4 until all notes have been added.

■ You can use the Record or Import buttons in the Sound Note area (see **Figure 39b**) to record or import sound notes.

To view cell notes

Choose Note from the Insert menu (see **Figure 39a**) and click on the cell containing the note in the Notes in Sheet list box. The note appears in the Text Note edit box (see **Figure 39b**).

Figure 39c. *A mark appears in the corner of a cell with a note.*

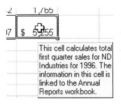

Figure 40.
Position the mouse pointer over any cell with a note to display the note as a CellTip.

or

Position the mouse pointer over a cell containing a note. A small box called a CellTip appears with the note inside it (see **Figure 40**).

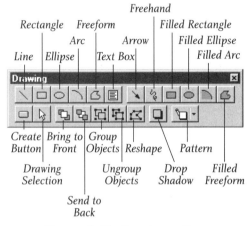

Freehand
Rectangle *Freeform* | *Filled Rectangle*
   Arc *Arrow* *Filled Ellipse*
Line | *Ellipse* | *Text Box* | *Filled Arc*

Create | *Bring to* | *Group*
Button | *Front* | *Objects* | *Reshape* \ *Pattern*
   Drawing *Ungroup* *Drop* *Filled*
   Selection *Objects* *Shadow* *Freeform*
     Send to
     Back

Figure 1. *The Drawing toolbar.*

Figure 2. *Click the Drawing button on the Standard toolbar.*

Figure 3. *If the Drawing toolbar is floating, you can hide it by clicking its close button.*

About Drawing Objects

Excel's Drawing toolbar (see **Figure 1**) includes a wide range of tools you can use to add lines, arrows, shapes, and text boxes to your worksheets and charts. Through creative use of these tools, you can add impact and improve appearance in all of your Excel documents.

To display the Drawing toolbar

Click the Drawing button on the Standard toolbar (see **Figure 2**). The Drawing toolbar appears (see **Figure 1**).

✔ Tip

- ■ If your Drawing toolbar doesn't look exactly like this one, don't panic. Although the Drawing toolbar is a floating toolbar by default, it may have been reshaped or anchored the last time it was used—Excel remembers the shape and position of all toolbars. I tell you more about toolbars in Chapter 14.

To hide the Drawing toolbar

Click the Drawing button on the Standard toolbar a second time.

or

If the Drawing toolbar's title bar is displayed, click its close button (see **Figure 3**).

Displaying & Hiding the Drawing Toolbar

About Objects

Many of the tools on the Drawing toolbar let you draw *objects* in worksheet or chart windows. An object can be any line or shape. Excel lets you draw lines, rectangles, squares, ellipses, circles, arcs, freeform shapes, and text boxes. Objects you draw can be selected, resized, moved, or copied at any time.

To draw a line or arrow

1. Click the appropriate Drawing toolbar button once to select it:

     Use the Line tool to draw straight lines.

     Use the Arrow tool to draw straight lines with arrowheads on either or both ends.

     Use the Arc tool to draw arcs. An arc is a quarter of a circle or an ellipse.

     Use the Freehand tool to draw lines in any shape. You can even use it to sign your name!

    When you click the tool's button the mouse pointer turns into a cross hair pointer (see **Figure 4**).

2. Position the cross hair where you want to begin drawing the line.

3. Press the mouse button down and drag. As you move the mouse, a line is drawn (see **Figure 5**).

4. Release the mouse button to complete the line. The line appears with selection handles on either end (see **Figures 6a** and **6b**) or around it (see **Figures 6c** and **6d**). I tell you more about selection handles later in this chapter.

Figure 4. *When you click a drawing tool, the mouse pointer changes into a cross hair.*

Figure 5. *Drag the cross hair pointer to draw a line.*

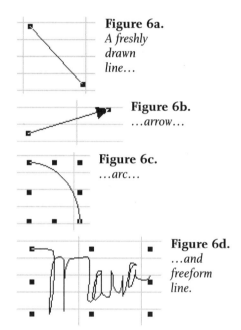

Figure 6a. *A freshly drawn line…*

Figure 6b. *…arrow…*

Figure 6c. *…arc…*

Figure 6d. *…and freeform line.*

✔ Tips

■ The Freehand tool's cross hair pointer turns into a pencil as you draw.

■ To draw a line or arrow that's perfectly vertical, horizontal, or at a 45° angle, hold down the Shift key as you press down the mouse button and draw.

■ To draw multiple lines with the same tool, double-click its button to select it. The tool remains active until you either click the button again, click another button, or press Esc.

To draw a rectangle, square, ellipse, or circle

1. Click the appropriate Drawing toolbar button once to select it:

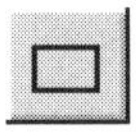

   Use the Rectangle tool to draw rectangles or squares.

   Use the Ellipse tool to draw ovals and circles.

   When you click the tool's button the mouse pointer turns into a cross hair pointer (see **Figure 4**).

2. Position the cross hair where you want to begin drawing the shape.

3. Press the mouse button down and drag. As you move the mouse, the shape begins to take form (see **Figure 7**).

4. Release the mouse button to complete the shape. The shape appears with selection handles around it (see **Figures 8a** and **8b**). I tell you more about selection handles later in this chapter.

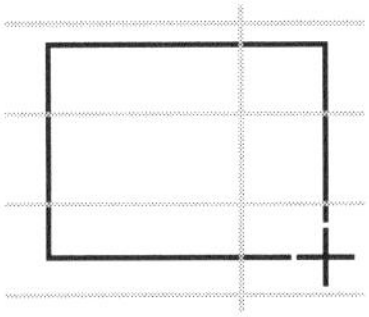

Figure 7.
Drag the cross hair pointer to draw a shape.

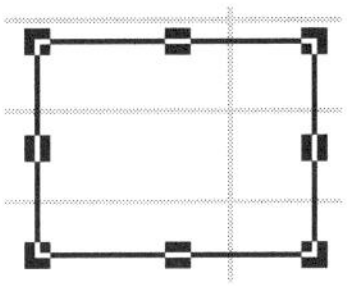

Figure 8a.
A freshly drawn rectangle...

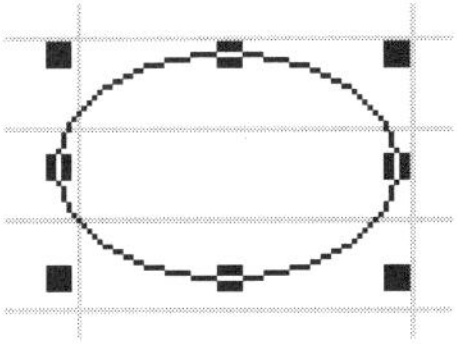

Figure 8b.
...and ellipse.

✔ Tips

- When you draw with the rectangle or ellipse tool, you draw from corner to corner.

- To draw a square or a circle, click the Rectangle or Ellipse button, then hold down the Shift key as you press down the mouse button and draw. The drawing movements are restricted so only perfectly square or perfectly round shapes can be drawn.

- To draw multiple shapes with the same tool, double-click its button to select it. The tool remains active until you either click the button again, click another button, or press Esc.

Drawing Shapes

To draw a freeform shape

1. Click the Freeform button on the Drawing toolbar once to select it. The mouse pointer turns into a cross hair pointer (see **Figure 4**).

2. Position the cross hair where you want to begin drawing the shape.

3. Press the mouse button down and drag to draw freehand lines (see **Figure 9a**).

   and/or

   Click where you want the corners of the shape to have Excel draw straight lines between them (see **Figure 9b**).

4. Click at the starting point of the shape to complete a closed shape (see **Figure 10a**).

   or

   Double-click at the ending point of the shape to complete an open shape (see **Figure 10b**).

   The finished shape appears with selection handles around it (see **Figures 10a** and **10b**). I tell you more about selection handles later in this chapter.

✔ Tips

- A freeform shape can combine the dragging and clicking techniques in step 3 above to make shapes that have straight and curved edges (see **Figure 11**).

- To draw multiple freeform shapes, double-click the Freeform button to select it. The Freeform tool remains active until you either click the button again, click another button, or press Esc.

- The best way to learn how to use the Freeform tool is by practicing!

Figure 9a. *With the Freeform tool selected, dragging draws freehand lines...*

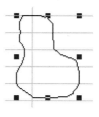

Figure 9b. *...while clicking specifies corners that Excel joins with straight lines.*

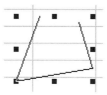

Figure 10a. *A freshly drawn closed freeform shape...*

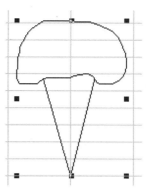

Figure 10b. *...and an open freeform shape.*

Figure 11. *An example of a freeform shape that combines straight lines with curves. Any resemblance to an ice cream cone is purely coincidental.*

About Filled Shapes

Four of Excel's Drawing toolbar buttons activate tools for drawing filled shapes:

 Use the Filled Rectangle tool to draw rectangles or squares.

 Use the Filled Ellipse tool to draw ovals and circles.

 Use the Filled Arc tool to draw arcs.

 Use the Filled Freeform tool to draw freeform shapes.

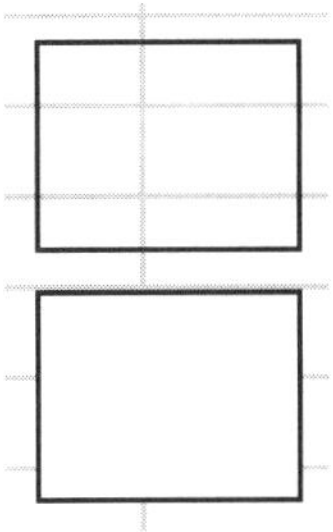

While an unfilled shape is simply a line with a specific form, a filled shape consist of an outline that defines the shape plus a fill color, pattern, and background color. **Figure 12** shows side-by-side examples of both an unfilled and filled shape.

You draw filled shapes the same way you draw unfilled shapes—I explain how to do that on the previous few pages.

Figure 12.
Two shapes: one unfilled, the other filled with the default color, white. See the difference?

✔ Tips

- The default fill color is white. I tell you how to change fill color later in this chapter.

- You can convert an unfilled shape to a filled shape by applying a fill color or pattern. You can also convert a filled shape to an unfilled shape by removing its fill color or pattern. I tell you how to do both of these things later in this chapter.

Understanding Filled Shapes

About Modifying Objects

Any object you draw in Excel can also be edited in Excel. You can resize and reshape objects, move and copy objects, and group objects together. You can also change the color and thickness of lines and the color and pattern of fill. If you decide you don't like the object, you can delete it.

In order to make any changes to an object, however, you must begin by selecting it.

To select an object

1. Position the mouse pointer on a line, on the border of an unfilled object, or anywhere on a filled object. The mouse pointer turns into a selection pointer (see **Figure 13a**) rather than the standard worksheet pointer (see **Figure 13b**).
2. Click. Selection handles appear around the object (see **Figure 14**).

✔ Tip

■ To convert the mouse pointer into a selection pointer so the standard worksheet pointer doesn't appear while you're working with drawing objects, click the Drawing Selection button on the Drawing toolbar. The button turns dark gray and the mouse pointer changes to an arrow. To get the regular pointer back, click the Drawing Selection button again, double-click any worksheet cell, or press Esc once or twice.

To deselect an object

Click on any other object or anywhere else in the window. The selection handles disappear.

Figure 13a. *This mouse pointer will select this object.*

Figure 13b. *This mouse pointer will only select the cell beneath the object.*

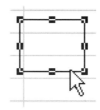

Figure 14. *Black boxes called selection handles appear around selected objects.*

Figure 15a.
Hold down the Shift key and click on each object…

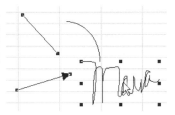

To select multiple objects

Follow steps 1 and 2 on the previous page to select the first object, then hold down the Shift key and continue to select objects (see **Figure 15a**) until all have been selected (see **Figure 15c**).

or

Figure 15b.
…or use the selection pointer to drag a rectangle around all objects.

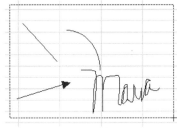

Click the Drawing Selection button on the Drawing toolbar to activate the selection pointer, then use the pointer to drag a rectangle that completely surrounds all the objects you want to select (see **Figure 15b**). When you release the mouse button, selection handles appear around each object (see **Figure 15c**).

✔ Tips

Figure 15c.
Selection handles appear around each object.

- To deselect specific objects from a multiple selection, hold down the Shift key while clicking on the objects you want to deselect.

- To deselect all objects from a multiple selection, make sure the Shift key is *not* held down, then click on any other object or anywhere else in the window.

To group objects

1. Select all the objects you want to include in the group.

2. Click the Group Objects button on the Drawing toolbar.

The objects are grouped together, with only one set of selection handles (see **Figure 16**).

Figure 16.
Grouped objects share one set of selection handles.

To ungroup objects

1. Select the grouped object you want to ungroup.

2. Click the Ungroup Objects button on the Drawing toolbar.

Separate selection handles appear for each object.

✔ Tips

- Grouping objects makes it easier to move, copy, or resize them when you want them to stay together.

- In addition to grouping separate objects, you can also group groups of objects.

To move an object

1. Position the mouse pointer on the object so that the selection pointer appears.

2. Press the mouse button down and drag. An outline of the object moves along with the mouse pointer (see **Figure 17**).

3. When the object's outline is in the desired position, release the mouse button. The object moves.

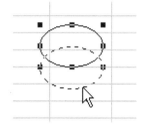

Figure 17.
To move an object, simply drag it.

✔ Tips

■ To restrict an object's movement so that it moves only horizontally or vertically, hold down the Shift key while dragging.

■ To restrict an object's movement so that it snaps to the worksheet grid, hold down the Alt key while dragging.

To copy an object with the Copy and Paste commands

1. Select the object you want to copy.

2. Choose Copy from the Edit menu, press Control+C, or click the Copy button on the Standard toolbar.

3. If you want to paste the object into a different worksheet or chart sheet, switch to that sheet.

4. Choose Paste from the Edit menu, press Control+V, or click the Paste button on the Standard toolbar.

✔ Tip

■ To remove the original object from the sheet, choose Cut from the Edit menu, press Control+X, or click the Cut button on the Standard toolbar in step 2 above.

To copy an object by dragging

1. Position the mouse pointer on the object so it turns into a selection pointer.

2. Hold down the Control key, press the mouse button down, and drag. A tiny plus sign appears beside the mouse pointer. As you drag, an outline of the object moves along with the mouse pointer (see **Figure 18**).

3. When you release the mouse button, a copy of the object appears at the outline's position.

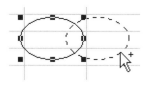

Figure 18. *If you hold down the Control key while dragging, a copy of the object is made.*

Figure 19.
Choosing All from the Clear submenu is only one way to delete a selected object.

To delete an object

1. Select the object(s) or group of objects you want to delete.

2. Press the Backspace key.

   or

   Press the Del key.

   or

   Choose All from the Clear submenu under the Edit menu (see **Figure 19**).

To resize an object

1. Select the object you want to resize.

2. Position the mouse pointer on a selection handle. The mouse pointer turns into a double-headed arrow (see **Figures 20a**, **20b**, and **20c**).

3. Press the mouse button down and drag to stretch or shrink the object. The mouse pointer turns into a cross hair and an outline of the edge of the object moves with your mouse pointer as you drag (see **Figure 21**).

4. When the outline of the object reflects the size you want, release the mouse button. The object is resized.

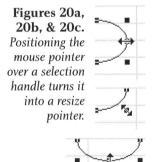

Figures 20a, 20b, & 20c.
Positioning the mouse pointer over a selection handle turns it into a resize pointer.

Figure 21. *To resize an object, drag one of its selection handles.*

✔ Tips

■ To resize an object or group proportionally, hold down the Shift key while dragging a corner selection handle.

■ To resize the object so that the handle you drag snaps to the worksheet gridlines, hold down the Alt key while dragging.

■ To resize multiple objects at the same time, select the objects, then resize one of them. All selected objects will stretch or shrink.

Deleting & Resizing Objects

To reshape an object

1. Select the object you want to reshape. The object must be a *polygon* (a multi-sided object).

2. Click the Reshape button on the Drawing toolbar. Handles for *vertices* appear at the ends of straight lines and along freehand curves (see **Figures 22a** and **22b**).

3. Position the mouse pointer on a vertex handle. The mouse pointer turns into a cross hair.

4. Press the mouse button down and drag (see **Figure 23a**). As you drag, an outline of the edge of the object moves with your mouse pointer.

5. When the vertex is in the proper position, release the mouse button. The object reshapes (see **Figure 23b**).

6. Repeat steps 3, 4, and 5 for any other vertices you need to move.

✔ Tips

■ The vertices will remain on the selected object (or will appear on any other polygon you select) until you click the Reshape button again.

■ To add a vertex, hold down the Control key and drag the edge of the polygon (see **Figure 24**). This inserts and positions the new vertex.

■ To delete a vertex, hold down the Control key and click on the vertex handle (see **Figure 25a**). The vertex is removed and the polygon reshapes accordingly (see **Figure 25b**).

Reshaping Objects

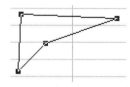

Figure 22a. *Vertices appear at the ends of straight lines…*

Figure 22b. *…and along freehand curves.*

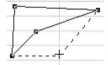

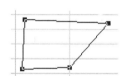

Figure 23a. *Drag a vertex to reshape an object.*

Figure 23b. *When you release the mouse button, the object reshapes.*

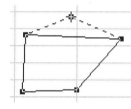

Figure 24. *Hold down the Control key and drag a polygon side to insert a vertex.*

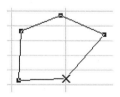

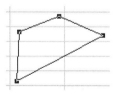

Figure 25a. *Hold down the Control key and click on a vertex handle.*

Figure 25b. *The vertex disappears and the shape of the polygon changes accordingly.*

To change the style, color, and weight of lines

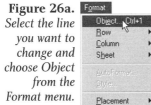

Figure 26a. *Select the line you want to change and choose Object from the Format menu.*

1. Click on the line you want to change to select it and choose Object from the Format menu (see **Figure 26a**) or press Control+1.

   or

   Double-click on the line you want to change.

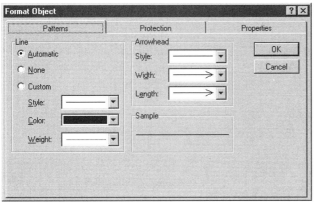

Figure 26b. *When a line or arrow is selected, the Patterns tab of the Format Objects dialog box offers these options.*

2. The Format Object dialog box appears. Click the Patterns tab if necessary to display its options (see **Figure 26b**).

3. To change the line style, choose a style from the Line Style drop-down list (see **Figure 26c**).

4. To change the line color, choose a color from the Line Color drop-down list (see **Figure 26d**).

5. To change the line weight or thickness, choose a weight from the Line Weight drop-down list (see **Figure 26e**).

Figure 26c. *Use the Line Style drop-down list to choose a line style.*

6. When the line in the Sample area looks like the line you want, click OK to apply the formatting.

✔ Tip

■ To return to default line formatting, select the Automatic option button in the Format Object dialog box.

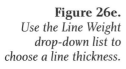

Figure 26d. *Use the Line Color drop-down list to choose a line color.*

Figure 26e. *Use the Line Weight drop-down list to choose a line thickness.*

Changing Line Style, Color, & Weight

To change or add arrowheads

1. Click on the line or arrowhead you want to change to select it and choose Object from the Format menu (see **Figure 26a**) or press Control+1.

   or

   Double-click on the line you want to change.

2. The Format Object dialog box appears. Click the Patterns tab if necessary to display its options (see **Figure 26b**).

3. To change the arrowhead style or add an arrowhead to a plain line, choose a style from the Style drop-down list (see **Figure 26f**).

4. To change the arrowhead width, choose a width from the Width drop-down list (see **Figure 26g**).

5. To change the arrowhead length, choose a length from the Length drop-down list (see **Figure 26h**).

6. If desired, make changes in the Style, Color, and Weight drop-down lists on the left side of the dialog box. I tell you how on the previous page.

7. When the arrow in the Sample area looks like the arrow you want, click OK to apply the formatting.

✔ Tips

■ To remove an arrowhead from a line, choose the first line style from the Arrowhead Style drop-down list (see **Figure 26f**).

■ When you draw an arrow, you always draw from the tail to the head. To switch arrowhead sides, drag the selection handle for the head around so that the arrow points in the opposite direction. Then drag the selection for the tail to adjust the line length.

Figure 26f. *Use the Arrowhead Style drop-down list to choose an arrowhead style.*

Figure 26g. *Use the Arrowhead Width drop-down list to choose an arrowhead width.*

Figure 26h. *Use the Arrowhead Length drop-down list to choose an arrowhead length.*

To change the style, color, and weight of shape borders

1. Click on the shape you want to change to select it and choose Object from the Format menu (see **Figure 26a**) or press Control+1.

   or

   Double-click on the shape you want to change.

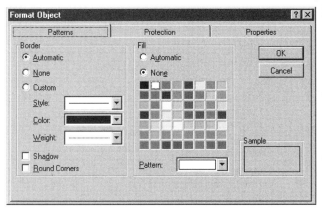

Figure 27. *When a shape is selected, the Patterns tab of the Format Object dialog box offers these options.*

2. The Format Object dialog box appears. Click the Patterns tab if necessary to display its options (see **Figure 27**).

3. To change the border style, choose a style from the Style drop-down list (see **Figure 26c**).

4. To change the border color, choose a color from the Color drop-down list (see **Figure 26d**).

5. To change the border weight or thickness, choose a weight from the Weight drop-down list (see **Figure 26e**).

6. To add a drop shadow border to the object, turn on the Shadow check box.

7. To round the corners of rectangles or squares, turn on the Round Corners check box. (This option is not available for ellipses and circles.)

8. When the border around the shape in the Sample area looks like the border you want, click OK to apply the formatting.

✔ Tips

- To add just a drop shadow border around a selected object, click the Drop Shadow button on the Drawing toolbar.

- To return to default border formatting, select the Automatic option button on the left side of the Format Object dialog box.

- To remove the border from the object, select the None option button on the left side of the Format Object dialog box.

To change or add fill colors and patterns to shapes

1. Click on the shape you want to change to select it and choose Object from the Format menu (see **Figure 26a**) or press Control+1.

   or

   Double-click on the shape you want to change.

2. The Format Object dialog box appears. Click the Patterns tab if necessary to display its options (see **Figure 27**).

3. To change or add the fill color, click the color you want on the Fill color palette. This is the foreground color.

4. To change the fill pattern and background color, choose a pattern and color from the Pattern drop-down list (see **Figure 28**).

5. If desired, make additional changes in the Border area of the dialog box. I tell you how on the previous page.

6. When the shape in the Sample area looks just the way you want it to, click OK to apply the formatting.

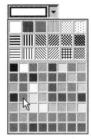

Figure 28.
Use the Fill Pattern drop-down list to choose a pattern and background color for object fill.

✔ Tips

■ To add or change just the fill pattern or background color for a selected object, use the Pattern menu/button on the Drawing toolbar. Click the button to apply the pattern and background color illustrated on it. Click the arrow on the right side of the button to display a menu identical to the Pattern drop-down list in the Format Object dialog box (see **Figure 28**).

■ To remove colors or patterns from the object fill, select the Automatic option button in the Fill area of the Format Object dialog box. This sets the fill to the default color—white.

■ To remove the fill color and pattern from the object, select the None option button in the Fill area of the Format Object dialog box.

Figure 29.
Each object you draw gets its own drawing layer.

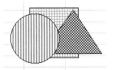

About Stacking Order

Each time you draw a shape, Excel puts it on a new drawing layer. So when you draw a shape that overlaps another shape, the first shape may be partially obscured by the one "on top" of it (see **Figure 29**).

To change stacking order

1. Select the object(s) you want to move to another layer (see **Figure 30a**).

Figure 30a.
Select the object you want to move to another layer…

2. To bring the object(s) to the top layer (see **Figure 30b**), click the Bring to Front button on the Drawing toolbar or choose Bring to Front from the Placement submenu under the Format menu (see **Figure 31**).

or

Figure 30b.
…then click the Bring to Front button…

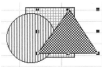

To send the object(s) to the bottom layer (see **Figure 30c**), click the Send to Back button on the Drawing toolbar or choose Send to Back from the Placement submenu under the Format menu (see **Figure 31**).

Figure 30c.
…or click the Send to Back button.

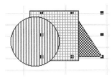

✔ Tips

■ Since there are no commands to move an object one layer at a time, you may need to move more than one object to achieve certain stacking orders.

■ Once you've gotten objects in the order you want, consider grouping them so they stay just the way you want them to. I tell you how to group objects earlier in this chapter.

Figure 31. *If you prefer, use the Bring to Front and Send to Back commands rather than the corresponding toolbar buttons.*

■ You cannot move graphic objects behind the worksheet layer.

About Text Boxes

A text box is like a little word processing document on an Excel sheet. Once created, you can enter and format text within it. Text boxes offer far more flexibility than worksheet cells when entering long passages of text.

To add a text box

1. Click the Text box button on the Drawing or Standard toolbar. The mouse pointer turns into a cross hair pointer.

2. Position the cross hair where you want to begin drawing the text box.

3. Press the mouse button down and drag. As you move the mouse, the text box begins to take form (see **Figure 32a**).

4. Release the mouse button to complete the text box. An insertion point appears within it (see **Figure 32b**).

5. Enter the text you want in the text box (see **Figure 32c**).

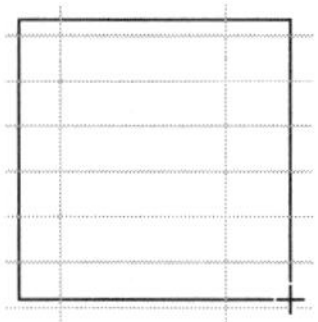

✔ Tips

■ You can move, copy, and resize a text box just like any other object.

■ To edit text in a text box, click on the box to select it, then click inside the text box to position an insertion point or drag over text in the text box to select it. Standard editing techniques apply.

■ To format text in a text box (see **Figure 32d**), select the text you want to change, then use keyboard shortcuts, toolbar buttons, or options in the Format Object dialog box to make the changes. All of these techniques and options are discussed in Chapter 6.

Figure 32a.
Drag with the text box tool to create a text box.

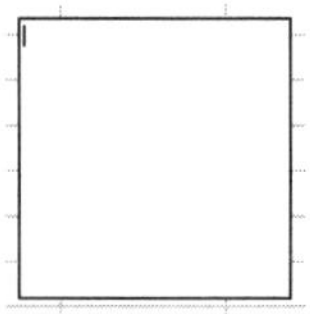

Figure 32b.
When you release the mouse button, an insertion point appears.

Figure 32c.
Enter the text you want in the box.

This is an example of a text box. It's just like a little word processing document!

This is an example of a **TEXT BOX** It's just like a little word processing document!

Figure 32d.
Select and format text as discussed in Chapter 6.

■ To change the border or fill of a text box, click on its border to select it and choose Object from the Format menu or press Control+1. I tell you how to use the Patterns tab options in the Format Object dialog box earlier in this chapter.

About External Graphics

You can add graphics created with other programs to your Excel sheets. You might find this handy if you need to include a company logo or other graphic in a file.

To paste in graphic objects

1. Use the Copy command in Excel or another application to copy the object (see **Figure 33a**).

2. If necessary, switch to the sheet in which you want to place the object.

3. Choose Paste from the Edit menu, press Control+V, or click the Paste button on the Standard toolbar. The object appears. You can drag it into position on the sheet. (see **Figure 33b**).

✔ Tip

■ Once you put a graphic object in an Excel sheet, it can be moved, copied, or resized just like any other graphic object.

Figure 33a.
Here's a company logo created in a drawing program and copied with the Copy command.

ND	ND INDUSTRIES			
	FIRST QUARTER SALES RESULTS			
	Jan	Feb	Mar	Total
Nancy	$ 443	$ 419	$ 841	$ 1,703
Bess	493	277	45	815
George	301	492	179	972
Ned	67	856	842	1,765
Total for all Salespeople	$ 1,304	$ 2,044	$ 1,907	$ 5,255

Figure 33b. *The logo can then be pasted into a worksheet to reinforce corporate identity.*

About Inserting Objects

The Object command on Excel's Insert menu (see **Figure 34a**) lets you *embed* objects created in other Microsoft applications into your Excel sheets. The types of objects you can embed depend on the applications installed in your computer. If you have Microsoft Word, PowerPoint, or Works installed, for example, you can embed objects created with those programs or clip art from the Microsoft ClipArt Gallery.

Figure 34a.
Choose Object from the Insert menu...

Figure 34b.
...choose Microsoft ClipArt Gallery in the Create New tab of the Object dialog box and click OK...

To insert Microsoft ClipArt

1. Choose Object from the Insert menu (see **Figure 34a**).

2. In the Object dialog box that appears, click the Create New tab to display its options (see **Figure 34b**).

3. Choose Microsoft ClipArt Gallery and click OK.

4. In the Microsoft ClipArt Gallery dialog box that appears (see **Figure 34c**), choose a category and then an image to insert in your sheet.

5. Click OK.

   After a moment, the image appears in your worksheet.

✔ Tips

- The Microsoft ClipArt Gallery must be installed in order to use this feature.

- You can move, copy, or resize ClipArt images like any other graphic image.

- ClipArt images are *embedded* into your sheets. This means there's a live link between the sheet and the image file. I tell you about links in Chapter 12.

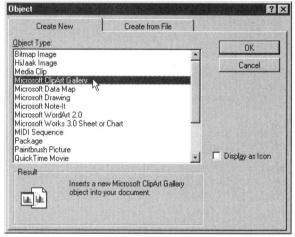

Figure 34c. *...then choose the category and image you want and click OK.*

Inserting ClipArt

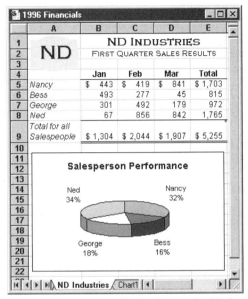

Figure 1. *Here's a 3-D pie chart embedded in a worksheet file.*

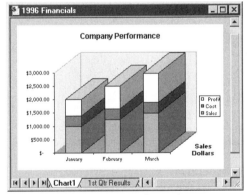

Figure 2. *Here's a 3-D column chart on a chart sheet of its own.*

About Charts

A chart is a graphic representation of data. A chart can be embedded on a worksheet (see **Figure 1**) or can be a chart sheet of its own (see **Figure 2**).

With Excel, you can create a wide variety of different chart types. The 3-D pie chart and 3-D column chart shown here (see **Figures 1** and **2**) are only two examples. Since each type of chart has at least one variation and you can customize any chart you create, there's no limit to the number of ways you can present data graphically with Excel.

✔ Tips

- ■ Include charts with worksheets whenever you want to emphasize worksheet results. Charts can often communicate information like trends and comparitive results better than numbers alone.

- ■ A skilled chartmaker can, through choice of data, chart format, and scale, get a chart to say almost anything about the data it represents!

About the ChartWizard

Excel's ChartWizard walks you step-by-step through the creation of a chart. It uses illustrated dialog boxes to prompt you for information. In the final steps of the ChartWizard, you get to see what your chart looks like. At any point, you can go back and make changes to selections. When you're finished, your chart appears. You can then use a variety of chart formatting commands and buttons to change the look of your chart.

Understanding Charts & the ChartWizard

To embed a chart on a worksheet

1. Select the data you want to chart (see **Figure 3a**). Your selection can include text to use as headings as well as the numbers the chart will represent.

	A	B	C	D	E	F	G
1	ND INDUSTRIES						
2	SALES RESULTS						
3							
4		Jan	Feb	Mar	Apr	May	Jun
5	Nancy	443	419	841	548	684	952
6	Bess	493	277	45	459	368	751
7	George	301	492	179	148	196	325
8	Ned	67	856	842	359	486	843
9	Total	1304	2044	1907	1514	1734	2871

2. Click the ChartWizard button on the Standard toolbar.

or

Figure 3a. *Select the data you want to chart.*

Choose On This Sheet from the Chart submenu under the Insert menu (see **Figure 3b**).

The mouse pointer turns into a cross hair with a chart icon beside it. The cells you selected become surrounded with a marquee. (See **Figure 3c**.)

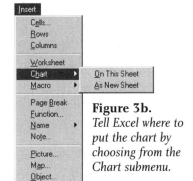

3. Use the mouse pointer to drag a box the size and shape of the chart you want (see **Figure 3d**).

4. Release the mouse pointer. The first dialog box of the ChartWizard appears. Follow the instructions on the next page to use the ChartWizard.

Figure 3b.
Tell Excel where to put the chart by choosing from the Chart submenu.

To insert a chart as a separate sheet

1. Select the data you want to chart (see **Figure 3a**). Your selection can include text to use as headings as well as the numbers the chart will represent.

		Jan	Feb	Mar	Apr	May	Jun
4		Jan	Feb	Mar	Apr	May	Jun
5	Nancy	443	419	841	548	684	952
6	Bess	493	277	45	459	368	751
7	George	301	492	179	148	196	325
8	Ned	67	856	842	359	486	843
9	Total	1304	2044	1907	1514	1734	2871
10							
11		+					
12							

2. Choose As a New Sheet from the Chart submenu under the Insert menu (see **Figure 3b**).

Figure 3c. *The mouse pointer changes and a marquee appears around selected cells.*

Excel inserts a chart sheet in front of the active sheet and displays the first dialog box of the ChartWizard. Follow the instructions on the next page to use the ChartWizard.

Figure 3d. *Drag a box the size and shape of the chart you want.*

To use the ChartWizard

Follow the steps on the previous page to tell Excel where to put the chart and activate the ChartWizard. Then:

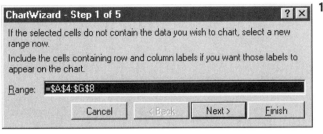

Figure 4a. *In Step 1, select the range(s) you want to chart.*

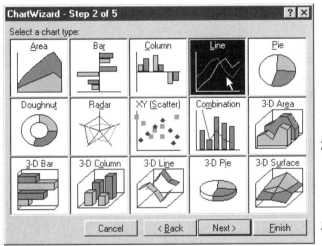

Figure 4b. *In Step 2, select a chart type.*

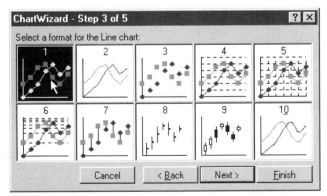

Figure 4c. *In Step 3, select a chart subtype or format.*

1. In the ChartWizard – Step 1 of 5 dialog box (see **Figure 4a**), check the contents of the Range edit box to assure that it indicates the data you want to chart. You can see which data range(s) will be charted by dragging the ChartWizard dialog box aside so you can see the sheet behind it. If incorrect, select the correct range(s). The ChartWizard window remains in the foreground as you make your changes, recording the new range(s) for you. When you're satisfied with your selection, click Next.

2. In the ChartWizard – Step 2 of 5 dialog box (see **Figure 4b**), select one of the 15 chart types by clicking it. Then click Next.

3. In the ChartWizard – Step 3 of 5 dialog box (see **Figure 4c**), select one of the formats for the chart by clicking it. The options offered vary depending on the selection you made in step 2. When you've made your selection, click Next.

Using the ChartWizard

Using the ChartWizard

4. In the ChartWizard – Step 4 of 5 dialog box (see **Figure 4d**), you get your first look at your chart. The options offered vary depending on the selections you made in steps 2 and 3. In **Figure 4d**, for example, I can change the data series and row(s) or column(s) containing text for labels or the chart legend. If I select the Columns option button under Data Series, I completely change the look of the sample chart (see **Figure 4e**). Experiment with the options that appear until the chart looks right, then click Next.

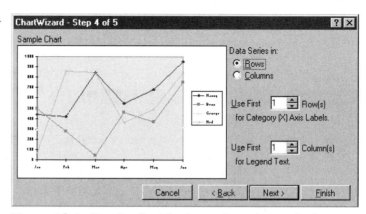

Figure 4d. *In Step 4, adjust the data series and text selections.*

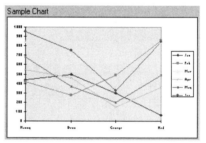

Figure 4e. *As this example illustrates, changing the data series in Step 4 can completely change the chart!*

5. In the ChartWizard – Step 5 of 5 dialog box (see **Figure 4f**), use option buttons to add or remove a chart legend and use text boxes to specify a chart title and axis labels. All of your changes are reflected in the Sample Chart area of the dialog box. When you're done, click Finish.

Excel inserts the chart you created with the ChartWizard's help (see **Figure 5a**).

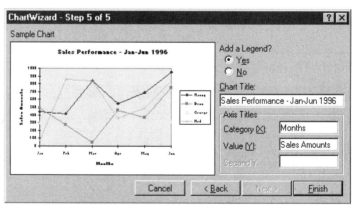

Figure 4f. *In Step 5, add or remove a legend, chart title, and axis labels.*

Selection Handles

Figure 5a. *The completed chart embedded in a worksheet file. If the information is packed so tightly that you can't read it...*

Figure 5b. *...drag one or more of its selection handles to stretch the box containing the chart so everything displays properly.*

✔ Tips

■ At any time while using the Chart-Wizard, you can click the Back button to move to a previous step. Any changes you make in a previous step are carried forward when you continue.

■ If your chart is too small to show everything it needs to display (see **Figure 5a**), you can resize it by dragging one of its selection handles. I tell you how to resize graphics in Chapter 7; resizing a chart works the same way. **Figure 5b** shows the chart from **Figure 5a** resized to display everything properly.

■ A chart is a special kind of graphic. You can move, copy, resize, or delete it just like any other graphic object. I tell you how to work with graphics in Chapter 7.

■ Although Excel will automatically include many formatting options in charts created with the ChartWizard, you can edit, move, format, or delete almost any chart element. I tell you how in Chapter 9.

■ Don't be afraid to experiment with the ChartWizard. Try different options to see what effects you can achieve. You can always delete the chart and start fresh. Deleting the chart does not change the data.

ChartWizard Tips

About Worksheet and Chart Links

When you create a chart based on worksheet data, the worksheet and chart are linked. Excel knows exactly which worksheet and cells it should look at to plot the chart. If the contents of one of those cells changes, the chart changes accordingly (see **Figures 6a** and **6b**).

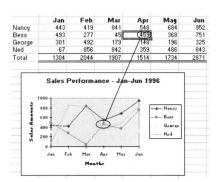

Figures 6a&b. *A linked worksheet and chart before (top) and after (bottom) a change to a cell's contents. When you change one, the other changes automatically.*

✔ Tips

■ The link works both ways. With some chart types, you can drag a data point to change the data in the source worksheet (see **Figure 7**). This makes a good planning tool for businesses interested in maintaining trends.

■ You can see (and edit) the links between a chart and a worksheet by activating the chart, selecting one of the data series, and looking at the formula bar. You should see a formula with a SERIES function that specifies the sheet name and absolute cell references for the range making up that series. **Figures 8a** and **8b** show an example.

■ If you delete worksheet data or an entire worksheet that is linked to a chart, Excel warns you with a dialog box like the one in **Figure 9**. If you removed the data by mistake, immediately choose Undo Delete Cells from the Edit menu, click the Undo button on the Standard toolbar, or press Control+Z to get the deleted data back.

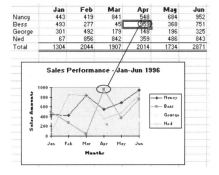

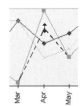

Figure 7. *Dragging a point on a chart also changes the corresponding value in a linked worksheet.*

Selected Series

Figure 8a. *When you select a chart series…*

`=SERIES('Sales Results'!$A$5,'Sales Results'!$B$4:$G$4,'Sales Results'! $B$5:$G$5,1)`

Figure 8b. *…you can see its link in the formula bar.*

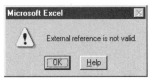

Figure 9. *If you delete data linked to a chart, you may get a warning dialog like this.*

To add or remove chart data with the ChartWizard

1. Activate the chart by switching to its chart sheet or, if it's an embedded chart, double-clicking it.

2. Click the ChartWizard button on the Standard or Chart toolbar.

3. In the ChartWizard – Step 1 of 2 dialog box (see **Figure 10a**), select the range(s) of cells that include all the data you want to chart. Then click Next.

4. In the ChartWizard – Step 2 of 2 dialog box (see **Figure 10b**), make changes as necessary to properly display your data in the Sample Chart area. Then click OK.

The revised chart appears, using the new data range(s) you selected.

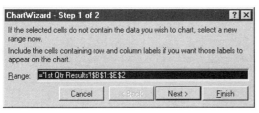

Figure 10a. *Use Step 1 of the ChartWizard to choose the range(s) to chart.*

✔ Tip

■ If all you're doing is adding or removing chart data, you shouldn't need to make any changes in the second step of the ChartWizard dialog box.

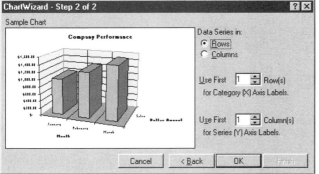

Figure 10b. *Then use Step 2 of the ChartWizard to fine-tune the revised chart if necessary.*

Adding or Removing Chart Data

To add chart data with the Copy and Paste commands

1. In the worksheet, select the data you want to add to the chart (see **Figure 11a**). Be sure to include column or row headings if they should be included as labels.

2. Choose Copy from the Edit menu.

   or

   Press Control+C.

   or

   Click the Copy button on the Standard toolbar.

   A marquee appears around the selected cells.

3. Activate the chart to which you want to add the data.

4. Choose Paste from the Edit menu.

   or

   Press Control+V.

   or

   Click the Paste button on the Standard toolbar.

5. If the Paste Special dialog box appears (see **Figure 11b**), select the option button to specify whether the data should be pasted in as a new series or new data points. Then click OK.

   The chart changes to include the additional data (see **Figure 11c**).

✔ Tip

- In order for this to work properly, the data you add must be the same kind of data originally charted. For example, if you originally plotted totals to create a pie chart, you can't successfully add a series of numbers that aren't totals to the chart.

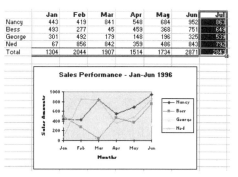

Figure 11a. *Select the range for the data you want to add to the chart and use the Copy command to copy it.*

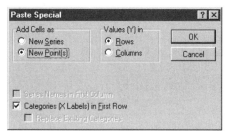

Figure 11b. *If the Paste Special dialog box appears, specify whether the cells should be added as a new series or new data points. Then click OK.*

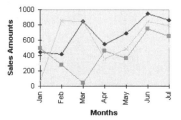

Figure 11c. *When you paste the data into the chart, the chart changes to include it.*

Adding Chart Data with Copy & Paste

To add chart data with drag and drop

1. In the worksheet, select the data you want to add to the chart (see **Figure 11a**). Be sure to include column or row headings if they should be included as labels.

2. Position the mouse pointer on the border of the selection. The mouse pointer turns into an arrow (see **Figure 12a**).

3. Press the mouse button down and drag the selection on top of the chart. The mouse pointer gets a little plus sign next to it and the chart border changes (see **Figure 12b**).

4. Release the mouse button.

   The chart changes to include the additional data (see **Figure 11c**).

✔ Tips

- This technique only works on charts that are embedded in the worksheet containing the original data. To add data from one worksheet to a chart on another, use the ChartWizard or Copy and Paste commands as discussed on the previous two pages.

- To add data contained in noncontiguous ranges, use the New Data command on the Edit menu, use the Copy and Paste commands as discussed on the previous page, or use the ChartWizard to reselect the data range(s) from scratch.

- In order for this technique to work properly, the data you add must be the same kind of data originally charted. For example, if you originally plotted totals to create a pie chart, you can't successfully add a series of numbers that aren't totals to the chart.

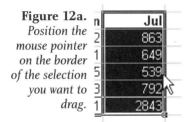

Figure 12a. *Position the mouse pointer on the border of the selection you want to drag.*

Figure 12b. *As you drag cells onto a chart, the mouse pointer changes and a striped border appears around the chart.*

Adding Chart Data with Drag & Drop

To remove a data series

1. Select the series you want to remove (see **Figure 13a**).

2. Choose Series from the Clear submenu under the Edit menu (see **Figure 13b**).

   or

   Press the Del key.

   The series disappears (see **Figure 13c**). If the chart included a legend, it is revised to exclude the deleted data.

✔ Tips

- ▪ Removing a series from a chart does not remove it from the source worksheet. It simply tells Excel that you no longer want it included in the chart.

- ▪ You can also remove a data series by using the ChartWizard to redefine the ranges you want to chart. I tell you how earlier in this chapter.

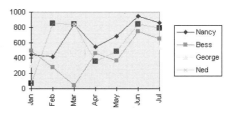

Figure 13a. *Select the series you want to remove…*

Figure 13b. *…then choose Series from the Clear menu under the Edit menu.*

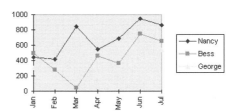

Figure 13c. *The series is removed and the legend (if any) is updated.*

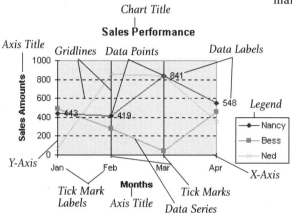

Chart Title

Sales Performance

Axis Title — *Gridlines* — *Data Points* — *Data Labels*

Legend

— Nancy
— Bess
— Ned

Y-Axis

X-Axis

Tick Mark Labels — **Months** — *Tick Marks*

Axis Title — *Data Series*

Figure 1. *The anatomy of a chart.*

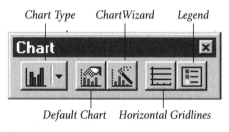

Chart Type — *ChartWizard* — *Legend*

Default Chart — *Horizontal Gridlines*

Figure 2. *The Chart toolbar.*

About Editing and Formatting Charts

Once you've created a chart, you can make a wide variety of changes to it.

- Add, remove, or change the text and formatting of titles and legends.
- Change the color, pattern, and background color of any chart item.
- Change the appearance, tick marks, and scale of axes.
- Move chart items almost anywhere within the chart area.
- Rotate 3-D charts to make charted data easier to view.

Figure 1 identifies most of the chart elements you'll work with.

About the Chart Toolbar

The Chart toolbar (see **Figure 2**) appears automatically whenever a chart is selected. It includes tools you can use to change the appearance of a chart. I tell you about Chart tools throughout this chapter.

✔ Tips

- The Chart toolbar only appears when a chart is selected. As soon as you click on a worksheet cell or switch to a sheet that does not contain a selected chart, the Chart toolbar disappears.
- You can move the Chart toolbar anywhere in the window by dragging its title bar. I tell you more about working with toolbars in Chapter 14.

Understanding Chart Editing & Formatting

About Activating Charts and Selecting Chart Items

To edit or format a chart, you *must* begin by activating it. Once a chart is activated, the chart commands and options are available (see **Figures 3a**, **3b**, **4a**, and **4b**). You can then select and modify various chart items or the entire chart.

To activate a chart

If the chart is embedded in a worksheet, double-click it. A thick, striped border appears around it (see **Figure 5**).

or

If the chart is on a chart sheet, activate it by clicking its sheet tab to display it.

To deactivate a chart

If the chart is embedded in a worksheet, click a worksheet cell. This deactivates the chart. Double-clicking a worksheet cell or pressing Esc several times also deselects the chart.

or

If the chart is on a chart sheet, click a different sheet tab.

To select a chart item

Once a chart has been activated, click on any chart item to select it. The name of the item appears in the name box on the left end of the formula bar.

✔ Tip

- You can often select separate items within groups. For example, if you click a data series, you select the whole series. If you then click one point in the series, you select just that point.

Figure 3a&b. *Here's the Insert menu with a worksheet active (left) and with a chart active (right).*

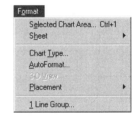

Figure 4a&b. *Here's the Format menu with a worksheet active (left) and with a chart active (right).*

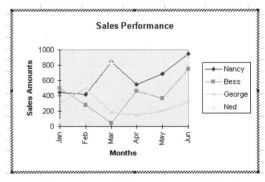

Figure 5. *An embedded chart gets a thick, striped border around it when activated.*

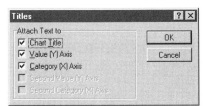

Figure 6. *Use the Titles dialog box to add a chart title or axis titles.*

Figure 7a.
Click the title to select it…

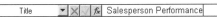

Figure 7b. *…then use standard editing techniques to change the text and click anywhere to accept it.*

Figure 7c. *…or enter new text in the formula bar and press Enter to accept it.*

Figure 8. *Use the All command under the Clear submenu to delete selected chart items like titles.*

To add titles

1. Choose Titles from the Insert menu (see **Figure 3b**).

2. In the Titles dialog box (see **Figure 6**), turn on the check boxes for the kinds of titles you want. The available options vary depending on the type and format of the chart.

3. Click OK.

To edit titles

1. If necessary, click on the title you want to edit to select it. A box with selection handles appears around it (see **Figure 7a**).

2. Click inside the box to position an insertion point or drag over the contents of the box to select all or part of its contents. The box disappears. Make changes using standard editing techniques (see **Figure 7b**). When you're finished, click elsewhere on the chart to accept the changes.

   or

   Enter new text. It appears in the formula bar (see **Figure 7c**) and overwrites the existing title. Press Enter or click the Enter button on the formula bar to accept the changes.

To remove titles

1. Choose Titles from the Insert menu (see **Figure 3b**).

2. In the Titles dialog box (see **Figure 6**), turn off the check boxes for the title(s) you want to remove.

3. Click OK.

   or

1. Select the title you want to remove.

2. Choose All from the Clear submenu under the Edit menu (see **Figure 8**) or press Del.

Adding, Editing, & Removing Titles

About Data Labels

A data label is text or a number that labels a data series. The options are:

- Value displays the number represented in the chart.
- Percent displays the percentage represented in the chart.
- Label displays the name of the item represented in the chart.
- Label and Percent displays both the percentage and label for the item represented in the chart.

✔ Tip

- The available options depend on the type and format of the chart. Percent, for example, is not available with line or bar charts.

To add data labels

1. Choose Data Labels from the Insert menu (see **Figure 3b**).
2. In the Data Labels dialog box (see **Figure 9a**), select the option button for the kind(s) of data labels you want.
3. Click OK.

   The data labels are applied (see **Figure 9b**).

✔ Tips

- To add data labels to only one data series or point (see **Figure 9c**), select that data series or point first. Otherwise, the labels will be applied to all data series in the chart (see **Figure 9b**).
- To display the legend color for the series beside its label, turn on the Show Legend Key next to Label check box in step 2 above.
- To turn off the data labels, select None in the Data Labels dialog box.

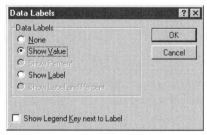

Figure 9a. *Use the Data Labels dialog box to choose a type of data label.*

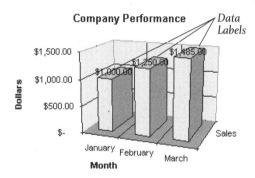

Figure 9b. *This chart has value data labels on all data series…*

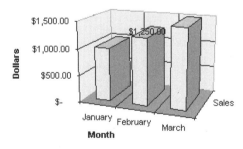

Figure 9c. *…while this chart has value data labels on only one data series.*

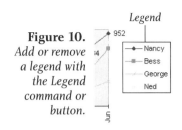

Figure 10.
Add or remove a legend with the Legend command or button.

To add a legend

Choose Legend from the Insert menu (see **Figure 3b**).

or

Click the Legend button on the Chart toolbar.

The legend appears (see **Figure 10**).

To remove a legend

Click the Legend button on the Chart toolbar.

or

Click the legend once to select it and choose All from the Clear submenu under the Edit menu (see **Figure 8**) or press Del.

✔ Tip

■ The Legend button on the chart toolbar looks pushed in when turned on.

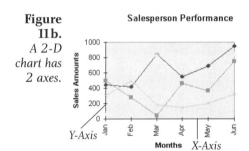

Figure 11a.
A 3-D chart has 3 axes.

About Axes

Most kinds of charts use two or three axes to plot the values (see **Figures 11a** and **11b**). Excel lets you decide which axes should display on your chart.

✔ Tip

■ Axes options depend on the type and format of the chart. Pie charts, for example, do not have axes.

Figure 11b.
A 2-D chart has 2 axes.

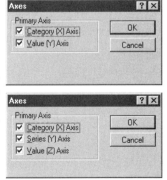

Figures 12a&b.
The Axes dialog box displays different options for 2-D (top) and 3-D (bottom) charts.

To add or remove axes

1. Choose Axes from the Insert menu (see **Figure 3b**).

2. In the Axes dialog box (see **Figures 12a** and **12b**), turn on the check box for the axis you want to display and turn off the check box for the axis you don't want to display.

3. Click OK.

Adding & Removing Legends & Axes

About Gridlines

Gridlines are solid, dashed, or dotted lines on the plot area of a chart. They help chart viewers follow the lines for values and labels. **Figures 13a, 13b,** and **13c** show examples of a chart with various gridline options turned on or off.

✔ Tip

■ Gridlines options depend on the type and format of the chart. Pie charts, for example, do not have gridlines.

To add or remove gridlines

1. Choose Gridlines from the Insert menu (see **Figure 3b**).

2. In the Gridlines dialog box (see **Figures 14a** and **14b**), turn on the check boxes for the kinds of gridlines you want to display and turn off the check boxes for the kinds of gridlines you don't want to display.

3. Click OK.

or

To turn only major horizontal gridlines on or off, click the Horizontal Gridlines button on the Chart toolbar.

✔ Tips

■ If you want to use both major and minor gridlines, format the lines differently. I tell you how to format gridlines later in this chapter.

■ The Horizontal Gridlines button on the Chart toolbar looks pushed in when turned on.

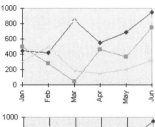

Figure 13a.
A chart with gridlines turned off.

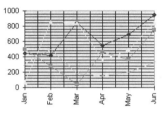

Figure 13b.
A chart with only major gridlines (on both axes) turned on.

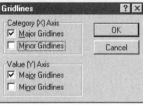

Figure 13c.
A chart with both major and minor gridlines (on both axes) turned on.

Figures 14a&b.
The Gridlines dialog box offers different options for 2-D (top) and 3-D (bottom) charts.

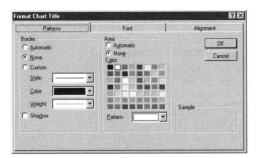

Figure 15. *The Format Chart Title and Format Axis Title dialog boxes let you format title text and the area around it.*

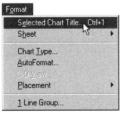

Figure 16a. *Select the title you want to format...*

Figures 16b&c.
...then choose Selected Chart Title or Selected Axis Title from the Format menu. (The command name changes depending on what's selected.)

About Formatting Titles

The Format Chart Title dialog box (see **Figure 15**) lets you format chart titles in the following ways:

■ Use the Patterns tab to add, remove, or format borders around titles and the area containing the title text.

■ Use the Font tab to change the font, size, style, and color of title text.

■ Use the Alignment tab to change the alignment and orientation of title text.

As you may have guessed, these tabs are almost identical to the ones I tell you about in Chapter 6, so if you need help using them, check the information I provide there.

To format titles

1. Select the title you want to format (see **Figure 16a**) and choose Selected Chart Title or Selected Axis Title from the Format menu (see **Figures 16b** and **16c**).

   or

   Double-click the border of the title you want to format.

2. In the Format Chart Title (see **Figure 15**) or Format Axis Title dialog box that appears, choose the tab corresponding to the type of formatting you want to do.

3. When you're finished making changes in the dialog box, click OK to accept them.

✔ Tip

■ You can also use buttons on the Formatting toolbar to format selected titles. I tell you how to use them in Chapter 6, too.

Formatting Titles

About Formatting Data Labels

The Format Data Labels dialog box (see **Figure 17**) lets you format data labels in the following ways:

■ Use the Patterns tab to add, remove, or format borders around data labels and the area around data label text.

■ Use the Font tab to change the font, size, style, and color of data label text.

■ Use the Number tab to change the number formatting of data label values.

■ Use the Alignment tab to change the alignment and orientation of data label text.

These tabs are almost identical to the ones I tell you about in Chapter 6, so if you need help using them, check the information I provide there.

To format data labels

1. Select the data label(s) you want to format (see **Figure 18a** and **18b**) and choose Selected Data Labels (see **Figure 18c**) from the Format menu.

   or

   Double-click one data label in the series you want to format.

2. In the Format Data Labels dialog box (see **Figure 17**), choose the tab corresponding to the type of formatting you want to do.

3. When you're finished making changes in the dialog box, click OK to accept them.

✔ Tip

■ You can also use buttons on the Formatting toolbar to format selected data labels. I tell you how to use them in Chapter 6, too.

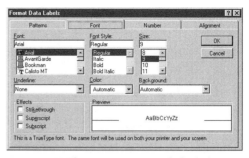

Figure 17. *The Format Data Labels dialog box lets you format data labels and the area around them.*

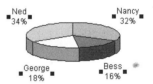

Figure 18a. *Select the data labels you want to format…*

Figure 18b. *…or one of the data labels in a data series…*

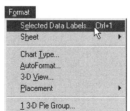

Figure 18c. *…and choose Selected Data Labels from the Format menu.*

Formatting Data Labels

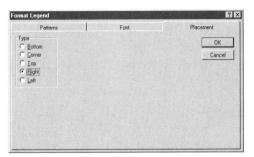

Figure 19. *The Format Legend dialog box lets you format the borders, fill, font, and placement of a legend.*

Figure 20. *The Bottom option changes the position and shape of the legend.*

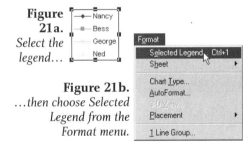

Figure 21a. *Select the legend...*

Figure 21b. *...then choose Selected Legend from the Format menu.*

Figure 22. *You can also reposition a legend by dragging it.*

✔ Tips

■ You can also use buttons on the Formatting toolbar to format the borders, fill, and text of a legend. I tell you how to use them in Chapter 6.

About Formatting Legends

The Format Legend dialog box (see **Figure 19**) lets you format legends in the following ways:

■ Use the Patterns tab to add, remove, or format borders around a legend and the area around legend text.

■ Use the Font tab to change the font, size, style, and color of legend text.

■ Use the Placement tab to change the positioning of a legend.

The Patterns and Font tabs are almost identical to the ones I tell you about in Chapter 6, so if you need help using them, check the information I provide there.

The Placement tab (see **Figure 19**), offers five options for positioning the legend in relation to the chart area. Select the option button for the option you want. **Figure 20** shows an example of a legend with the Bottom option button selected.

To format a legend

1. Select the legend (see **Figure 21a**) and choose Selected Legend (see **Figure 21b**) from the Format menu.

    or

    Double-click the legend.

2. In the Format Legend dialog box (see **Figure 19**), choose the tab corresponding to the type of formatting you want to do.

3. When you're finished making changes in the dialog box, click OK to accept them.

■ You can also change the placement of a legend by dragging it into a new position (see **Figure 22**). This is not the same as using options in the Placement tab.

About Formatting Axes

The Format Axis dialog box (see **Figures 23**, **28a**, and **28b**) lets you format axes in the following ways:

- Use the Patterns tab to change the appearance of the axis and its tick marks and tick mark labels.

- Use the Scale tab to change the scale or units for the axis.

- Use the Font tab to change the font, size, style, and color of axis tick mark text.

- Use the Number tab to change the number formatting of axis tick mark value text.

- Use the Alignment tab to change the alignment of axis tick mark text.

The Font, Number, and Alignment tabs are almost identical to the ones I tell you about in Chapter 6, so if you need help using them, check the information I provide there. I tell you about the Patterns and Scale tabs on the next two pages.

To format an axis

1. Select the axis you want to format (see **Figure 24a**) and choose Selected Axis (see **Figure 24b**) from the Format menu.

   or

   Double-click the axis.

2. In the Format Axis dialog box (see **Figures 23**, **28a**, and **28b**), choose the tab corresponding to the type of formatting you want to do.

3. When you're finished making changes in the dialog box, click OK to accept them.

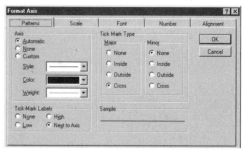

Figure 23. *The Patterns tab of the Format Axis dialog box is just one of five formatting tabs.*

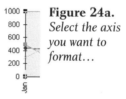

Figure 24a.
Select the axis you want to format…

Figure 24b.
…then choose Selected Axis from the Format menu.

✔ Tip

- You can also use buttons on the Formatting toolbar to format the text of axis tick marks. I tell you how to use them in Chapter 6.

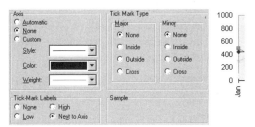

Figure 25a&b. *This example takes the standard settings and removes the axis line.*

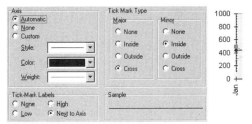

Figure 26a&b. *This example adds minor tick marks.*

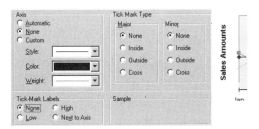

Figure 27a&b. *This example, for minimalists, removes tick marks, tick mark labels, and the axis line.*

To change the appearance of an axis and its tick marks

1. Select the axis you want to format (see **Figure 24a**) and choose Selected Axis (see **Figure 24b**) from the Format menu.

   or

   Double-click the axis.

2. In the Format Axis dialog box, click the Patterns tab (see **Figure 23**).

3. To change the appearance of the axis line, choose options from the Style, Color, and Weight drop-down lists. These lists are identical to the ones in the Patterns tab of the Format Cells dialog box. I tell you about that in Chapter 6.

4. To change the positioning of the tick mark labels in relation to the tick marks, select one of the option buttons in the Tick-Mark Labels area.

5. To change the positioning of the major and minor tick marks in relation to the axis, select option buttons in the Major and Minor areas.

6. When you're finished making changes, click OK.

Figures 25a&b, **26a&b**, and **27a&b** show examples of some of the effects you can achieve with the Patterns tab of the Format Axis dialog box.

To change the axis scale

1. Select the axis whose scale you want to change (see **Figure 24a**) and choose Selected Axis (see **Figure 24b**) from the Format menu.

   or

   Double-click the axis.

2. In the Format Axis dialog box, click the Scale tab (see **Figures 28a** and **28b**).

3. Enter values in the text boxes for the scale elements you want to change. These elements vary depending on whether the axis is a value axis (see **Figure 28a**) or a category axis (see **Figure 28b**). To have Excel automatically assign values for any of these elements, turn on its Auto check box.

4. If desired, turn on check boxes for additional scale-related options at the bottom of the dialog box. These options will affect the tick marks and axis position.

5. When you're finished making changes, click OK.

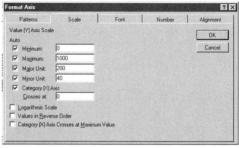

Figure 28a. *The Scale tab offers value-related options for value axes…*

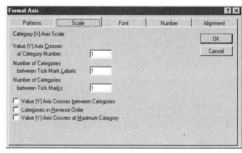

Figure 28b. *…and category-related options for category axes.*

✔ Tips

■ To make results look more dramatic, set the minimum and maximum values the same as the minimum and maximum values of the data. **Figures 29a** and **29b** show a before and after example.

■ You can make results look even more dramatic by stretching the chart so it's long and narrow. **Figure 29c** shows an example.

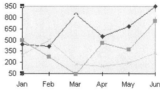

Figure 29b. *Changing the scale makes the lines a little steeper.*

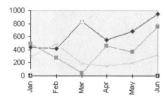

Figure 29a. *Here's a chart with automatic scale options set.*

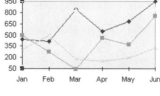

Figure 29c. *Stretching the chart makes the lines even steeper!*

Changing Axis Scale

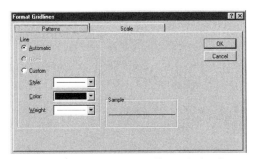

Figure 30. *The Format Gridlines dialog box lets you change the look and the scale of gridlines.*

About Formatting Gridlines

The Format Gridlines dialog box (see **Figure 30**) lets you format gridlines in the following ways:

- Use the Patterns tab to change the appearance of the gridlines.

- Use the Scale tab to change the scale or units for the gridlines.

The Patterns tab (see **Figure 30**) is an abbreviated version of the Patterns tab in the Format Axis dialog box. The Line options are the same as the Axis options. I tell you about them earlier in this chapter. The Scale tab is identical to the Scale tab for the Format Axis dialog box. I tell you about that on the previous page.

To format gridlines

1. Select one of the major or minor horizontal or vertical gridlines you want to format (see **Figure 31a**) and choose Selected Gridlines (see **Figure 31b**) from the Format menu.

    or

    Double-click the gridline.

2. In the Format Gridlines dialog box (see **Figure 30**), choose the tab corresponding to the type of formatting you want to do.

3. When you're finished making changes in the dialog box, click OK to accept them.

✔ Tip

- While gridlines can make it easier to read a chart, they can also obscure it. Formatting gridlines as dotted, dashed, or lightly colored lines can prevent them from cluttering the chart with lines and overpowering other chart elements.

Figure 31a. *Select a horizontal or vertical gridline…*

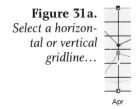

Figure 31b. *…then choose Selected Gridlines from the Format menu.*

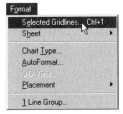

Formatting Gridlines

About Formatting the Chart Area

The *chart area* is the area around the chart. The Format Chart Area dialog box (see **Figure 32**) lets you format the chart area in the following ways:

■ Use the Patterns tab to change the appearance of the border and fill for the chart area.

■ Use the Font tab to change the font, size, and style for chart text.

These two tabs are almost identical to the ones I tell you about in Chapter 6, so if you need additional help using them, check the information I provide there.

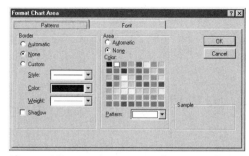

Figure 32. *Use the Format Chart Area dialog box to change the border, fill, and font formatting of the area around a chart.*

To format the chart area

1. Select the chart area (see **Figure 33a**) and choose Selected Chart Area (see **Figure 33b**) from the Format menu.

   or

   Double-click the chart area.

2. In the Format Chart Area dialog box (see **Figure 32**), choose the tab corresponding to the type of formatting you want to do.

3. When you're finished making changes in the dialog box, click OK to accept them.

✔ Tips

■ If you decide to use a fill color or pattern in the chart area, choose a color or pattern that contrasts with the chart elements that will appear against it.

■ To add floating text to the chart area, activate the chart, make sure the formula area of the formula bar is empty, and type in the text you want. You can then drag the text anywhere within the chart area.

Figure 33a. *Select the chart area...*

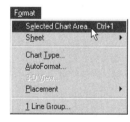

Figure 33b. *...then choose Selected Chart Area from the Format menu.*

(vertical sidebar) Formatting the Chart Area

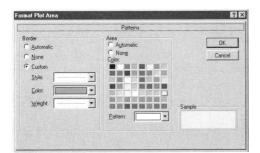

Figure 34. *Use the Format Plot Area dialog box to change the border, color, and pattern of the area between chart axes. For 3-D charts, use the Format Chart Walls dialog box, which is identical (except for title bar name) to this one.*

Figures 35a&b. *Select the plot area on a 2-D chart (top) or select the chart walls on a 3-D chart (bottom)…*

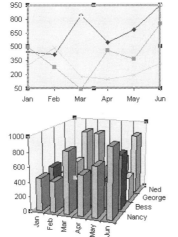

Figure 35c&d. *…then choose Selected Plot Area or Selected Walls from the Format menu.*

About Formatting the Plot Area and Chart Walls

The *plot area* is the area within the axes of the chart. In a 3-D chart, this area is referred to as the *chart walls*.

The Format Plot Area (see **Figure 34**) and Format Chart Walls dialog boxes let you change the border, fill, and pattern for the plot area and chart walls. These two dialog boxes are identical and offer the same options you'll find in the Patterns tab of dialog boxes I tell you about earlier in this chapter and in Chapter 6. If you need additional help using them, check the information I provide there.

To format the plot area or chart walls

1. Select the plot area (see **Figure 35a**) or chart walls (see **Figure 35b**) and choose Selected Plot Area (see **Figure 35c**) or Selected Walls (see **Figure 35d**) from the Format menu.

   or

   Double-click the plot area or a chart wall.

2. In the Format Plot Area (see **Figure 34**) or Format Chart Walls dialog box, make changes in the Borders and Area sections.

3. Click OK to accept your changes.

✔ Tip

- If you decide to use a fill color or pattern in the plot area or chart walls, choose a color or pattern that contrasts with the chart elements that will appear against it.

Formatting the Plot Area & Chart Walls

About Formatting a Data Series or Data Point

A *data series* is a group of numbers plotted on a chart. A *data point* is one number plotted on a chart. Some charts, like pie charts, have only one data series. Other charts, like line and column charts, can have multiple data series. Most charts have multiple data points.

The Format Data Series (see **Figure 36**) and Format Data Point (see **Figure 39**) dialog boxes let you change a wide variety of options for a data series or data point. The options offered vary depending on the type and format of the chart. Some of these options are for advanced chartmakers and beyond the scope of this book. Others can be accomplished with other methods discussed elsewhere in this book.

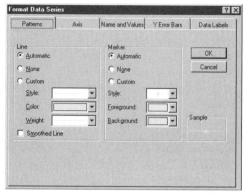

Figure 36. *Use the Format Data Series dialog box to make a wide variety of changes to a data series.*

To change the appearance of lines and markers

1. Select the data series for the line you want to format (see **Figure 37a**) and choose Selected Data Series (see **Figure 37b**) from the Format menu.

   or

   Double-click the data series you want to format.

2. In the Format Data Series dialog box (see **Figure 36**), click the Patterns tab to display its options.

3. Make selections in the Line area to change the Style (shape), Color, and Weight of the line.

4. Make selections in the Marker area to change the Style, Foreground Color, and Background Color of the marker.

5. Click OK to accept your changes.

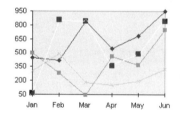

Figure 37a. *Select the data series for the line you want to change...*

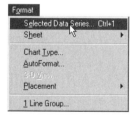

Figure 37b. *...then choose Selected Data Series from the Format menu.*

✔ Tip

■ If you change the color of a line, choose a color that will stand out against the color of the plot area.

Figure 38a. *Select the data point for the bar, column, or pie slice you want to change...*

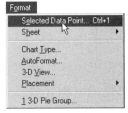

Figure 38b. *...then choose Selected Data Point from the Format Menu.*

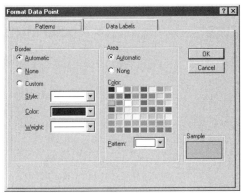

Figure 39. *The Patterns tab of the Format Data Point dialog box lets you change the appearance of a single data point.*

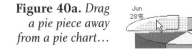

Figure 40a. *Drag a pie piece away from a pie chart...*

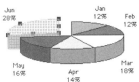

Figure 40b. *...for an "exploded" pie chart effect.*

To change the appearance of bars, columns, or pie slices

1. Select the data point for the bar, column, or pie slice you want to format (see **Figure 38a**) and choose Selected Data Point (see **Figure 38b**) from the Format menu.

    or

    Select and then double-click the data point you want to format.

2. In the Format Data Point dialog box (see **Figure 39**), click the Patterns tab to display its options.

3. Make selections in the Border section to change the style, color, and weight of the border.

4. Make selections in the Area section to change the color, pattern, and background color of the bar, column, or pie slice.

5. Click OK to accept your changes.

✔ Tip

■ If you change the color of a bar, column, or pie slice, choose a color that will stand out against the color of the plot area or chart walls.

To "explode" a pie chart

1. Select the data point for the pie piece you want to move.

2. Drag the pie piece away from the pie (see **Figure 40a**).

When you release the mouse button, the piece moves away from the pie and the pie gets smaller (see **Figure 40b**).

✔ Tip

■ The farther away you move the pie piece, the smaller the pie gets.

To rotate a 3-D chart

1. Activate the chart you want to rotate (see **Figure 41a**).

2. Choose 3-D View from the Format menu (see **Figure 41b**).

3. In the Format 3-D View dialog box (see **Figure 41c**), click the Elevation and Rotation buttons to change the perspective and rotate the chart.

4. When you're finished making changes, click OK to apply them (see **Figure 41d**) and close the dialog box.

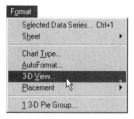

Figure 41a. *Start by selecting a 3-D chart...*

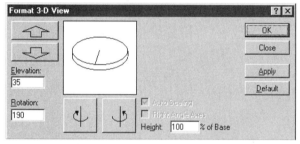

Figure 41b. *...choose 3-D View from the Format menu...*

✔ Tips

- You can click the Apply button in the Format 3-D View dialog box (see **Figure 41c**) to get a first-hand look at the modified chart without closing the dialog box. You may have to drag the Format 3-D View dialog box out of the way to see your chart.

- Some changes in the Format 3-D View dialog box will change the size of the chart.

Figure 41c. *...make changes like these in the Format 3-D View dialog box.*

To move a chart item

1. With the chart activated, select the chart item you want to move.

2. Position the mouse pointer on the border of the item, press the mouse button down, and drag the item (see **Figure 42**) to a new position.

   When you release the mouse button, the item moves.

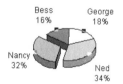

Figure 41d. *...and you'll end up with a modified 3-D chart like this.*

Figure 42. *To move a chart item, simply drag it to a new position.*

To change the chart type

1. Activate the chart you want to change.

2. Choose Chart Type from the Format menu (see **Figure 43a**).

3. In the Chart Type dialog box (see **Figure 43b**), select a Chart Dimension option button for the kind of chart you want. Then select the icon representing the chart type and click OK.

or

1. Activate the chart you want to change.

2. Click the arrow on the right side of the Chart Type button on the Chart toolbar to display a menu of chart types (see **Figure 44**) and choose the one you want.

The chart changes immediately to an unformatted chart of the type you chose.

Figure 43a. *Choose Chart Type from the Format menu.*

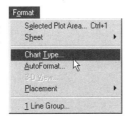

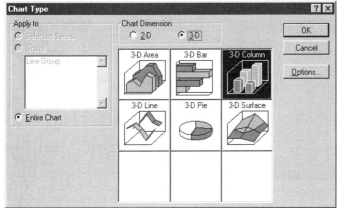

Figure 43b. *Use the Chart Type dialog box to choose the Chart Dimension and new chart type for the selected chart.*

Figure 44. *Or use the Chart Type menu on the Chart toolbar to select a new chart type.*

✔ Tips

■ To change to the default chart type, click the Default Chart button on the Chart toolbar.

■ To apply the chart type illustrated on the Chart Type button on the Chart toolbar, click the button.

Changing the Chart Type

To Use AutoFormat

1. Activate the chart you want to change.

2. Choose AutoFormat from the Format menu (see **Figure 45a**).

3. In the AutoFormat dialog box (see **Figure 45b**), select a chart type from the Galleries list box. Then choose a Format by clicking on a format illustration.

4. Click OK to apply the format.

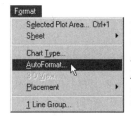

Figure 45a. *Choose AutoFormat from the Format dialog box…*

✔ Tip

■ You can use the AutoFormat dialog box to create your own custom formats. Select the User-Defined option button to display a list of your formats, then click the Customize button. Use the dialog box that appears to add the format of the active chart or delete formats you've already added.

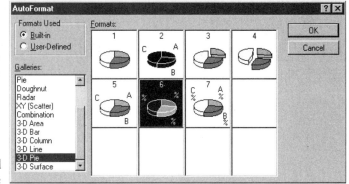

Figure 45b. *…then choose a chart type and format to apply.*

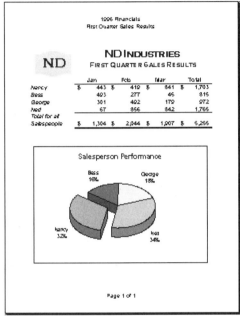

Figure 1. *Print Preview lets you see your reports before you commit them to paper.*

About Printing

In most cases, when you create a worksheet or chart, you'll want to print it. With Excel, you can print all or part of a sheet, multiple sheets, or an entire workbook—all at once. Excel gives you control over page size, margins, headers, footers, page breaks, orientation, scaling, page order, and content. Its Print Preview feature (see **Figure 1**) shows you what your report will look like when printed, so you can avoid wasteful, time consuming reprints.

Printing is basically a four-step process:

1. Prepare the report for printing by setting page breaks and selecting print ranges. You can skip this step if you don't need to insert manual page breaks or specify a print range.

2. Use the Page Setup dialog box to set up your report for printing. You can skip this step if you set the report up the last time you printed it and don't need to change the setup.

3. Use the Print Preview feature to take a look at your report before committing it to paper. You can skip this step if you already know what the report will look like.

4. Use the Print command to send the desired number of copies to the printer for printing.

✔ Tip

■ Before you can print a document from any Windows 95 application, you must set up your printer. This chapter assumes you have already done this. If you haven't, consult the documentation that came with Windows 95 for instructions.

Understanding Printing

About the Page Setup dialog box

The Page Setup dialog box (see **Figure 2**) lets you set up a document for printing. Setup options are organized under the following tabs:

- Page (see **Figure 2**) lets you set the orientation, scaling, paper size, print quality, and first page number.

- Margins lets you set the page margins, the distance the header and footer should be from the edge of the paper, and the positioning of the sheet on the paper.

- Header/Footer lets you select a standard header and footer or create custom ones.

- Sheet lets you specify the print area, print titles, items to print, and page order. If a chart sheet is active when you choose Page Setup, you'll see a Chart tab (see **Figure 8**) rather than a Sheet tab. Use it to specify the printed chart size and print quality.

✔ Tip

- The Options button in the Page Setup dialog box opens the Properties dialog box for your default printer (see **Figure 3**). The options in this dialog box vary depending on your printer and its capabilities. Normally, you won't have to change any of these options to print Excel sheets.

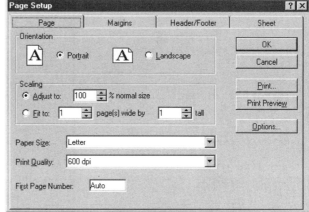

Figure 2. *The Page tab is only one of four tabs in the Page Setup dialog box, which you use to set up your sheets and charts for printing.*

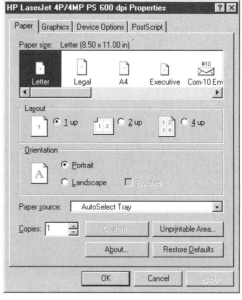

Figure 3. *The Printer Properties dialog box lets you set specific options for your printer.*

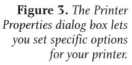

Understanding Page Setup Options

Figure 4.
*Choose
Page Setup
from the
File menu.*

Figure 5. *The Paper Size drop-
down list lets you select from
among all the paper sizes supported by your printer.*

Figure 6. *Use the Orientation area of the Page
Setup dialog box to choose Portrait or
Landscape orientation.*

To set the paper size

1. Choose Page Setup from the File menu (see **Figure 4**). The Page Setup dialog box appears.
2. If necessary, click the Page tab to display its options (see **Figure 2**).
3. Choose a paper size from the Paper Size drop-down list (see **Figure 5**).
4. Click OK.

✔ Tips

■ The Paper Size drop-down list will include all paper sizes supported by your printer.

■ If you prefer, you can change this option in the Printer Properties dialog box (see **Figure 3**). If you do, it will automatically change in the Page Setup dialog box.

To set the page orientation

1. Choose Page Setup from the File menu (see **Figure 4**).
2. If necessary, click the Page tab to display its options (see **Figure 2**).
3. In the Orientation area (see **Figure 6**), select the option button for Portrait or Landscape.
4. Click OK.

✔ Tip

■ If you prefer, you can change this option in the Printer Properties dialog box (see **Figure 3**). If you do, it will automatically change in the Page Setup dialog box.

Setting Paper Size & Orientation

To reduce or enlarge a worksheet report

1. Choose Page Setup from the File menu (see **Figure 4**).

2. If necessary, click the Page tab to display its options (see **Figure 2**).

3. To reduce or enlarge a report by a certain percentage, select the Adjust to option button and enter a value between 10 and 400 in the text box beside it (see **Figure 7a**).

    or

    To force a long report to fit on a certain number of pages, select the Fit To option button and enter the number of pages you want it to fit on in the text boxes beside it (see **Figure 7a**).

4. Click OK.

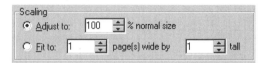

Figure 7a&b. *The Scaling area on the Page tab for a worksheet (top) and for a chart sheet (bottom).*

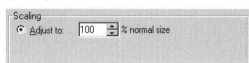

✔ Tip

■   Both scaling options size your report proportionally, so you don't have to worry about stretched text or charts.

To reduce or enlarge a chart

1. Choose Page Setup from the File menu (see **Figure 4**).

2. If necessary, click the Chart tab to display its options (see **Figure 8**).

3. Choose the option button under Printed Chart Size for the scaling you want. If you choose Custom, you must enter a value between 10 and 400 in the Adjust to text box on the Page tab (see **Figure 7b**).

4. Click OK.

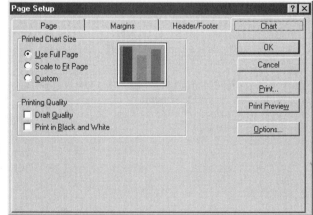

Figure 8. *The Chart tab of the Page Setup dialog box lets you set the size of the printed chart.*

Scaling a Report or Chart

To set margins in the Page Setup dialog box

1. Choose Page Setup from the File menu (see **Figure 4**).

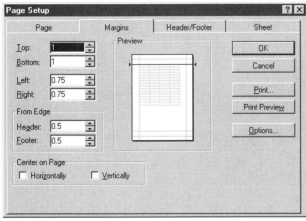

2. If necessary, click the Margins tab to display its options (see **Figure 9**).

3. Enter margin measurements in the Top, Bottom, Left, and Right text boxes.

4. Click OK.

Figure 9. *The Margins tab of the Page Setup dialog box lets you set margins, header and footer locations, and page position.*

✔ Tips

- If a chart sheet rather than a worksheet is active, the preview area displays a chart (see **Figure 10**).

- You can also set margins in the Print Preview window. I tell you how later in this chapter.

- To center the report horizontally or vertically on the page, turn on the Horizontally and/or Vertically check boxes in the Center on Page area of the Margins tab (see **Figure 9**). The preview area picture changes accordingly (see **Figure 11**).

- Do not set margins to smaller values than the Header and Footer values or Excel will print your report over the header or footer.

- Some printers cannot print close to the edge of the paper. If part of your report is cut off when printed, increase your margins.

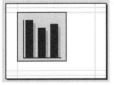

Figure 10. *The preview area of the Margins tab when a chart sheet is active.*

Figure 11. *If you turn on the Horizontally and Vertically check boxes in the Center on Page area, the preview illustration shows the report centered on the page.*

About Page Breaks

Page Break

When you make changes in the Page Setup dialog box, Excel recalculates page breaks. It displays page breaks as dashed lines between columns and rows (see **Figure 12**). Page breaks between columns are often called *vertical* page breaks while page breaks between rows are called *horizontal* page breaks.

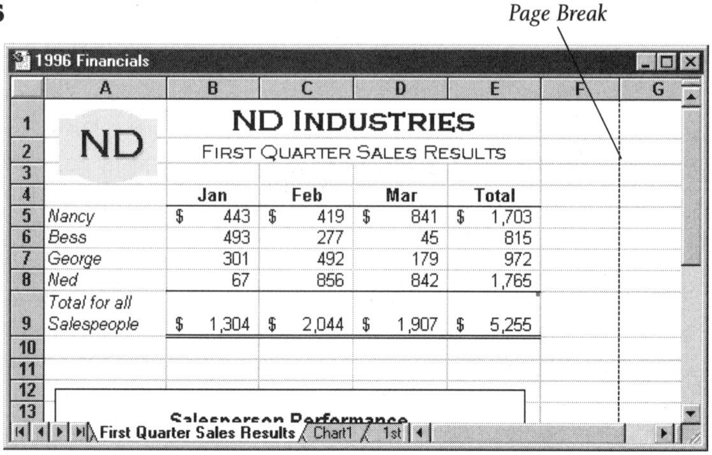

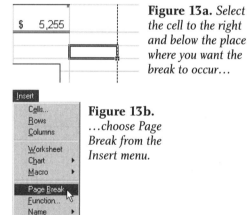

Figure 12. *Excel automatically calculates and displays page breaks.*

You can override Excel's automatic page breaks by inserting manual page breaks.

To insert a page break

1. Select the cell immediately to the right of and immediately below the place you want the break to occur (see **Figure 13a**).

2. Choose Page Break from the Insert menu (see **Figure 13b**).

A manual page break appears to the left of or above the selected cell (see **Figure 13c**) and any automatic page breaks nearby may disappear.

✔ Tips

■ You can insert both a horizontal and a vertical page break at the same time by selecting the cell at the intersection of where you want the breaks to occur (see **Figure 13a** and **13c**).

■ Excel ignores manual page breaks when you use the Fit to option on the Page tab of the Page Setup dialog box. I tell you about the Fit to feature earlier in this chapter.

Figure 13a. *Select the cell to the right and below the place where you want the break to occur...*

Figure 13b. *...choose Page Break from the Insert menu.*

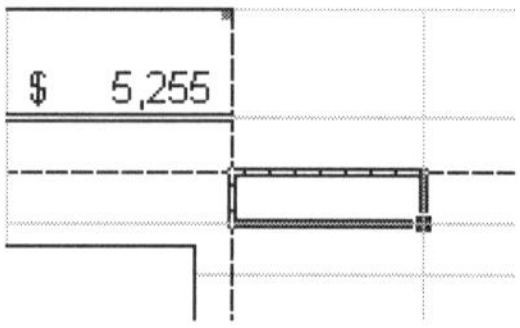

Figure 13c. *The manual page break appears.*

Setting Page Breaks

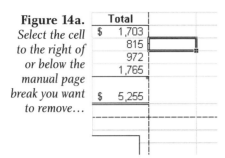

Figure 14a.
Select the cell to the right of or below the manual page break you want to remove…

Total	
$	1,703
	815
	972
	1,765
$	5,255

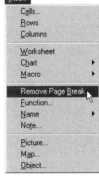

Figure 14b.
…then choose Remove Page Break from the Insert menu.

Insert
- Cells...
- Rows
- Columns
- Worksheet
- Chart ▶
- Macro ▶
- Remove Page Break
- Function...
- Name ▶
- Note...
- Picture...
- Map...
- Object...

Figure 14c.
The page break disappears and an automatic page break (if necessary) appears nearby.

Total	
$	1,703
	815
	972
	1,765
$	5,255

Manual Page Break

Automatic Page Break

To remove a page break

1. Select the cell immediately to the right of or immediately below the manual page break (see **Figure 14a**).

2. Choose Remove Page Break from the Insert menu (see **Figure 14b**).

The manual page break disappears and an automatic page break (if required) may appear nearby (see **Figure 14c**).

✔ Tips

- You can use the Remove Page Break command (see **Figure 14b**) to remove manual page breaks only.

- If you try to remove a manual page break and the Remove Page Break command doesn't appear on the Insert menu (see **Figure 14b**), you either have the wrong cell selected or the page break is an automatic page break.

- You can remove both horizontal and vertical page breaks at the same time by selecting the cell at the intersection of the two page breaks (see **Figure 13c**).

- To remove all manual page breaks in a worksheet, select the entire worksheet and choose Remove Page Break from the Insert menu (see **Figure 14b**).

- If you have sharp eyes, you can see the difference between a manual and an automatic page break: The manual page break has longer dashes. **Figure 14c** shows a manual horizontal page break and an automatic vertical page break. Can you see the difference?

Removing Page Breaks

About Headers and Footers

A *header* is text that appears at the top of every page. A *footer* is text that appears at the bottom of every page. **Figure 15** shows an example of a page with both a header and footer.

Excel lets you set the distance from the header and the footer to the edge of the paper, as well as the contents of the header and footer.

To set header and footer locations

1. Choose Page Setup from the File menu (see **Figure 4**).

2. If necessary, click the Margins tab to display its options (see **Figure 9**).

3. Enter a value in the Header and Footer text boxes (see **Figure 16**) to position the header and footer in relation to the edge of the paper.

4. Click OK.

✔ Tips

■ You can also set header and footer locations in the Print Preview window. I tell you how later in this chapter.

■ Do not set the Header and Footer values larger than the margin values or Excel will print your report on top of the header or footer.

■ Some printers cannot print close to the edge of the paper. If your header or footer is cut off when printed, increase the values in the Header and Footer text boxes in step 3 above.

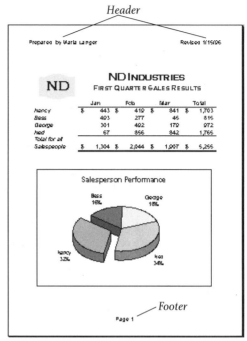

Figure 15. *A page with both a header and a footer.*

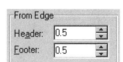

Figure 16. *Enter new values in the Header and Footer edit boxes to specify the distance from the top of the header and the bottom of the footer to the edge of the page.*

To use built-in headers and footers

1. Choose Page Setup from the File menu (see **Figure 4**).

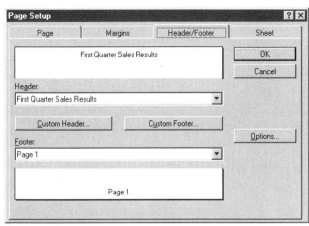

Figure 17. *The Header/Footer tab of the Page Setup dialog box lets you set the contents and formatting of the header and footer.*

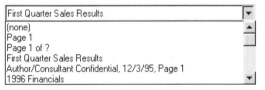

Figure 18. *Excel's built-in headers and footers offer many useful options, some of which include your name and company name (or title, in my case).*

2. If necessary, click the Header/Footer tab to display its options (see **Figure 17**).

3. Choose an option from the Header drop-down list (see **Figure 18**) to set the header.

4. Choose an option from the Footer drop down list to set the footer.

5. Click OK.

✔ Tips

- The drop-down list for Footer is identical to the one for Header.

- Excel gets your name and company name from entries you made when you installed Excel. You can change the name by choosing Options from the Tools menu, entering a new User Name in the General tab, and clicking OK. You cannot change the company name without reinstalling Excel.

- To change the formatting of text in the header or footer, you need to use the Custom Header or Custom Footer button in the Header/Footer tab of the Page Setup dialog box. I tell you about that on the next page.

Using Built-In Headers & Footers

To create custom headers and footers

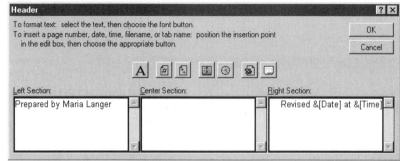

1. Choose Page Setup from the File menu (see **Figure 4**).

2. If necessary, click the Header/ Footer tab to display its options (see **Figure 17**).

Figure 19a. *The Header dialog box lets you create and format a custom header. The Footer dialog box is identical.*

3. Click the Custom Header or Custom Footer button.

4. In the Header (see **Figure 19a**) or Footer dialog box, enter the text or codes you want in the Left Section, Center Section, and Right Section text boxes. Use the buttons listed in **Table 1** to format selected text or insert codes for dynamic information.

5. Click OK.

6. The Page Setup dialog box preview area and Header or Footer drop-down list reflect your changes (see **Figure 19b**). Click OK to accept them.

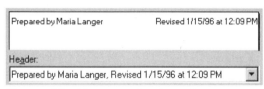

Figure 19b. *The custom header or footer appears in the Page Setup dialog box.*

✔ Tips

■ The dialog box for Footer is identical to the one for Header.

■ To enter an ampersand (&) character in a header or footer, type *&&* where you want it to appear in step 4 above.

■ To specify the starting page number to be printed in the header or footer, enter a value in the First Page Number edit box of the Page tab of the Page Setup dialog box (see **Figure 2**).

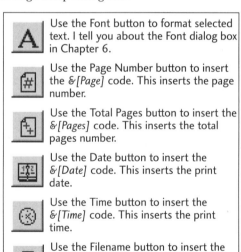

A	Use the Font button to format selected text. I tell you about the Font dialog box in Chapter 6.
	Use the Page Number button to insert the *&[Page]* code. This inserts the page number.
	Use the Total Pages button to insert the *&[Pages]* code. This inserts the total pages number.
	Use the Date button to insert the *&[Date]* code. This inserts the print date.
	Use the Time button to insert the *&[Time]* code. This inserts the print time.
	Use the Filename button to insert the *&[File]* code. This inserts the workbook name.
	Use the Sheet Name button to insert the *&[Tab]* code. This inserts the sheet name.

Table 1. *Use these buttons to insert codes for dynamic information.*

Creating Custom Headers & Footers

About the Print Area

The *print area* is the portion of a work-book that you want to print. If you do not specify a print area, Excel prints all of the selected sheet(s).

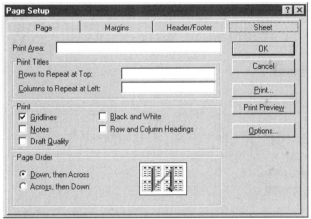

Figure 20. *Use the Sheet tab of the Page Setup dialog box to tell Excel what to print.*

Print Area:	$A$1:$E$9

Figure 21a. *Enter the cell references for the range you want to print in the Print Area edit box or…*

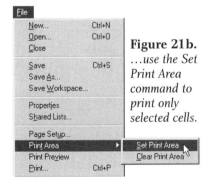

Figure 21b. *…use the Set Print Area command to print only selected cells.*

✔ Tip

■ You can set multiple non-adjacent print areas by entering the cell refer-ences for each range in the Print Area edit box separated by commas.

To set the print area for a worksheet

1. Choose Page Setup from the File menu (see **Figure 4**).

2. If necessary, click the Sheet tab to display its options (see **Figure 20**).

3. Enter the cell references for the range you want to print in the Print Area text box (see **Figure 21a**). If you pre-fer, you can position the insertion point in the Print Area text box and select the cells you want to print in the worksheet window.

4. Click OK.

or

1. In the worksheet window, select the range of cells you want to print.

2. Choose Set Print Area from the Print Area submenu under the File menu (see **Figure 21b**).

To clear a print area

1. Choose Page Setup from the File menu (see **Figure 4**).

2. If necessary, click the Sheet tab to dis-play its options (see **Figure 20**).

3. Clear the contents of the Print Area text box (see **Figure 21**).

or

Choose Clear Print Area from the Print Area submenu under the File menu.

About Print Titles

Print titles are worksheet columns and/or rows that are repeated on every page of the report. This is useful if the print area does not fit on one page and you want to repeat column or row titles on subsequent pages (see **Figures 22a**, **22b**, and **22c**).

To set print titles

1. Choose Page Setup from the File menu (see **Figure 4**).

2. If necessary, click the Sheet tab to display its options (see **Figure 20**).

3. To set column titles to repeat on each page, click in the Rows to Repeat at Top text box and enter the reference for the rows that contain column titles (see **Figure 23**).

   or

   To set row titles to repeat on each page, click in the Columns to Repeat at Left text box and enter the reference for the columns that contain row titles (see **Figure 23**).

4. Click OK.

✔ Tip

■ If you prefer, in step 3 above, you can position the insertion point in the appropriate text box and select the rows or columns in the worksheet window by clicking or dragging over their headings.

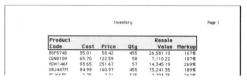

Figure 22a. *The first page of a long report will include column titles as part of the print area...*

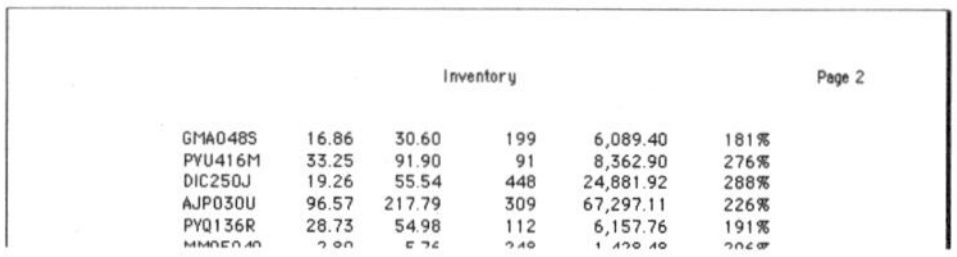

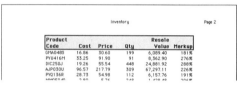

Figure 22b. *...but subsequent pages won't.*

Figure 22c. *By setting print titles, you can include column or row titles on every single page of a report.*

Print Titles	
Rows to Repeat at Top:	$1:$2
Columns to Repeat at Left:	$A:$A

Figure 23. *In this example, Row 1 of the worksheet will be printed on every page.*

About other Print Options

The Sheet tab of the Page Setup dialog box (see **Figure 20**) gives you control over several other print options:

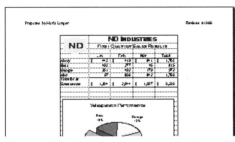

Figure 24a. *Printing a worksheet with Gridlines turned on.*

Figure 24b. *The last page of a report with Notes turned on.*

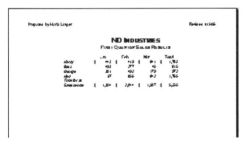

Figure 24c. *Draft Quality turns off most graphic elements—even charts!*

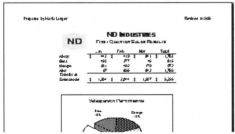

Figure 24d. *Black and White strips the color out of the report when printing.*

- The Gridlines option prints cell gridlines like those that appear in the worksheet window (see **Figure 24a**). I tell you how to turn off the display of gridlines in the worksheet window in Chapter 14.

- The Notes option prints cell notes on a separate page at the end of the report (see **Figure 24b**). I tell you about cell notes in Chapter 6. To print cell notes along with the corresponding cell references, turn on both the Notes and Row and Column Headings check boxes.

- The Draft Quality option prints fewer graphics and omits gridlines (see **Figure 24c**) to speed up printing.

- The Black and White option converts the Excel elements of the worksheet to black or white (see **Figure 24d**).

- The Row and Column Headings option prints the row and column headings in the worksheet window (see **Figure 24e**). Don't confuse this with print titles, which I tell you about on the previous page.

- Page Order specifies the print order for the pages of long, wide reports.

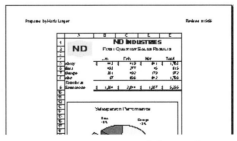

Figure 24e. *Printing a worksheet with Row and Column Headings turned on.*

About Print Preview

Excel's Print Preview feature lets you see what a report will look like before you print it. If a report doesn't look perfect, Page Setup and Margins buttons right inside the Print Preview dialog box let you make adjustments. When you're ready to print, click the Print button.

To preview a report

Choose Print Preview from the File menu (see **Figure 25a**).

or

Click the Print Preview button on the Standard toolbar.

or

Click the Print Preview button in the Page Setup or Print dialog box.

A preview of the current sheet appears (see **Figure 25b**). It reflects all Page Setup dialog box settings.

✔ Tips

- To view the other pages of the report, click the Next or Previous button.

- To zoom in to see report detail, click the Zoom button or click the mouse pointer (a magnifying glass) on the area you want to magnify.

- To open the Print dialog box and print, click the Print button. I tell you about the Print dialog box later in this chapter.

- To change Page Setup dialog box options, click the Setup button.

- To close the Print Preview dialog box, click the Close button.

Figure 25a.
Choose Print Preview from the File menu.

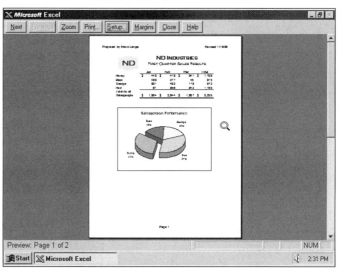

Figure 25b. *The Print Preview dialog box lets you see your report before you print it.*

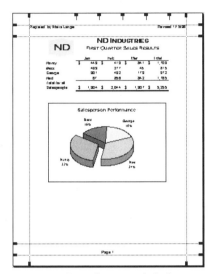

Figure 26a. *When you click the Margins button, handles for margins, header, footer, and columns appear.*

Figure 26b.
Position the mouse pointer over a handle and drag to change the width.

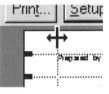

To change margins, header and footer locations, and column widths in Print Preview

1. In the Print Preview dialog box, click the Margins button.

   Handles for margins, header and footer locations, and column widths appear around the report preview (see **Figure 26a**).

2. Position the mouse pointer over the handle or guideline for the margin, header, footer, or column you want to change. The mouse pointer turns into a line with two arrows coming out of it (see **Figure 26b**).

3. Press the mouse button down and drag to make the change. A measurement for your change appears in the status bar as you drag.

4. Release the mouse button to complete the change. The report reformats automatically.

✔ Tips

■ The changes you make by dragging handles in the Print Preview dialog box will be reflected in the appropriate text boxes of the Page Setup and Column Width dialog boxes.

■ I tell how to change margins and header and footer locations with the Page Setup dialog box earlier in this chapter. I tell you how to change column widths in the worksheet window or with the Column Width dialog box in Chapter 6.

To print a report

1. Choose Print from the File menu (see **Figure 27a**).

   or

   Press Control+P.

   The Print dialog box appears (see **Figure 27b**).

2. If necessary, choose a different printer from the Name drop-down list. All installed printers appear on this list. You can also use the Properties button to change printer settings.

3. If necessary, select the Print What option button for the print area. By default, Excel uses Selected Sheet(s), but you can print only selected cells (Selection) or every sheet in the work-book (Entire Workbook).

4. To print more than one copy of the report, enter the num-ber of copies you want in the Number of Copies text box.

5. To print only certain pages, enter a starting and ending page number in the Page Range area's from and to text boxes.

6. Click OK.

   The report is sent or *spooled* to the printer. A dialog box like the one in **Figure 28** appears while it's being sent. When the dialog box disappears, you can continue working with Excel.

Figure 27a. *Choose Print from the File menu.*

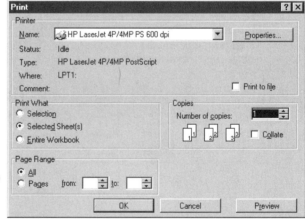

Figure 27b. *Use the Print dialog box to set final print options and send the print job to the printer.*

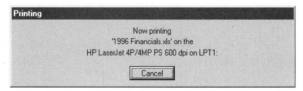

Figure 28. *A dialog box like this appears while a docu-ment is being spooled to the printer for printing.*

✔ Tip

■ If you click the Print button on the Standard toolbar, Excel sends the report to the printer without displaying the Print dialog box.

WORKING WITH DATABASES

About Databases

Excel's database features and functions help make it a flexible tool for creating, maintaining, and reporting data. With Excel, you can use a form to enter data into a list, filter information, sort records, and automatically generate subtotals. You can use Excel's calculating, formatting, charting, and printing features on your database, too.

In Excel, a *database* is any list of information with unique labels in the first row. You don't need to do anything special to identify a database—Excel is smart enough to know one when it sees it. **Figure 1**, for example, shows the first few rows of a list that Excel can recognize as a database.

Understanding Databases

	A	B	C	D	E	F	G	H	I
1	Product Code	Department	Cost	Selling Price	Order Point	Qty on Hand	Time to Order?	Total Resale Value	Markup
2	JZR-245	Sound Acc.	120.95	429.45	20	35		15,030.75	255%
3	HHQ-146	Keyboards	51.68	106.55	40	70		7,458.50	106%
4	CUR-75	Computers	1,238.28	4,680.75	30	11	X	51,488.25	278%
5	EPU-283	Software	282.10	702.45	40	65		45,659.25	149%
6	ISM-S1	Sound Acc.	32.62	79.55	40	90		6,913.40	247%

Figure 1. *The first few rows of a list that Excel can automatically recognize as a database.*

A database is organized into fields and records. A *field* is a category of information. In **Figure 1**, *Product Code*, *Department*, and *Cost* are the first three fields. A *record* is a collection of fields for one thing. In **Figure 1**, *row 2* shows the record for the item with product code *JZR-245* and *row 3* shows the record for *HHQ-146*.

✔ Tip

- Fields are always in columns while records are aways in rows.

To create a list

1. In a worksheet window, enter unique column titles for each of the fields in your list (see **Figure 2a**). These will be the field names.

2. Beginning with the row immediately after the one containing the column titles, enter the data for each record (see **Figure 2b**). Be sure to put the proper information in each column.

✔ Tips

■ Use only one cell for each column title. If the field name is too long to fit in the cell, use the Alignment tab in the Font dialog box to wrap text in the cell (see **Figure 3**). I tell you about alignment options in Chapter 6.

■ Do not skip rows when entering information. A blank row indicates the end of the database above it.

■ Excel's AutoComplete automatically completes entries for you based on other entries you've made in that column. In **Figure 4**, for example, typing the first three characters of the word "Software" completes the entry.

■ To enter data in a field by choosing from a list of existing entries, double-click the cell and press Alt+Down Arrow. Choose a value from the drop-down list that appears (see **Figure 5**).

■ You can format your list any way you like. The formatting will not affect the way Excel recognizes and works with the list data.

■ Your list can include formulas. Excel treats the results of the formulas like any other field.

■ When working with a long list, use the Freeze Panes (see **Figure 4**) or Split Window command to keep the field names on screen. I tell you about splitting the window in Chapter 4.

	A	B	C
1	First Name	Last Name	Phone Number
2			
3			

Figure 2a. *Begin by entering unique field names in the first row of the list...*

	A	B	C
1	First Name	Last Name	Phone Number
2	Nancy	Drew	555-4521
3	Sherlock	Holmes	555-6859
4	Lew	Archer	555-7846
5	Sam	Spade	555-9685
6	Peter	Wimsey	555-3248
7	Jessica	Fletcher	555-6941
8	John	Aabbott	555-6937

Figure 2b. *...then enter the data, one record per row.*

	A	B	C
1	First Name	Last Name	Phone Number
2	Nancy	Drew	555-4521
3	Sherlock	Holmes	555-6859

Figure 3. *Formatting a list doesn't affect the way Excel works with its data.*

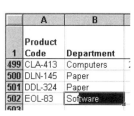

Figure 4.
The AutoComplete feature finishes an entry based on the contents of other cells in the same column.

Figure 5. *You can also enter data in a field by choosing an existing value from a drop-down list. Excel automatically maintains this sorted list of values for you.*

Creating a List

Figure 6. *The data form offers another way to enter, edit, delete, and find records.*

Figure 7. *Choose Form from the Data menu.*

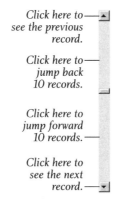

Click here to see the previous record.

Click here to jump back 10 records.

Click here to jump forward 10 records.

Click here to see the next record.

Figure 8. *Use the scroll bar in the data form to browse records.*

✔ Tips

■ Excel records your changes when you move to another record or click the Close button to close the form.

■ If a field should contain a formula, Excel automatically carries the formula forward from the previous record and performs the calculation.

About the Data Form

Excel automatically creates a dialog box with a custom data form (see **Figure 6**) when you choose Form from the Data menu. You can use this form to browse, enter, edit, delete, and find records.

To browse, enter, edit, and delete records with the data form

1. Select any cell in the list.

2. Choose Form from the Data menu (see **Figure 7**). The data form appears (see **Figure 6**).

3. To browse through the records, use the scroll bar (see **Figure 8**):
   - ■ To see the next record, click the down arrow on the scroll bar.
   - ■ To see the previous record, click the up arrow on the scroll bar.
   - ■ To jump ahead 10 records, click the scroll bar beneath the scroll box.
   - ■ To jump back 10 records, click the scroll bar above the scroll box.

4. To create a new record, click the New button and enter the information into the empty edit boxes for each field.

5. To edit a record, locate the record you want to edit and make changes in the appropriate edit boxes.

6. To delete a record, locate the record you want to delete and click the Delete button.

7. When you're finished working with the records, click the Close button. Any changes you made to the data will be reflected in the list.

To find records with the data form

1. Select any cell in the list.

2. Choose Form from the Data menu (see **Figure 7**). The data form appears (see **Figure 6**).

3. Click the Criteria button. A criteria form appears (see **Figure 9a**).

4. Enter search criteria in the field(s) in which you expect to find a match (see **Figure 9b**).

5. Click the Find Next button to move forward through the list for records that match the criteria or click the Find Prev button to move backward through the list for records that match the criteria. Excel beeps when it reaches the end or beginning of the matches.

✔ Tips

■ You can enter criteria in any combination of fields. If you enter criteria into multiple fields, Excel looks for records that match all criteria.

■ The more fields you enter data into, the more specific you make the search and the fewer matches you'll find.

■ You can use comparison operators (see **Table 1**) and wildcard characters (see **Table 2**) in conjunction with criteria. For example, *>100* finds records with values greater than 100 in the field in which the criteria is entered.

■ You can also use Excel's AutoFilter feature to quickly locate and display all records that match search criteria. I tell you how next.

Figure 9a. *The data form turns into a criteria form when you click the Criteria button.*

Cost:	<100

Figure 9b. *Enter the search criteria in the field(s) in which you expect to find a match.*

Operator	Meaning
=	Equal To
<>	Not Equal To
>	Greater Than
>=	Greater Than or Equal To
<	Less Than
<=	Less Than or Equal To

Table 1. *Comparison operators.*

Character	Meaning
?	Any single character
*	Any group of characters

Table 2. *Wildcard characters.*

About AutoFilter

The AutoFilter feature puts drop-down lists in the titles of each column (see **Figure 10b**). You can use these lists to choose criteria in the column and display only those records that match the criteria.

To find records with AutoFilter

1. Select any cell in the list.

2. Choose AutoFilter from the Filter submenu under the Data menu (see **Figure 10a**). Excel creates drop-down lists for each field (see **Figure 10b**).

Figure 10a. *The Filter submenu under the Data menu offers several filtering options.*

	A	B	C	D	E	F	G	H	I
1	Product Code	Department	Cost	Selling Price	Order Poi	Qty on Hai	Time to Orde	Total Resale Value	Marki
2	JZR-245	Sound Acc.	120.95	429.45	20	35		15,030.75	255%
3	HHQ-146	Keyboards	51.68	106.55	40	70		7,458.50	106%
4	CUR-75	Computers	1,238.28	4,680.75	30	11	X	51,488.25	278%

Figure 10b. *The AutoFilter feature creates a drop-down list for each field.*

3. Use a drop-down list to select criteria in a specific field (see **Figure 10c**). When you make your choice, only the records matching the criteria are displayed (see **Figure 10d**).

Figure 10c. *Choose criteria from a drop-down list…*

(All)
(Top 10...)
(Custom...)
Accessories
Books
CD-ROMs
Computers
Keyboards

✔ Tips

■ To display all of the records again, choose Show All from the Filter submenu under the Data menu (see **Figure 10a**) or choose (All) from the drop-down list you used to filter the data (see **Figure 10c**).

■ You can select criteria for more than one field at a time. When you do, Excel displays records that match *all* criteria in its filtered list.

■ Excel filters the list by hiding the rows that contain data that do not match criteria. Data is not removed from the list.

	A	B	C	D	E	F	G	H	I
1	Product Code	Department	Cost	Selling Price	Order Poi	Qty on Hai	Time to Orde	Total Resale Value	Marki
12	ADV-189	Accessories	31.74	119.75	20	37		4,430.75	277%
24	AGA-287	Accessories	19.34	38.95	50	41	X	1,596.95	101%
33	ATR-425	Accessories	13.35	27.65	10	69		1,907.85	107%
41	AOC-172	Accessories	49.62	101.75	40	100		10,175.00	105%
58	ALE-498	Accessories	6.16	10.95	30	50		547.50	78%
78	AWC-198	Accessories	21.89	37.05	40	49		1,815.45	69%
100	AAY-24	Accessories	17.35	74.45	20	18	X	1,340.10	329%
102	AYL-27	Accessories	25.29	88.85	30	43		3,820.55	251%
112	AUK-177	Accessories	6.39	20.85	50	99		2,064.15	226%
120	ABQ-140	Accessories	21.52	57.25	20	76		4,351.00	166%
128	ATE-259	Accessories	22.22	70.75	30	82		5,801.50	218%
133	ATA-9	Accessories	9.94	38.05	50	54		2,054.70	283%

Figure 10d. *…and Excel displays only the records that match the criteria.*

To use the Top 10 AutoFilter

1. With AutoFilters turned on, choose Top 10 from the drop-down list for the field you want to filter (see **Figure 11a**).

2. In the Top 10 AutoFilter dialog box that appears (see **Figure 11b**), use the drop-down lists and text box to specify which records to show.

3. Click OK. Excel filters the list to match the criteria you specified (see **Figure 11c**).

To use a custom AutoFilter

1. Choose Custom from the drop-down list for the field you want to filter.

2. In the Custom AutoFilter dialog box (see **Figure 12**), use the drop-down lists to choose comparison operators and criteria.

3. Select the And or Or option button to tell Excel whether it should match both criteria (And) or either criteria (Or).

4. Click OK. Excel filters the list to match the criteria you specified.

✔ Tip

- Criteria can include wildcard characters (see **Table 2**).

To use multiple AutoFilters

Choose filters from the drop-down lists for each of the fields for which you want to set criteria. Excel will display only the records that match all of the filters (see **Figure 13**).

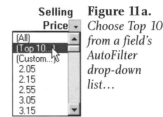

Figure 11a. *Choose Top 10 from a field's AutoFilter drop-down list...*

Figure 11b. *Then set options in the Top 10 AutoFilter dialog box to specify which records to show.*

	A	B	C	D	E	F	G	H	I
1	Product Code	Department	Cost	Selling Price	Order Poi	Qty on Ha	Time to Orde	Total Resale Value	Mark
39	CKF-42	Computers	2,073.37	7,339.75	20	88		645,898.00	254%
45	CAI-194	Computers	2,468.53	7,504.35	30	21	X	157,591.35	204%
148	CMA-131	Computers	1,889.82	7,370.35	30	26	X	191,629.10	290%
242	CCV-12	Computers	2,485.40	9,543.95	10	64		610,812.80	284%
255	CVM-125	Computers	1,964.48	7,209.65	50	95		684,916.75	267%
331	CQD-387	Computers	2,162.15	8,605.45	40	91		783,095.95	298%
372	CFV-458	Computers	2,312.52	9,458.25	40	72		680,994.00	309%
483	IPH-130	Monitors	1,483.23	6,244.45	20	92		574,489.40	321%
496	CPY-441	Computers	2,307.07	7,221.15	40	46		332,172.90	213%
499	CLA-413	Computers	2,547.51	9,425.85	40	58		546,699.30	270%

Figure 11c. *The list that results based on the criteria in Figure 11b.*

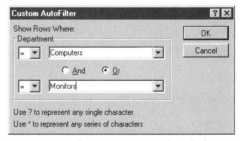

Figure 12. *The Custom AutoFilter dialog box lets you set multiple criteria for a field.*

	A	B	C	D	E	F	G	H	I
1	Product Code	Department	Cost	Selling Price	Order Poi	Qty on Ha	Time to Orde	Total Resale Value	Mark
270	BHT-56	Books	12.13	19.25	30	13	X	250.25	59%
273	BGO-247	Books	12.45	42.05	50	17	X	714.85	238%
299	BLX-376	Books	4.87	12.05	40	36	X	433.80	147%

Figure 13. *In this example, three filters were used: Department=Books, Selling Price<=50, and Time to Order?=X.*

About Advanced Filters

With advanced filters you can specify even more criteria than with AutoFilters. First set up a criteria range, then use the Advanced Filter dialog box to perform the search.

To use advanced filters

1. Create a criteria range by copying the data labels in the list to a blank area of the worksheet and then entering the criteria in the cells beneath it (see **Figure 14a**).

2. Choose Advanced Filter from the Filter submenu under the Data menu (see **Figure 10a**).

3. In the Advanced Filter dialog box (see **Figure 14b**), select an option button to specify whether the matches should replace the original list (Filter the List, in-place) or a new list should be created elsewhere (Copy to Another Location).

4. In the List Range text box, confirm that the correct cell references for your list have been entered.

5. In the Criteria Range text box, enter the cell references for the range containing your criteria (including the field labels).

6. If you selected the Copy option button in step 3 above, enter a cell reference for the first cell of the new list in the Copy to text box.

7. Click OK.

   Excel searches for records that match the criteria and either replaces the original list or creates a new list with the matches (see **Figure 14c**).

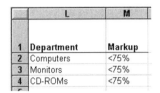

Figure 14a. *Create a criteria range with field names and values you want to match.*

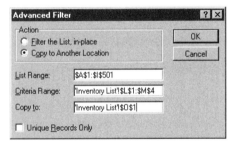

Figure 14b. *Then use the Advanced Filter dialog box to tell Excel where the List Range, Criteria Range, and Copy to locations are.*

	O	P	Q	R	S	T	U	V	W
1	Product Code	Department	Cost	Selling Price	Order Point	Qty on Hand	Time to Order?	Total Resale Value	Markup
2	KKS-494	CD-ROMs	9.46	14.65	20	30		439.50	55%
3	ICX-437	Monitors	618.18	1,007.65	20	32		32,244.80	63%
4	CRU-360	Computers	2,069.72	3,228.85	20	65		209,875.25	56%
5	CMX-198	Computers	1,580.34	2,607.65	40	86		224,257.90	65%
6	CUV-122	Computers	1,065.33	1,736.55	20	52		90,300.60	63%
7	IOF-471	Monitors	325.53	559.95	40	84		47,035.80	72%
8	IGG-5	Monitors	1,206.11	2,038.35	40	48		97,840.80	69%
9	IJW-301	Monitors	593.86	1,003.65	10	19		19,069.35	69%
10	CUP-54	Computers	2,606.36	4,430.85	20	47		208,249.95	70%
11	CMO-337	Computers	2,879.49	4,549.65	50	41	X	186,535.65	58%
12	INH-439	Monitors	1,128.10	1,895.25	30	28	X	53,067.00	68%

Figure 14c. *The criteria in Figure 14a yielded these results.*

Using Advanced Filters

About Sorting

You can sort lists by any column(s). Excel will quickly put database information in the order you specify.

To sort a list

1. Select any cell in the list.

2. Choose Sort from the Data menu (see **Figure 15a**).

3. In the Sort dialog box (see **Figure 15b**), choose a primary sort field from the Sort By drop-down list (see **Figure 15c**). Then select an option button to specify whether the sort should be in Ascending (lowest to highest) or Descending (highest to lowest) order.

4. If desired, choose a secondary and tertiary sort field from each of the Then By drop-down lists. Be sure to select a sort order option button beside each field.

5. Select an option button at the bottom of the dialog box to tell Excel whether this list has a Header Row (column titles) or No Header Row.

6. Click OK.

   Excel sorts the list as you specified (see **Figure 15d**).

   or

1. Select any cell in the list column by which you want to sort.

2. Click the Sort Ascending button to sort from lowest to highest value or the Sort Descending button to sort from highest to lowest value. Both buttons are on the Standard toolbar.

Figure 15a.
Choose Sort from the Data menu...

Figure 15b. *...choose sort fields in the Sort dialog box...*

Figure 15c.
...by choosing from drop-down list of field names.

Sorting Lists

✔ Tips

■ The two Then By fields in the sort dialog box are "tie-breakers" and are only used if the primary sort field has more than one record with the same value.

■ If the results of a sort are not what you expected, choose Undo from the Edit menu, press Control+Z, or click the Undo button on the Standard toolbar to restore the original sort order.

■ If you make the wrong selection in the My List Has area at the bottom of the dialog box, you could sort column titles along with the rest of the list. If you see that you've done that, choose Undo from the Edit menu, press Control+Z, or click the Undo button on the Standard toolbar to restore the original order and try again.

■ If you select a cell anywhere in the column by which you want to sort before choosing Sort from the Data menu, that column is automatically referenced in the Sort dialog box.

■ To sort by more than three columns, sort by the least important columns first, then by the most important ones. For example, to sort a list by *columns A, B, C, D,* and *E,* you'd sort first by *columns D* and *E,* then by *columns A, B,* and *C.*

■ In order to use Excel's Subtotal feature, you must first sort the data by the column for which you want subtotals. I tell you about the Subtotal feature next.

Sorting Tips

	O	P	Q	R	S	T	U	V	W
1	Product Code	Department	Cost	Selling Price	Order Point	Qty on Hand	Time to Order?	Total Resale Value	Markup
2	KKS-494	CD-ROMs	9.46	14.65	20	30		439.50	55%
3	CMO-337	Computers	2,879.49	4,549.65	50	41	X	186,535.65	58%
4	CMX-198	Computers	1,580.34	2,607.65	40	86		224,257.90	65%
5	CRU-360	Computers	2,069.72	3,228.85	20	65		209,875.25	56%
6	CUP-54	Computers	2,606.36	4,430.85	20	47		208,249.95	70%
7	CUV-122	Computers	1,065.33	1,736.55	20	52		90,300.60	63%
8	ICX-437	Monitors	618.18	1,007.65	20	32		32,244.80	63%
9	IGG-5	Monitors	1,206.11	2,038.35	40	48		97,840.80	69%
10	IJW-301	Monitors	593.86	1,003.65	10	19		19,069.35	69%
11	INH-439	Monitors	1,128.10	1,895.25	30	28	X	53,067.00	68%
12	IOF-471	Monitors	325.53	559.95	40	84		47,035.80	72%

Figure 15d. *The sort order in Figure 15b yields this report of data filtered from Figure 14c.*

About Subtotal and the SUBTOTAL Function

Excel's Subtotal feature enters formulas with the SUBTOTAL function in sorted database lists. The SUBTOTAL function (see **Figure 16d**) returns a subtotal for a sorted list. It uses the following syntax:

SUBTOTAL(function_num,ref)

The *function_num* argument is a number that specifies which function to use. **Table 3** shows the valid values. I tell you about most of these functions in Chapter 5. The *ref* argument is the range of cells to subtotal.

To subtotal a list

1. Sort the list by the field(s) for which you want subtotals and position the cellpointer in the list.

2. Choose Subtotals from the Data menu (see **Figure 16a**) to display the Subtotal dialog box (see **Figure 16b**).

3. From the At Each Change In drop-down list, choose the field to be grouped for subtotaling. This may be the same field you sorted by.

4. Choose a function from the Use Function drop-down list (see **Figure 16c**).

5. In the Add Subtotal To list box, use the check boxes to choose the field(s) to subtotal.

6. If desired, use the check boxes at the bottom of the dialog box to set other options.

7. Click OK.

Excel turns the list into an outline and enters row titles and subtotals (see **Figure 16d**).

Figure 16a. *Choose Subtotals from the Data menu.*

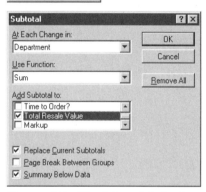

Figure 16b. *The Subtotal dialog box lets you choose the field to group data for, the function, and the field(s) to subtotal.*

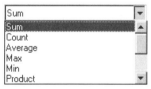

Figure 16c. *The Use Function drop-down list offers a variety of subtotal functions to choose from.*

✔ Tip

■ To remove subtotals, click the Remove All button in the Subtotal dialog box.

About Outlines

Excel's outline feature groups calculated information into different levels. You can then show or hide information based on its level:

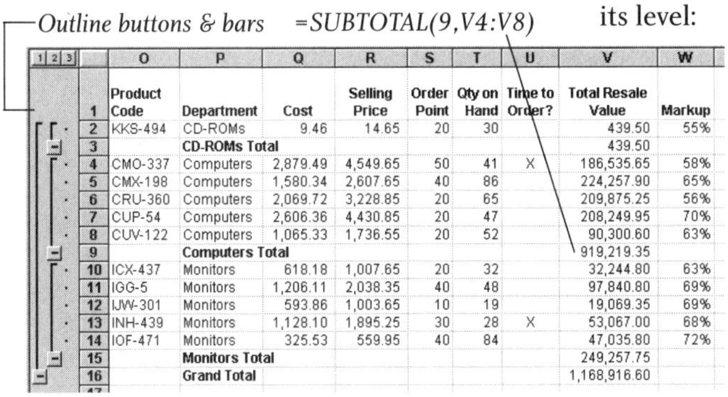

Outline buttons & bars   =SUBTOTAL(9,V4:V8)

Figure 16d. *Here's the information sorted in Figure 15d with subtotals.*

- Click a minus sign button to collapse the outline for that section.

- Click a plus sign button to expand the outline for that section.

- Click one of the outline level numbers to collapse or expand the entire outline to that level.

Figure 17 shows an outline created by the Subtotal command partially collapsed. Note how the outline buttons and bars are set to the left of the data.

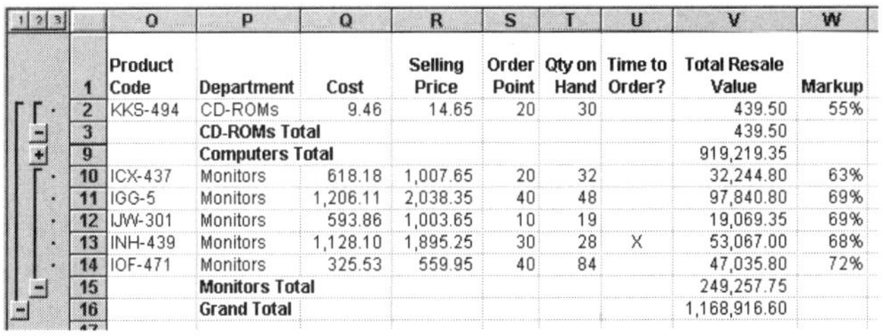

Figure 17. *Here's the outline from Figure 16d partially collapsed to hide some of the detail.*

✔ Tip

- Creating outlines is beyond the scope of this book, but here's a hint to get you started if you decide to explore this feature: Use commands on the Group and Outline submenu under the Data menu to create and clear groups and outlines.

Understanding Subtotals & Outlines

Table 3. *Valid function_num values for the SUBTOTAL function.*

Number	Function Name
1	AVERAGE
2	COUNT
3	COUNTA
4	MAX
5	MIN
6	PRODUCT
7	STDEV
8	STDEVP
9	SUM
10	VAR
11	VARP

About Database Functions

Excel includes over a dozen database and list management functions. Here are a few of the most commonly used ones, along with their syntax:

DSUM(database,field,criteria)
DAVERAGE(database,field,criteria)
DCOUNT(database,field,criteria)
DCOUNTA(database,field,criteria)
DMAX(database,field,criteria)
DMIN(database,field,criteria)

The *database* argument is the cell references for a range containing the database or list. The *field* argument is the name of the field you want to summarize. The *criteria* argument is either the data you want to match or a range containing the data you want to match.

Figure 18 shows an example of these database functions in action.

✔ Tips

■ Each database function corresponds to a mathematical or statistical function and performs the same kind of calculation—but on records matching criteria only. I tell you about other functions in Chapter 5.

■ You can enter database functions with the Function Wizard. I tell you how to use the Function Wizard in Chapter 5.

DSUM	1,168,916.60	—=DSUM(A1:I501,H1,L1:M4)
DAVERAGE	106,265.15	—=DAVERAGE(A1:I501,H1,L1:M4)
DCOUNT	11	—=DCOUNT(A1:I501,H1,L1:M4)
DCOUNTA	11	—=DCOUNTA(A1:I501,H1,L1:M4)
DMAX	224,257.90	—=DMAX(A1:I501,H1,L1:M4)
DMIN	439.50	—=DMIN(A1:I501,H1,L1:M4)

Figure 18. *These formulas use database functions to summarize information based on criteria. The database is the 500-record list used throughout this chapter. The field is the Department field, which is found in cell H1 of the database. The criteria range is the range illustrated in Figure 14a.*

ADVANCED FORMULA TECHNIQUES 12

About Excel's Advanced Formula Techniques

Excel's advanced formula techniques include:

- ■ Names that let you assign easy-to-remember names to cell references (see **Figure 1**). You can then use the names in place of cell references in formulas.

- ■ 3-D cell references that let you write formulas with links to other worksheets and workbooks (see **Figure 2**).

- ■ Consolidations that let you summarize information from several source areas into one destination area (see **Figure 3**), with or without live links.

In Chapter 2, I tell you how to write formulas. In Chapter 3, I tell you how to copy and move formulas and I explain relative and absolute cell references. In Chapter 5, I tell you how to use functions in formulas. In this chapter, I tell you how to take what those chapters cover a step further with advanced formula techniques.

✔ Tip

- ■ To get the most out of the information in this chapter, you should have a solid understanding of the information in Chapters 2, 3, and 5.

	A	B	C	D	E	F	G	H
1	ND INDUSTRIES							
2	SALES RESULTS							
3								
4		Jan	Feb	Mar	Apr	May	Jun	Total
5	Nancy	443	419	841	548	684	952	3887
6	Bess	493	277	45	459	368	751	2393
7	George	301	492	179	148	196	325	1641
8	Ned	67	856	842	359	486	843	3453
9	Total	1304	2044	1907	1514	1734	2871	11374

Figure 1. *The reference to the selected range would be a lot easier to remember if it had a name like NancySales rather than just B5:G5.*

=SUM('1st Qtr Results:4th Qtr Results'!E9)

	A	B
1	Total Sales	$ 29,949
2	Total Costs	14,685
3	Total Profits	$ 15,264

Figure 2. *3-D cell references make it possible to link information between worksheets or workbooks.*

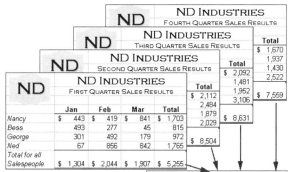

Figure 3. *Excel's consolidation feature lets you combine information in multiple source areas into one destination area—with or without live links.*

About Names

The trouble with using cell references in formulas is that they're difficult to remember. To make matters worse, cell references can change if cells above or to the left of them are inserted or deleted.

The Names feature of Excel eliminates both problems by letting you assign easy-to-remember names to cells in your worksheets. The names don't change, no matter how much worksheet editing you do.

✔ Tips

- ■ Names can apply to single cells or cell ranges.

- ■ Names can be up to 255 characters long and can include letters, numbers, periods, question marks, and underscore characters (_). The first character must be a letter. Names cannot contain spaces or "look" like cell references.

To define a name

1. Select the cell(s) you want to name (see **Figure 4a**).

2. Choose Define from the Name submenu under the Insert menu (see **Figure 4b**).

3. In the Define Name dialog box (see **Figure 4c**), Excel may suggest a name in the Names in Workbook edit box. You can use that name or enter a name you prefer.

4. The cell reference in the Refers To text box should reflect the range you selected in step 1. You can type in a new range or highlight the contents of the text box and reselect the cell(s) in the worksheet window.

5. Click OK to define the name.

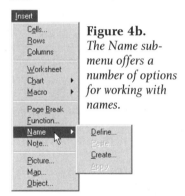

Figure 4a. *Select the cell(s) you want to name.*

Figure 4b. *The Name submenu offers a number of options for working with names.*

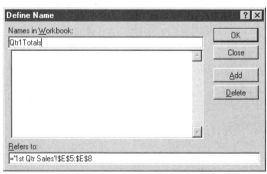

Figure 4c. *Use the Define Name dialog box to set a name for one or more cells. As you can see, the name of the worksheet is part of the cell reference.*

Defining Names

	A	B	C	D	E	F	G	H
3								
4		Jan	Feb	Mar	Apr	May	Jun	Total
5	Nancy	443	419	841	548	684	952	3887
6	Bess	493	277	45	459	368	751	2393
7	George	301	492	179	148	196	325	1641
8	Ned	67	856	842	359	486	843	3453
9	Total	1304	2044	1907	1514	1734	2871	11374

Figure 5a. *To use the Create Names dialog box, you must first select the cells you want to name as well as adjoining cells with text you want to use as names...*

Figure 5b.
...then tell Excel which cells contain the text for names.

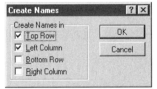

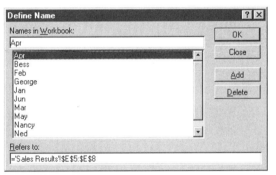

Figure 5c. *Look inside the Define Name dialog box to see how many names were added.*

To create a name

1. Select the cells containing the ranges you want to name as well as text in adjoining cells that you want to use as names (see **Figure 5a**).

2. Choose Create from the Name submenu under the Insert menu (see **Figure 4b**).

3. In the Create Names dialog box (see **Figure 5b**), turn on the check box(es) for the cells that contain the text you want to use as names.

4. Click OK.

   Excel uses the text in the cells you indicated as names for the adjoining cells. You can see the results if you open the Define Names dialog box (see **Figure 5c**).

✔ Tip

■ This is a quick way to create a lot of names all at once.

To delete a name

1. Choose Define from the Name submenu under the Insert menu (see **Figure 4b**).

2. In the Define Name dialog box (see **Figure 5c**), select the name you want to delete from the list box under Names in Workbook.

3. Click the Delete button.

4. Click OK.

✔ Tip

■ Deleting a name does not delete the cells to which the name refers.

Creating & Deleting Names

185

To enter a name in a formula

1. Select the cell in which you want to write the formula.

2. Type in the formula, replacing any cell reference with the corresponding name (see **Figure 6**).

3. Press Enter or click the Enter button on the formula bar.

   Excel performs the calculation just as if you'd typed in a cell reference.

	A	B
3		
4		Jan
5	Nancy	443
6	Bess	493
7	George	301
8	Ned	67
9	Total	=SUM(JAN)

Figure 6.
Once a range has been named, it can be used instead of a cell reference in a formula.

✔ Tips

■ You can use the Paste Name command to enter a name for you. Follow the steps above, but when it's time to type in the name, choose Paste from the Name submenu under the Insert menu (see **Figure 7a**). Use the Paste Name dialog box that appears (see **Figure 7b**) to select and paste in the name you want. The Paste Name command even works when you use the Function Wizard to write formulas. I tell you about the Function Wizard in Chapter 5.

■ To create a list of all names and their corresponding cell references, select a cell in an empty area of a worksheet, choose Paste from the Name submenu under the Insert menu (see **Figure 7a**), and click the Paste List button in the Paste Name dialog box (see **Figure 7b**).

■ When you delete a name, Excel responds with a *#NAME?* error in each cell that contains a formula referring to that name (see **Figure 8**). These formulas must be rewritten.

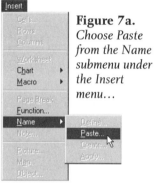

Figure 7a.
Choose Paste from the Name submenu under the Insert menu...

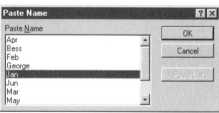

Figure 7b. *...then use the Paste Name dialog box to select and paste in a name.*

	A	B
3		
4		Jan
5	Nancy	443
6	Bess	493
7	George	301
8	Ned	67
9	Total	#NAME?

Figure 8.
If you delete a name used in a formula, a #NAME? error results.

To apply names to existing formulas

1. Select the cells containing formulas for which you want to apply names. If you want to apply names throughout the worksheet, click any single cell.

2. Choose Apply from the Name submenu under the Insert menu (see **Figure 4b**).

3. In the Apply Names dialog box (see **Figure 9a**), select the names that you want to use in place of the cell reference. To select or deselect a name, click on it.

4. Click OK.

    Excel rewrites the formulas with the appropriate names from those you selected. **Figure 9b** shows an example of formulas changed by selecting the names for salespeople in **Figure 9a**.

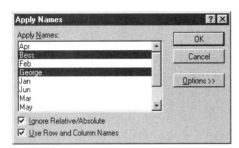

Figure 9a. *Select the names that you want to apply to formulas in your worksheet.*

	A	B	C	D	E	F	G	H
3								
4		Jan	Feb	Mar	Apr	May	Jun	Total
5	Nancy	443	419	841	548	684	952	3887
6	Bess	493	277	45	459	368	751	2393
7	George	301	492	179	148	196	325	1641
8	Ned	67	856	842	359	486	843	3453
9	Total	1304	2044	1907	1514	1734	2871	11374

Before	*After*
=SUM(B5:G5)	=SUM(Nancy)
=SUM(B6:G6)	=SUM(Bess)
=SUM(B7:G7)	=SUM(George)
=SUM(B8:G8)	=SUM(Ned)

Figure 9b. *Excel applies the names you selected to formulas that reference their ranges.*

✔ Tips

■ If only one cell is selected, Excel applies names based on your selection(s) in the Apply Names dialog box, not the selected cell.

■ If you turn off the Ignore Relative/Absolute check box in the Apply Names dialog box (see **Figure 9b**), Excel matches the type of reference. I tell you about relative and absolute references in Chapter 3.

Applying Names to Formulas

To select named cells

Use the name box's drop-down list on the left end of the formula bar to choose a name for the cells you want to select (see **Figure 10**).

or

1. Click the name box at the left end of the formula bar to select its contents.

2. Type in the cell name or reference for the cells you want to select (see **Figure 11**).

3. Press Enter.

or

1. Choose Go To from the Edit menu (see **Figure 12a**).

   or

   Press F5 or Control+G.

2. In the Go To dialog box (see **Figure 12b**), select the name of the cells you want to select from the Go To list box.

3. Click OK.

✔ Tip

■ When named cells are selected, the name appears in the name box at the left end of the formula bar—even if you didn't use the name box to select the cells.

Figure 10.
The name box on the left end of the formula bar offers a drop-down list of all named ranges.

Figure 11. *If you prefer, you can type a name (or cell reference) in the Name box and press Enter to select cells.*

Figure 12a.
Choose Go To from the Edit menu...

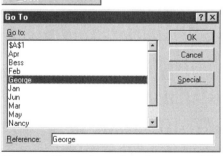

Figure 12b. *...then select the name of the cells you want to select from the Go To list box.*

About 3-D References

3-D cell references let you write formulas that reference cells in other worksheets or workbooks. The links are *live*—when a cell's contents change, the results of formulas in cells that reference it change.

Excel offers several ways to write formulas with 3-D cell references:

- Use cell names. I tell you about cell names in the first part of this chapter. **Figure 13** shows an example.

- Type them in. When you type in a 3-D cell reference, you must include the name of the sheet (in single quotes, if the name contains a space), followed by an exclamation point (!) and cell reference. If the reference is for a cell in another workbook, you must also include the workbook name, in brackets. **Figures 14a**, **14b**, and **14c** show examples.

- Click on them. You'll get the same results as if you had typed the references, but Excel does all the typing for you.

- Use the Paste Special command. The Paste Link button in the Paste Special dialog box lets you paste a link between cells in different sheets of a workbook or different workbooks.

```
=SUM(Nancy,Bess,George,Ned)
```

Figure 13. *This example uses the SUM function to add the contents of the cells named* Nancy, Bess, George, *and* Ned *in the same workbook.*

```
='Results for Year'!$B$9
```

Figure 14a. *This example refers to cell B9 in a worksheet called* Results for Year *in the same workbook.*

```
=SUM('1st Qtr Results:4th Qtr Results1'!E9)
```

Figure 14b. *This example uses the SUM function to add the contents of cell E9 in worksheets starting with* 1st Qtr Results *and ending with* 4th Qtr Results *in the same workbook.*

```
='[Drew Industries Reports]1st Qtr Results'!$E$9
```

Figure 14c. *This example refers to cell E9 in a worksheet called* 1st Qtr Results *in a workbook called* Drew Industries Reports.

✔ Tips

- When you delete a cell, Excel displays a *#REF!* error in any cells that referred to it. The cells containing these errors must be revised to remove the error.

- Do not make references to an unsaved file. If you do and you close the file with the reference before saving (and naming) the file it refers to, Excel won't be able to update the link.

Understanding 3-D References

To reference a named cell or range in another worksheet

1. Select the cell in which you want to enter the reference.

2. Type an equal sign (=).

3. If the sheet containing the cells you want to reference is in another workbook, type the name of the workbook (within single quotes, if the name contains a space) followed by an exclamation point (!).

4. Type the name of the cell(s) you want to reference (see **Figures 15a** and **15b**).

5. Press Enter or click the Enter button on the formula bar.

✔ Tip

■ If the name you want to reference is in the same workbook, you can paste it in by choosing Paste from the Name submenu under the Insert menu. I tell you how earlier in this chapter.

To reference a cell or range in another worksheet by clicking

1. Select the cell in which you want to enter the reference.

2. Type an equal sign (=).

3. If the sheet containing the cells you want to reference is in another workbook, switch to that workbook.

4. Click on the sheet tab for the worksheet containing the cell you want to reference.

5. Select the cell(s) you want to reference (see **Figure 16**).

6. Press Enter or click the Enter button on the formula bar.

Figures 15a&b. *Two examples of 3-D references utilizing names. The first example references a name in the same workbook. The second example refers to a name in a different workbook.*

Figure 16. *After typing an equal sign in the cell in which you want the reference to go, you can select the cell(s) you want to reference.*

To reference a cell or range in another worksheet by typing

1. Select the cell in which you want to enter the reference.

2. Type an equal sign (=).

3. If the sheet containing the cells you want to reference is in another workbook, type the name of the workbook within brackets ([ ]).

4. Type the name of the sheet followed by an exclamation point (!).

5. Type the cell reference for the cell(s) you want to reference.

6. Press Enter or click the Enter button on the formula bar.

✔ Tip

■ If the name of the sheet includes a space character, it must be enclosed within single quotes in the reference. See **Figures 14a**, **14b**, and **14c** for examples.

To reference a cell with the Paste Special command

1. Select the cell you want to reference.

2. Choose Copy from the Edit menu, press Control+C, or click the Copy button on the Standard toolbar.

3. Switch to the worksheet in which you want to put the reference.

4. Select the cell in which you want the reference to go.

5. Choose Paste Special from the Edit menu (see **Figure 17a**).

6. In the Paste Special dialog box (see **Figure 17b**), click the Paste Link button.

Figure 17a. *Choose Paste Special from the Edit menu...*

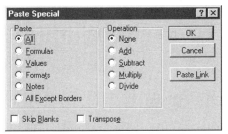

Figure 17b. *...then click the Paste Link button in the Paste Special dialog box.*

✔ Tips

■ Do not press Enter after using the Paste Special command! Doing so pastes what you originally copied into the cell, overwriting the link.

■ Using the Paste Link button to paste a range of cells creates a special range called an *array*. Each cell in an array shares the same cell reference and cannot be changed unless all cells in the array are changed.

Referencing Cells in other Worksheets

To write a formula with 3-D references

1. Select the cell in which you want to enter the formula.

2. Type an equal sign (=).

3. Use any combination of the following techniques until the formula is complete.

   ■ To enter a function, use the Function Wizard or type in the function. I tell you how to use the Function Wizard in Chapter 5.

   ■ To enter an operator, type it in. I tell you about using operators in Chapter 2.

   ■ To enter a cell reference, select the cell(s) you want to reference or type the reference in. If typing the reference, be sure to include single quotes, brackets, and exclamation points as discussed on the previous page.

4. Press Enter or click the Enter button on the formula bar.

About Opening Worksheets with Links

When you open a worksheet that has a link to another workbook file, a dialog box like the one in **Figure 18** appears.

■ If you click Yes, Excel checks the other file and updates linked information. If Excel can't find the other workbook, it displays a standard Open dialog box so you can find it.

■ If you click No, Excel does not check the data in the other file.

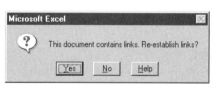

Figure 18. *This dialog box appears if you open a workbook that contains links to another workbook.*

To write a formula that sums the same cell on multiple, adjacent sheets

1. Select the cell in which you want to enter the formula.

2. Type *=SUM(* (see **Figure 19a**).

3. If the cells you want to add are in another workbook, switch to that workbook.

4. Click the sheet tab for the first worksheet containing the cell you want to sum.

5. Hold down the Shift key and click on the sheet tab for the last sheet containing the cell you want to sum. All tabs from the first to the last become selected (see **Figure 19b**). The formula in the formula bar looks something like the one in **Figure 19c**.

6. Click the cell you want to sum (see **Figure 19d**). The cell reference is added to the formula (see **Figure 19e**).

7. Type).

8. Press Enter or click the Enter button on the formula bar.

Figure 19a.
Type the beginning of a formula with the SUM function...

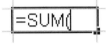

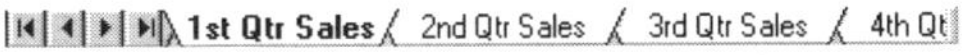

Figure 19b. *...select all of the tabs for sheets containing the cell you want to sum...*

1st Qtr Sales / 2nd Qtr Sales / 3rd Qtr Sales / 4th Qt

=SUM('1st Qtr Sales:4th Qtr Sales'!

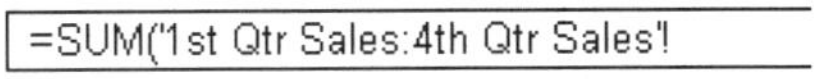

Figure 19c. *...so the sheet names are appended as a range in the formula bar...*

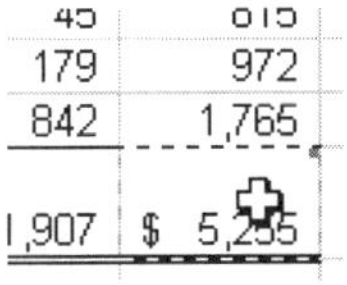

Figure 19d. *...then click on the cell you want to add...*

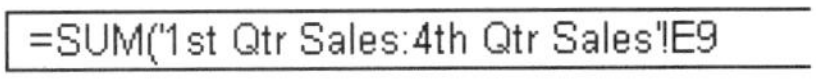

4つ	015
179	972
842	1,765
1,907	$ 5,255

=SUM('1st Qtr Sales:4th Qtr Sales'!E9

Figure 19e. *...so that its reference is appended to the formula in the formula bar.*

✔ Tips

■ Use this technique to link cells of identically arranged worksheets. This results in a "3-D worksheet" effect.

■ Although you can use this technique to consolidate data, the Consolidate command, which I begin discussing on the next page, automates consolidations with or without links.

Writing Formulas with 3-D References

About Consolidations

The Consolidate command lets you combine data from multiple sources. Excel lets you do this in two ways:

■ Consolidate based on the arrangement of data. This is useful when data occupies the same number of cells in the same arrangement in multiple locations (see **Figure 3**).

■ Consolidate based on identifying labels or categories. This is useful when the arrangement of data varies from one source to the next.

Excel can even create links to the source information so the consolidation changes automatically when linked data changes.

To consolidate based on the arrangement of data

1. Select the cell(s) where you want the consolidated information to go (see **Figure 20a**).

2. Choose Consolidate from the Data menu (see **Figure 20b**).

3. In the Consolidate dialog box (see **Figure 20c**), choose a function from the Function drop-down list.

4. Switch to the worksheet containing the first cell(s) to be included in the consolidation. The worksheet reference is entered into the Reference text box.

5. Select the cell(s) you want to include in the consolidation (see **Figure 20d**). The cell reference is entered into the Reference text box.

6. Click Add.

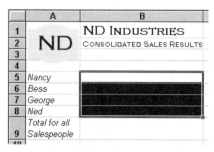

Figure 20a. *Select the cells in which you want the consolidated data to go...*

Figure 20b. *...and choose Consolidate from the Data menu.*

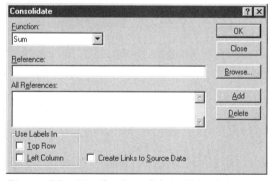

Figure 20c. *Use the Consolidate dialog box to identify the cells you want to combine.*

D	E
Mar	**Total**
841	$ 1,703
45	815
179	972
842	1,766
1,907	$ 5,255

Figure 20d.
Enter references for cells in the Consolidate dialog box by selecting them.

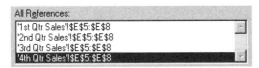

All References:

'1st Qtr Sales'!$E$5:$E$8
'2nd Qtr Sales'!$E$5:$E$8
'3rd Qtr Sales'!$E$5:$E$8
'4th Qtr Sales'!$E$5:$E$8

Figure 20e. *The cells you want to consolidate are listed in the All References area of the Consolidate dialog box.*

	A	B
1	**ND**	**ND INDUSTRIES**
2		CONSOLIDATED SALES RESULTS
3		
4		
5	Nancy	$ 5,907
6	Bess	4,780
7	George	4,803
8	Ned	6,900
9	Total for all Salespeople	
10		

Figure 20f. *Excel combines the data in the cell(s) you originally selected.*

	A	B
1	**ND**	**ND INDUSTRIES**
2		CONSOLIDATED SALES RESULTS
3		
4		
8	Nancy	$ 5,907
9		815
10		2,484
11		1,481
12	Bess	4,780
16	George	4,803
20	Ned	6,900
21	Total for all Salespeople	
22		

Figure 21. *If you turn on the Create Links to Source Data check box, Excel links all source data to the consolidation and creates an outline. In this illustration, the outline is partially expanded to show detail for Bess.*

7. Repeat steps 4, 5, and 6 for all cells you want to include in the consolidation. When you're finished, the All References area of the Consolidate dialog box might look something like **Figure 20e**.

8. To create links between the source data and destination cell(s), turn on the Create Links to Source Data check box.

9. Click OK.

Excel consolidates the information in the originally selected cell(s) (see **Figure 20f**).

✔ Tips

■ In order for this technique to work, each source range must have the same number of cells with data arranged in the same way.

■ If the Consolidate dialog box contains references when you open it, you can clear them by selecting each one and clicking the Delete button.

■ If you turn on the Create Links to Source Data check box, Excel creates an outline with links to all source cells (see **Figure 21**). You can expand or collapse the outline by clicking the outline buttons. I tell you more about outlines in Chapter 11.

To consolidate based on labels

1. Select the cell(s) in which you want the consolidated information to go. As shown in **Figure 22a**, you can select just a single starting cell.

2. Choose Consolidate from the Data menu (see **Figure 20b**).

3. In the Consolidate dialog box (see **Figure 22c**), choose a function from the Function drop-down list.

4. Switch to the worksheet containing the first cell(s) to be included in the consolidation. The worksheet reference is entered into the Reference text box.

5. Select the cell(s) you want to include in the consolidation, including any text that identifies data (see **Figure 22b**). The text must be in cells adjacent to the data. The cell reference is entered into the Reference text box.

6. Click Add.

7. Repeat steps 4, 5, and 6 for all cells you want to include in the consolidation. **Figures 22c** and **22d** show the other two ranges included for the example. When you're finished, the Consolidate dialog box might look something like **Figure 22e**.

8. Turn on the appropriate check box(es) in the Use Labels In area to tell Excel where identifying labels for the data are.

9. Click OK.

   Excel consolidates the information in the originally selected cell(s) (see **Figure 22f**).

Figure 22a.
Select the destination cell(s).

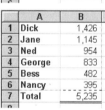

Figures 22b,c,&d.
Select the cell(s) you want to include in the consolidation.

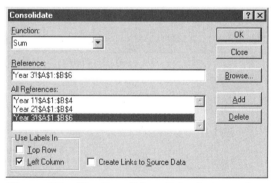

Figure 22e. *The Consolidate dialog box records all selections.*

Figure 22f.
The final consolidation accounts for all data.

Consolidating Based on Labels

ADD-INS & MACROS

About Add-ins

An add-in is a special kind of file that, when installed, adds features to Excel. Excel comes with several add-ins.

While many add-ins provide advanced features for Excel "power users," some add-ins provide basic features that any Excel user can benefit from. In this chapter, I tell you about three add-ins I think are useful: AutoSave, View Manager, and Report Manager.

Figure 1a.
Choose Add-Ins from the Tools menu.

✔ Tips

- Once installed, an add-in is fully integrated with the Excel program. It may add a menu command to one of Excel's menus or a function to the Function Wizard dialog box.

- The add-ins available for installation and use depend on the setup options you chose when installing Excel on your computer. You can see what add-ins are available by choosing Add-Ins from the Tools menu (see **Figure 1a**) and checking the Add-Ins Available list box in the Add-Ins dialog box (see **Figure 1b**). **Figure 1b** shows the add-ins that are available when you do a "Typical" installation of Excel. If the add-in you want to use is not one of those listed, you'll have to use Excel's Setup program to add it. I tell you how on the next page.

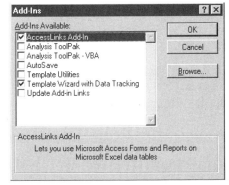

Figure 1b. *The Add-Ins dialog box displays a list of all available add-ins.*

To add add-in files with Setup

1. If Excel is running, choose Exit from the File menu.

2. Insert the Excel disk labeled "Disk 1 - Setup" in your disk drive. Click the Start button and then click the Run button. In the dialog box that appears, enter *A:\Setup.exe* and click OK. (If installing from the Microsoft Office CD-ROM, follow the instructions that came with it to launch the Setup program.)

3. In the main Setup window (see **Figure 2a**), click the Add/Remove button.

4. In the Maintenance dialog box that appears (see **Figure 2b**), click Add-ins in the list box to select it. Then click Change Options.

5. In the Add-Ins dialog box (see **Figure 2c**), turn on the check boxes for the add-ins you want to install and turn off the check boxes for the add-ins you want to remove. Then click OK.

6. In the Maintenance dialog box, click Continue.

7. Insert disks as prompted by the Setup program.

8. When the Successful Installation dialog box appears, click OK.

The add-ins you added will now appear in the Add-Ins dialog box in Excel (see **Figure 3**).

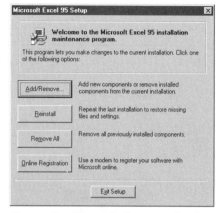

Figure 2a. *The main Setup window lets you tell Setup what you want to do.*

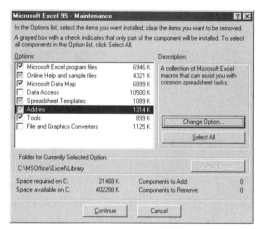

Figure 2b. *Select Add-ins and click Change Options…*

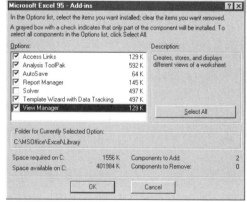

Figure 2c. *…then turn check boxes on or off to install or remove add-ins.*

Adding Add-In Files with Setup

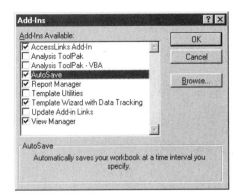

Figure 3. *Turn on the check box(es) for add-in(s) you want to install and turn off the check box(es) for add-in(s) you want to remove.*

To install add-ins

1. Choose Add-Ins from the Tools menu (see **Figure 1a**).

2. In the Add-Ins dialog box (see **Figure 3**), turn on the check box(es) for the add-in(s) you want to install.

3. Click OK.

✔ Tips

■ If you're not sure what an add-in does, in step 2, click the add-in name to select it. The name and a description appears at the bottom of the dialog box (see **Figure 3**).

■ Add-ins remain installed until you remove them.

To remove add-ins

1. Choose Add-Ins from the Tools menu (see **Figure 1a**).

2. In the Add-Ins dialog box (see **Figure 3**), turn off the check box(es) for the add-in(s) you want to remove.

3. Click OK.

✔ Tips

■ Add-ins you remove are not disabled until you quit Excel. Once removed, they remain removed until you install them again.

■ The more add-ins you install, the more RAM Excel requires to operate.

Installing and Removing Add-ins

About AutoSave

The AutoSave add-in, when installed and activated, automatically saves your work at a time interval you specify. This is especially useful for people who can't remember to save their Excel documents periodically as they work.

To use AutoSave

1. Install the AutoSave add-in as discussed on the previous page.

2. Pull down the Tools menu. You'll see a new command named AutoSave (see **Figure 4a**). A check mark beside it indicates that it is turned on. Choose the AutoSave command to configure the add-in.

3. In the AutoSave dialog box (see **Figure 4b**), make sure the check box beside Automatic Save is turned on. Then enter the number of minutes you want Excel to wait before each save in the Minutes edit box beside it.

4. Under Save Options, select the appropriate option button to tell Excel whether it should save just the active workbook or all open workbooks.

5. If you want Excel to display a dialog box like the one in **Figure 4c** before it saves a workbook, turn on the check box beside Prompt Before Saving.

6. Click OK to accept your settings.

✔ Tip

■ The settings you enter in the AutoSave dialog box (see **Figure 4b**) remain in effect until you change them or remove the AutoSave add-in.

Figure 4a. *The AutoSave add-in puts an AutoSave command under the Tools menu when installed.*

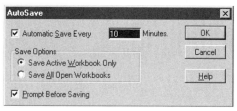

Figure 4b. *The AutoSave dialog box lets you set options for the automatic saving of workbooks.*

Figure 4c. *If you want to, you can have Excel display a dialog box like this before it automatically saves a workbook.*

	A	B	C	D	E	F	G	H	I
1	Product Code	Department	Cost	Selling Price	Order Poi	Qty on Hai	Time to Orde	Total Resale Value	Marki
5	EPU-283	Software	282.10	702.45	40	65		45,659.25	149%
14	EXY-468	Software	185.97	373.85	30	35		13,084.75	101%
26	EZC-376	Software	107.13	422.15	50	80		33,772.00	294%
30	EJZ-70	Software	267.40	497.45	40	46		22,882.70	86%
55	EHS-219	Software	121.12	189.05	30	18	X	3,402.90	56%
56	EXI-88	Software	57.64	188.55	40	69		13,009.95	227%
72	EVR-452	Software	54.28	182.45	20	19	X	3,466.55	236%
84	EZO-100	Software	273.15	860.45	50	35	X	30,115.75	215%
110	ETT-154	Software	120.63	474.15	40	27	X	12,802.05	293%
115	EKY-171	Software	263.09	797.25	20	10	X	7,972.50	203%
121	EGL-468	Software	26.34	104.65	10	79		8,267.35	297%

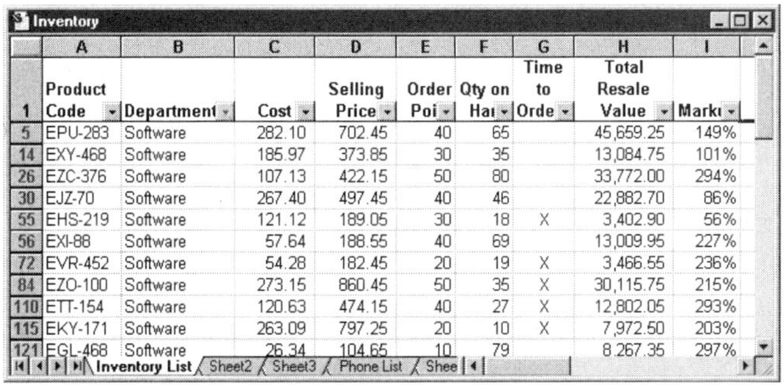

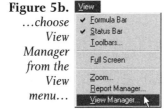

Figure 5a. *Create a view you'd like to save...*

Figure 5b. *...choose View Manager from the View menu...*

Figure 5c. *...click Add in the View Manager dialog box...*

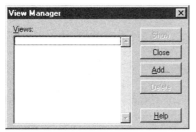

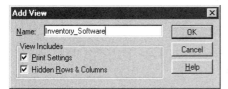

Figure 5d. *...then enter a name and set options for the view and click OK.*

About View Manager

The View Manager add-in lets you create several *views* of a workbook file. A view includes the window size and position, the active cell, the zoom percentage, and most Page Setup and Options dialog box settings. Once you've set up a view, you can choose it from a dialog box to see it quickly.

✔ Tip

- Views are stored for each sheet in a workbook. That means the View Manager dialog box will only display the views for the active sheet.

To add a view with View Manager

1. Install the View Manager add-in as discussed earlier in this chapter.
2. Create the view you want to save. **Figure 5a** shows an example.
3. Choose View Manager from the View menu (see **Figure 5b**). (This command only appears when the View Manager add-in is installed.)
4. In the View Manager dialog box (see **Figure 5c**), click the Add button.
5. In the Add View dialog box (see **Figure 5d**), enter a name for the view in the Name edit box.
6. Turn on the appropriate check boxes if you want the view to include all current Print Settings and Hidden Rows & Columns.
7. Click OK.
8. Repeat steps 2 through 7 for all of the views you want to create.

To switch to a view with View Manager

1. Switch to the sheet containing the view you want to see.

2. Choose View Manager from the View menu (see **Figure 5a**).

3. In the View Manager dialog box (see **Figure 6**), select the view you want to see from the Views list box.

4. Click Show.

   Excel changes the sheet so it looks just like it did when you created the view.

To delete a view

1. Switch to the sheet containing the view you want to delete.

2. Choose View Manager from the View menu (see **Figure 5a**).

3. In the View Manager dialog box (see **Figure 6**), select the view you want to delete from the Views scrolling list.

4. Click Delete.

5. In the confirmation dialog box that appears (see **Figure 7**), click OK.

6. Repeat steps 3 through 5 for each view you want to delete.

7. Click Close to dismiss the View Manager dialog box.

✔ Tip

■ Deleting a view does not delete the information contained in the view. It simply removes the reference to the information from the View Manager.

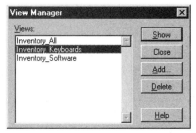

Figure 6. *To see or delete a view, select the name of the view in the View Manager dialog box, then click Show or Delete.*

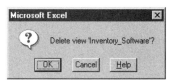

Figure 7. *Excel lets you confirm that you really do want to delete a view.*

Working with View Manager Views

About Report Manager

With the Report Manager add-in, you can automate the printing of reports. Set up reports with sections that include different sheets, views, and scenarios, then choose a report when it's time to print.

✔ Tips

■ To get the most out of Report Manager, use View Manager to set up views that include Page Setup options for report sections you want to print.

■ Excel's Scenarios feature changes cell contents as you specify to show different results. To explore this advanced feature on your own, choose Scenarios from the Tools menu.

To add a report with Report Manager

1. Install the Report Manager add-in as discussed earlier in this chapter.

2. Choose Report Manager from the View menu (see **Figure 8a**). (This command only appears when the Report Manager add-in is installed.)

3. In the Report Manager dialog box (see **Figure 8b**), click the Add button.

4. In the Add Report dialog box (see **Figure 8c**), enter a name for the report in the Report Name edit box.

5. Use the drop-down lists in the Section to Add area to select the Sheet, View, and Scenario for a report section. Then click Add. The information is added to the Sections in this Report list box (see **Figure 8c**).

6. Repeat step 5 for each section of the report.

7. If desired, turn on the Use Continuous Page Numbers check box.

8. Click OK.

Figure 8a. *Choose Report Manager from the View menu...*

Figure 8b. *...click Add in the Report Manager dialog box...*

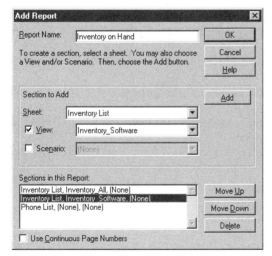

Figure 8c. *...name the report and use the drop-down lists and Add button to add sections to it.*

To print a report with Report Manager

1. Choose Report Manager from the View menu (see **Figure 8a**).

2. In the Report Manager dialog box (see **Figure 9a**), select the report you want to print from the Reports list box.

3. Click Print.

4. A small Print dialog box like the one in **Figure 9b** appears. Enter the number of copies you want to print and click OK.

   Excel begins sending report sections to the printer. A dialog box reports its progress. When the dialog box disappears, you can continue working with Excel.

To delete a report

1. Choose Report Manager from the View menu (see **Figure 8a**).

2. In the Report Manager dialog box (see **Figure 9a**), select the report you want to delete from the Reports list box.

3. Click Delete.

4. In the confirmation dialog box that appears (see **Figure 10**), click OK.

5. Repeat steps 2 through 4 for each view you want to delete.

6. Click Close to dismiss the Print Report dialog box.

✔ Tip

■ Deleting a report does not delete sheet data. It simply removes the report information from the Report Manager.

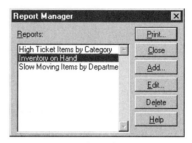

Figure 9a. *Select the report you want to print from the Reports scrolling list.*

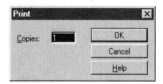

Figure 9b. *Enter the number of copies you want to print and click OK.*

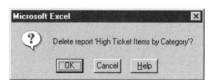

Figure 10. *Excel lets you confirm that you really do want to delete the report.*

About Macros

A macro is a series of commands that Excel can perform automatically. You can create simple macros to automate repetitive tasks, like entering data or formatting cells.

Although macros are stored as Visual Basic modules, you don't need to be a Visual Basic programmer to create them. Excel's Macro Recorder will record your keystrokes, menu choices, and dialog box settings as you make them and will write the programming code for you. This makes macros useful for all Excel users, even raw beginners.

To record a macro with the Macro Recorder

1. Choose Record New Macro from the Record Macro submenu under the Tools menu (see **Figure 11a**).

2. In the Record New Macro dialog box (see **Figure 11b**), enter a name for the macro in the Macro Name edit box. If desired, you can also edit the description automatically entered in the Description edit box.

3. Click OK.

4. Perform all the steps you want to include in your macro. Excel records them all—even the mistakes—so be careful!

5. When you're finished recording macro steps, click the Stop Macro button on the tiny Stop Recording toolbar (see **Figure 11c**).

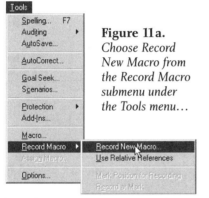

Figure 11a. *Choose Record New Macro from the Record Macro submenu under the Tools menu...*

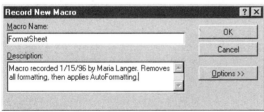

Figure 11b. *...enter a macro name and description in the Record New Macro dialog box, and click OK.*

Figure 11c. *When you're finished recording your macro, click the Stop Macro button on the tiny Stop Recording toolbar.*

To run a macro

1. Choose Macro from the Tools menu (see **Figure 12a**).
2. In the Macro dialog box (see **Figure 12b**), select the macro you want to run from the list box.
3. Click Run.

   Excel performs each macro step, just the way you recorded it.

✔ Tips

■ Save your workbook before running a macro for the first time. You may be surprised by the results and need to revert the file to the way it was before you ran the macro.

■ Excel stores each macro in a module sheet at the end of the workbook. View a macro by clicking the tab for its sheet (see **Figure 13**). You can edit a module to change the way it works.

■ More advanced uses of macros include the creation of custom functions and applications that work within Excel. Add-ins, which I discuss earlier in this chapter, are just complex macros.

Figure 12a.
Choose Macro from the Tools menu...

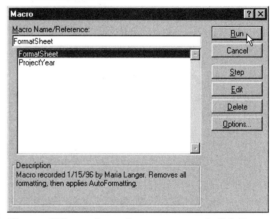

Figure 12b. *...then select a macro and click Run.*

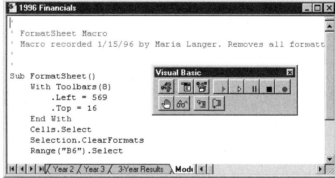

Figure 13. *This Visual Basic Module sheet changes cell formatting.*

CUSTOMIZING EXCEL 14

About Customization

Excel offers a number of ways to customize the way it looks and works:

- Changing general options like your name, the default font, and whether Excel should display a list of recently opened files on the File menu.

- Modifying editing options to enable or disable editing features.

- Changing display options to show or hide gridlines, column and row headings, formulas, and other elements (see **Figure 1**).

- Turning automatic recalculation on or off.

- Creating custom AutoFill lists (see **Figures 2a** and **2b**).

- Customizing existing toolbars or creating your own from scratch (see **Figure 3**).

In this chapter, I tell you how to make all of these customization changes so Excel looks and works the way you want it to.

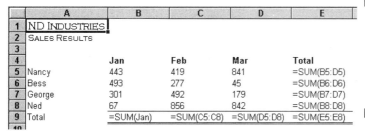

Figure 1. *In this example, display options were changed to hide gridlines and display formulas instead of values.*

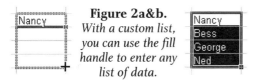

Figure 2a&b. *With a custom list, you can use the fill handle to enter any list of data.*

Figure 3. *You can create a custom toolbar with buttons for commands you like to keep handy.*

About General Options

The options available under the General tab of the Options dialog box (see **Figure 4b**), control basic Excel settings. Here's a list of the ones you'll find most useful:

- Recently Used File List displays a list of the four most recently opened files under the File menu.

- Prompt for File Properties displays the File Properties dialog box the first time you save a file.

- Sheets in New Workbook lets you change the default number of worksheets in new workbooks you create.

- Standard Font and Size let you change the default font and font size used in worksheets.

- User Name lets you change the default user name that appears in various places when you work with Excel.

To change General options

1. Choose Options from the Tools menu (see **Figure 4a**).

2. In the Options dialog box, click the General tab to display its options (see **Figure 4b**).

3. Make changes as desired to options.

4. Click OK to accept your changes.

Figure 4a. *To display the Options dialog box, choose Options from the Tools menu.*

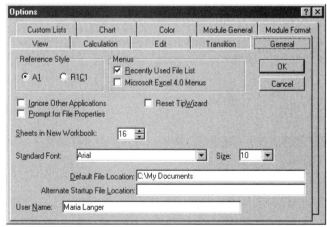

Figure 4b. *The General tab of the Options dialog box.*

About Editing Options

The options available under the Edit tab of the Options dialog box (see **Figure 5**), let you turn certain editing features on or off. Here's what each option does:

- Edit Directly in Cell controls whether you can edit the contents of a cell by double-clicking it.

- Allow Cell Drag and Drop controls whether you can move or copy cells by dragging them to another location.

- Alert before Overwriting Cells controls whether Excel warns you about overwriting a cell's contents when you drag another cell on top of it.

- Move Selection after Enter controls whether Excel moves the cell pointer to the next cell when you press Enter.

- Fixed Decimal lets you set a fixed number of decimal places for all numbers that are entered or calculated.

- Cut, Copy, and Sort Objects with Cells controls whether objects stay with cells when you cut, copy, or sort the cells.

- Ask to Update Automatic Links controls whether Excel asks you about updating links to other documents when you open a document with links.

- Animate Insertion and Deletion controls whether Excel displays an animation when you insert or delete cells, columns, or rows.

- Enable AutoComplete for Cell Values toggles the AutoComplete feature, which can automatically complete entries based on the contents of other cells in the same column.

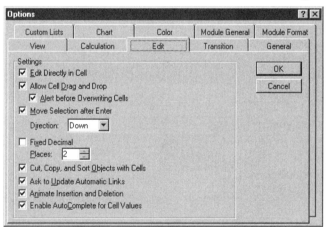

Figure 5. *The Edit tab of the Options dialog box.*

To change Editing options

1. Choose Options from the Tools menu (see **Figure 4a**).

2. In the Options dialog box, click the Edit tab to display its options (see **Figure 5**).

3. Make changes as desired to options.

4. Click OK to accept your changes.

Changing Editing Options

About View Options

The options available under the View tab of the Options dialog box (see **Figure 9**), control what is displayed in Excel windows. Here's what each option does:

■ The four Show options let you toggle the display of the Formula Bar, Status Bar, Note Indicator, and Info Window (see **Figure 6**).

■ The Objects option buttons specify how Excel displays objects. Placeholders show only boxes the size of the objects that would appear (see **Figure 7**).

■ Automatic Page Breaks lets you toggle the display of dashed lines at automatic page breaks.

■ Formulas lets you switch between displaying formula results (the default) or formulas (see **Figure 1**) in cells.

■ Gridlines lets you toggle the display of gridlines (see **Figure 1**). The Color drop-down list (see **Figure 8**) lets you select a gridline color.

■ Row & Column Headers toggles the display of the letters and numbers that appear at the top of each column and the left side of each row.

■ Outline Symbols toggles the display of outline buttons and bars when an outline appears on screen.

■ Zero Values toggles the display of 0s in cells. When turned off, any cell containing the value 0 appears empty.

■ Horizontal Scroll Bar and Vertical Scroll Bar toggle the display of scroll bars on the right side or bottom of the window.

■ Sheet Tabs toggles the display of sheet tabs at the bottom of the window.

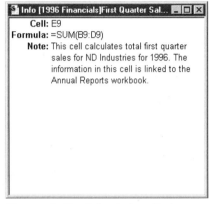

Figure 6. *The Info window displays the cell reference, contents, and note for the active cell.*

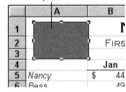

Figure 7. *When you display placeholders rather than actual objects, only gray boxes are displayed on screen.*

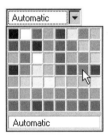

Figure 8. *Change the color of the gridlines with the Color drop-down list.*

Changing View Options

✔ Tips

■ Displaying only placeholders in a worksheet containing graphics can speed up the scrolling and displaying of windows by reducing the amount of detail that must be drawn on screen.

■ To help troubleshoot a complex worksheet, use the View options to display formulas and check your cell references.

■ When you print a worksheet that has formulas displayed, the formulas print.

To change View options

1. Choose Options from the Tools menu (see **Figure 4a**).

2. In the Options dialog box, click the View tab to display its options (see **Figure 9**).

3. Make changes as desired to options.

4. Click OK to accept your changes.

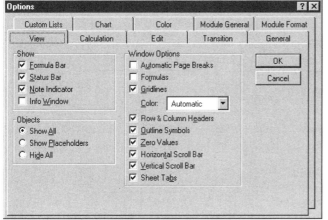

Figure 9. *The View tab of the Options dialog box.*

About Calculation Options

The options available under the Calculation tab of the Options dialog box (see **Figure 10**) control the way Excel calculates formulas. Of these options, the Calculation area option buttons, which set calculation frequency, are the most useful:

- Automatic, which is the default, tells Excel to recalculate each time you enter or change information.

- Automatic Except Tables calculates all formulas automatically except those in data tables.

- Manual calculates only when you click the Calculate Now button in the Options dialog box or press F9. When you select Manual, you can turn on the Recalculate before Save check box to ensure that worksheets are completely recalculated before being saved.

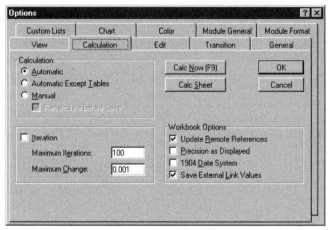

Figure 10. *The Calculation tab of the Options dialog box.*

✔ Tips

- If a worksheet has not been calculated but needs to be, a reminder message appears in the status bar at the bottom of the screen (see **Figure 11**).

- If your worksheet is long and complex, selecting Manual calculation could make it faster to work with by reducing the frequency of recalculations.

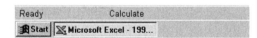

Figure 11. *If you set Calculation to Manual, Excel reminds you to recalculate by putting the word* Calculate *in the status bar.*

To change Calculation options

1. Choose Options from the Tools menu (see **Figure 4a**).

2. In the Options dialog box, click the Calculation tab to display its options (see **Figure 10**).

3. Make changes as desired to options.

4. Click OK to accept your changes.

About Custom Lists

The custom list feature of Excel lets you create your own lists of information to be entered with the fill handle (see **Figures 2a** and **2b**) or Series command. (I discuss AutoFill and the Series command in Chapter 3.) This can speed up data entry when you're creating a worksheet.

To create a custom list

1. Choose Options from the Tools menu (see **Figure 4a**).

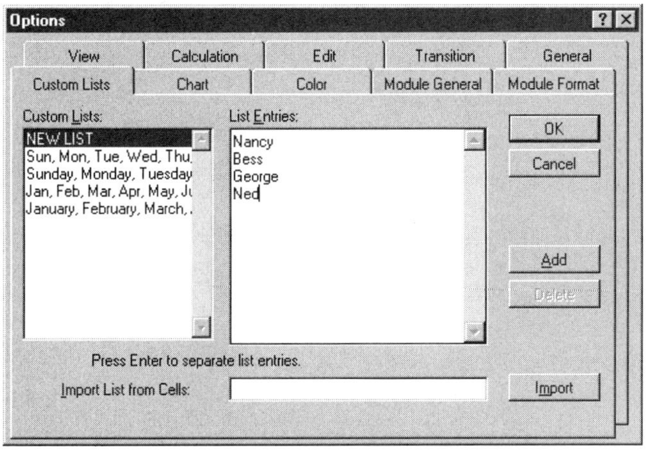

Figure 12. *The Custom Lists tab of the Options dialog box.*

2. In the Options dialog box, click the Custom Lists tab to display its options (see **Figure 12**).

3. With *NEW LIST* selected in the Custom Lists scrolling list, enter each value you want in your list in the List Entries list box. Be sure to press Enter after each entry to separate them.

4. Click the Add button.

5. Repeat steps 2 through 4 for each list you want to create.

6. Click OK.

✔ Tips

■ If the list has already been entered into a worksheet, enter the cell references for the cells containing the list in the Import List from Cells edit box in step 3. Then click Import instead of Add in step 4.

■ To delete a custom list, select it from the Custom Lists scrolling list and click the Delete button. Then click OK in the confirmation dialog box that appears.

About Toolbars

Excel has a variety of toolbars, each with its own collection of buttons. You can show or hide toolbars, change the way their buttons look, move them around your screen, and customize them.

To show or hide toolbars

1. Choose Toolbars from the View menu (see **Figure 13a**).

2. In the Toolbars dialog box (see **Figure 13b**), turn on the check box for the name of a toolbar you want to show or turn off the check box for the name of a toolbar you want to hide.

3. Click OK.

or

1. Position the mouse pointer on any part of the toolbar.

2. Press the right mouse button to display the Toolbars shortcut menu (see **Figure 14**).

3. Choose the toolbar you want to show or hide.

✔ Tips

■ If a toolbar is floating, you can hide it by clicking its close button. I tell you about floating toolbars on the next page.

■ Turn on the Large Buttons check box in the Toolbars dialog box to increase the size of the buttons (see **Figure 15**).

■ Toggle the ToolTips feature on or off by clicking the Show ToolTips check box in the Toolbars dialog box.

Figure 13a.
Choose Toolbars from the View menu.

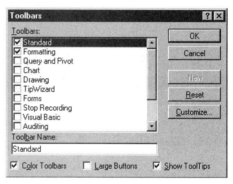

Figure 13b. *Use the Toolbars dialog box to show, hide, customize, or create new toolbars.*

Figure 14.
Point to any toolbar and press the right mouse button to display the Toolbar short-cut menu.

Figure 15.
A standard size button and a large button — both shown at actual size.

Figure 16. *A floating toolbar appears on top of a window and can be moved or resized.*

Figure 17a. *Position the mouse pointer on the edge of the toolbar...*

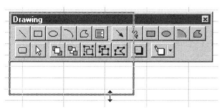

Figure 17b. *...press the mouse button down and drag.*

Figure 17c.
When you release the mouse button, the toolbar is resized and reshaped.

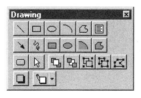

Docked vs. floating toolbars

Toolbars can be *docked* or *floating*. Docked (or anchored) toolbars appear along the edge of the window, like the Standard and Formatting toolbars. Floating toolbars appear in separate, moveable windows on top of the main window (see **Figure 16**). Floating toolbars can be moved or resized.

To move a toolbar

1. Position the mouse pointer on any part of the toolbar that is not a button.
2. Press your mouse button down, and drag.

✔ Tips

- If the toolbar is docked, you can move it anywhere within the window to float it.
- If the toolbar is floating, you can move it against any side of the window to dock it.

To resize a floating toolbar

1. Position the mouse pointer on the edge of the toolbar (see **Figure 17a**).
2. Press the mouse button down and drag to change the toolbar's size and shape (see **Figure 17b**). You'll find that you're restricted to sizes that display all of the buttons.
3. When you release the mouse button, the toolbar resizes and reshapes itself (see **Figure 17c**).

Moving & Resizing Toolbars

To customize a toolbar

1. Choose Toolbars from the View menu (see **Figure 13a**).

2. In the Toolbars dialog box (see **Figure 13b**), make sure the check box beside the toolbar you want to customize is turned on. (The toolbar must be displayed to customize it.) Then click the Customize button.

3. To add a button to a toolbar, in the Customize dialog box (see **Figure 18**), select a toolbar button category from the Categories list box. Then drag the button you want to add to the toolbar from the Buttons area of the dialog box to the toolbar. When you release the button, it's added to the toolbar.

4. To remove a button from a toolbar, drag the button off of the toolbar. When you release it, it disappears.

5. To change a toolbar button's position, drag it to a new position on the toolbar.

6. When you're finished making changes to the toolbar(s), click the Close button.

✔ Tip

■ To find out what a button does, click it while the Customize dialog box is open. A description of the button appears at the bottom of the dialog box (see **Figure 18**).

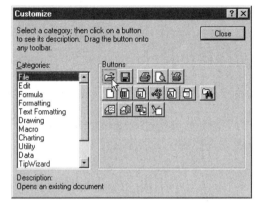

Figure 18. *Use the Customize dialog box to add or remove toolbar buttons.*

To reset a toolbar

1. Choose Toolbars from the View menu (see **Figure 13a**).

2. In the Toolbars dialog box (see **Figure 13b**), select the toolbar you want to reset from the Toolbars scrolling list.

3. Click Reset. The toolbar is restored to its "factory defaults."

✔ Tip

■ You can only reset Excel's toolbars, not ones you create from scratch.

To create a toolbar

1. Choose Toolbars from the View menu (see **Figure 13a**).

2. In the Toolbars dialog box (see **Figure 13b**), type the name of your new toolbar in the Toolbar Name edit box (see **Figure 19a**).

3. Click New. A tiny, empty, floating toolbar appears (see **Figure 19b**).

4. In the Customize dialog box (see **Figure 18**), select a toolbar button category from the Categories list box. Then drag the button you want to add to the toolbar from the Buttons area of the dialog box to the toolbar. When you release the button, it is added to the toolbar (see **Figure 19c**).

5. Repeat step 4 until the toolbar contains all of the buttons you want.

6. Click the Close button in the Customize dialog box.

Figure 19a. *Enter a name for the toolbar you want to create.*

Figure 19b. *A newborn toolbar.*

Figure 19c. *Drag buttons onto the toolbar to build it.*

✔ Tips

■ Once a toolbar has been created, it appears in the Toolbars scrolling list inside the Toolbars dialog box (see **Figure 13b**) and on the Toolbars shortcut menu (see **Figure 14**).

■ You customize a toolbar that you created from scratch just as you would customize any other toolbar.

Resetting & Creating Toolbars

To delete a toolbar

1. Choose Toolbars from the View menu (see **Figure 13a**).

2. In the Toolbars dialog box (see **Figure 13b**), select the toolbar you want to delete from the Toolbars list box.

3. Click Delete.

4. In the confirmation dialog box that appears (see **Figure 20**), click OK.

✔ Tip

■ You can only delete toolbars you created. Excel's built-in toolbars cannot be deleted.

Figure 20. *Excel asks you to confirm that you really do want to delete the toolbar.*

Deleting Toolbars

SHORTCUT KEYS

About Shortcut Keys

This appendix provides a list of shortcut keys for Excel menu commands and tasks. To use a shortcut key, hold down the modifier key(s) while pressing the shortcut key. Using shortcut keys is discussed in Chapter 1.

Modifier Keys

Ctrl	Control Key
Shift	Shift Key
Alt	Alt Key

General-Purpose Menu Commands

F10	Activate menu bar
Shift+F10	Display Shortcut menu
Up Arrow	Select previous command in open menu
Down Arrow	Select next command in open menu
Right Arrow	Select menu to right or open submenu
Left Arrow	Select menu to left or close submenu.

Document Control Menu Commands

Alt+Space	Display application Control menu
Ctrl+F5	Restore
Ctrl+F7	Move
Ctrl+F8	Size
Ctrl+F9	Minimize
Ctrl+F10	Maximize
Ctrl+W	Close

File Menu Commands

Alt+F	Display File Menu
Ctrl+N	New
Ctrl+O	Open
Ctrl+F12	Open
Ctrl+W	Close
Ctrl+F4	Close
Ctrl+S	Save
Shift+F12	Save
F12	Save As
Ctrl+P	Print
Control+Shift+F12	Print
Alt+F4	Exit (Close application)

Edit Menu Commands

Alt+E	Display Edit menu
Ctrl+Z	Undo
F4	Repeat
Shift+F4	Repeat Find or Go To
Ctrl+X	Cut
Ctrl+C	Copy
Ctrl+V	Paste
Ctrl+D	Fill Down
Ctrl+R	Fill Right
Del	Clear Contents
Ctrl+-	Delete
Ctrl+F	Find
Shift+F5	Find
Ctrl+H	Replace
Ctrl+G	Go To
F5	Go To

View Menu Commands

Alt+V	Display View menu
Ctrl+7	Toggle Standard toolbar

Insert Menu Commands

Alt+I	Display Insert menu
Ctrl+Shift+=	Cells
Alt+Shift+F1	Worksheet
Shift+F3	Function
Alt+=	Insert SUM Function
Atrl+A	Display Step 2 of Function Wizard for entered function
Ctrl+Shift+A	Insert argument names for entered function
Ctrl+F3	Define Name
F3	Paste Name
Ctrl+Shift+F3	Create Name
Shift+F2	Note

Format Menu Commands

Ctrl+1	Cells
Ctrl+Shift+~	Apply General number format
Ctrl+Shift+4	Apply Currency style
Ctrl+Shift+5	Apply Percent style
Ctrl+Shift+1	Apply Comman style
Ctrl+Shift+6	Apply Exponential format
Ctrl+Shift+3	Apply Date format
Ctrl+Shift+2	Apply Time format
Ctrl+B	Toggle bold
Ctrl+I	Toggle italic
Ctrl+U	Toggle underline
Ctrl+5	Toggle strikethrough
Ctrl+Shift+7	Apply outline border
Ctrl+Shift+-	Remove all borders
Ctrl+9	Hide Rows
Ctrl+Shift+9	Unhide Rows
Ctrl+0	Hide Columns
Ctrl+Shift+0	Unhide Columns
Alt+'	Style

Insert & Format Menu Commands

Tools Menu Commands

Alt+T	Display Tools menu
F7	Spelling
F9	Calculate all sheets
Ctrl+=	Calculate all sheets
Shift+F9	Calculate active sheet
Ctrl+6	Toggle obejct display
Ctrl+`	Toggle formula display
Ctrl+8	Toggle outline symbol display
Ctrl+F2	Display Info window

Data Menu Commands

Alt+D	Display Data menu
Alt+Shift+Left Arrow	Ungroup rows or columns
Alt+Shift+Right Arrow	Group rows or columns

Window Menu Commands

Alt+W	Display Window menu
Ctrl+F6	Display next workbook
Ctrl+Shift+F6	Display previous workbook

Help Menu Commands

Alt+H	Display Help menu
F1	Microsoft Excel Help Topics

Movement Keys with only one cell active

Arrow	Move one cell in direction of arrow
Ctrl+Arrow	Move to edge of current data region
Tab	Move left to right between unlocked cells
Shift+Tab	Move right to left between unlocked cells
Home	Move to beginning of row
Ctrl+Home	Move to beginning of worksheet (A1)
Ctrl+End	Move to last cell in worksheet (lower-right corner)
Page Down	Move one screen down
Page Up	Move one screen up
Alt+Page Down	Move one screen to right
Alt+Page Up	Move one screen to left
Ctrl+Page Down	Move to next sheet in workbook
Ctrl+Page Up	Move to previous sheet in workbook
F6	Move to next pane
Shift+F6	Move to previous pane

Movement Keys within a Selection

Enter	Move to next cell in selection
Shift+Enter	Move to previous cell in selection
Tab	Move left to right in selection
Shift+Tab	Move right to left in selection
Ctrl+.	Move clockwise to next corner of selection
Ctrl+Alt+Right Arrow	Move to right between nonadjacent selections
Ctrl+Alt+Left Arrow	Move to left between nonadjacent selections

Movement Keys in Print Preview

Arrow	Move around page when zoomed in
Page Down	Move to next page when zoomed out
Page Up	Move to previous page when zoomed out
Ctrl+Up Arrow	Move to first page when zoomed out
Ctrl+Left Arrow	Move to first page when zoomed out
Ctrl+Down Arrow	Move to last page when zoomed out
Ctrl+Right Arrow	Move to last page when zoomed out

Movement Keys

Selection Keys

Ctrl+A	Select entire work-sheet
Ctrl+Shift+Space	Select all objects on sheet (with an object selected)
Ctrl+Space	Select entire column
Shift+Space	Select entire row
Ctrl+Shift+8	Select current region
Shift+Backspace	Collapse selection to active cell
F8	Extend selection
Shift+Arrow	Extend selection by one cell
Shift+Home	Extend selection to beginning of row
Ctrl+Shift+Home	Extend selection to beginning of work-sheet
Ctrl+Shift+End	Extend selection to last cell in worksheet
Ctrl+Shift+Arrow	Extend selection to edge of current data region
Shift+Page Down	Extend selection down one screen
Shift+Page Up	Extend selection up one screen
Ctrl+Shift+/	Select cells contain-ing a note
Ctrl+[	Select direct prece-dent cells
Ctrl+Shift+[	Select precedent cells
Ctrl+]	Select direct depen-dent cells
Ctrl+Shift+]	Select dependent cells
Alt+;	Select visible cells in selection
Ctrl+/	Select current array

Ctrl+\	Select cells that differ from comparison cell in row
Ctrl+Shift+\	Select cells that differ from comparison cell in column
Up Arrow	Select next group of chart items
Down Arrow	Select previous group of chart items
Right Arrow	Select next chart item within selected group
Left Arrow	Select previous chart item within selected group

Data Entry & Editing Keys

F2	Activate active cell
=	Start a formula
Backspace	Activate and clear formula bar for active cell
Backspace	Delete character to left of insertion point
Del	Delete character to right of insertion point
Ctrl+Del	Delete text to end of line
Arrow	Move one character in direction of arrow
Home	Move to beginning of line
Shift+Left Arrow	Select character to left of insertion point
Shift+Right Arrow	Select character to right of insertion point.
Alt+Down Arrow	Display AutoComplete list
Ctrl+;	Enter the date
Ctrl+Shift+;	Enter the time
Ctrl+Shift+"	Copy value from cell above active cell
Ctrl+Alt+Tab	Insert tab character in cell
Alt+Enter	Insert line break in cell
Enter	Complete entry and move down in selection
Shift+Enter	Complete entry and move up in selection
Tab	Complete entry and move right in selection
Shift+Tab	Complete entry and move left in selection
Ctrl+Enter	Fill selection with current entry
Ctrl+Shift+Enter	Enter formula as array formula
Esc	Cancel entry

Dialog Box Keys

Enter	Choose default button
Esc	Choose the Cancel or Close button
Ctrl+Tab	Switch to next tab
Ctrl+Page Down	Switch to next tab
Ctrl+Shift+Tab	Switch to previous tab
Ctrl+Page Up	Switch to previous tab
Tab	Move to next option
Shift+Tab	Move to previous option
Arrow	Move within active list box or group of option buttons
Letter key	Move to next item begining with that letter in active list box
Alt+Letter key	Select item with that underlined letter
Space	Select active button or check box
Alt+Down Arrow	Display drop-down list
Esc	Close drop-down list

Data Form Keys

Alt+Letter key	Select field or button for that underlined letter
Down Arrow	Move to same field in next record
Up Arrow	Move to same field in previous record
Tab	Move to next field
Shift+Tab	Move to previous field
Enter	Move to first field in next record
Shift+Enter	Move to first field in previous record
Page Down	Move to same field 10 records forward
Page Up	Move to same field 10 records back
Ctrl+Page Down	Move to new record
Ctrl+Page Up	Move to first record
Home	Move to beginning of field
End	Move to end of field
Left Arrow	Move one character to left in field
Right Arrow	Move one character to right in field
Shift+Home	Select from insertion point to beginning of field
Shift+End	Select from insertion point to end of field
Shift+Left Arrow	Select character to left of insertion point
Shift+Right Arrow	Select character to right of insertion point

AutoFilter Keys

Alt+Down Arrow	Display list for selected column
Alt+Up Arrow	Close list for selected column
Up Arrow	Select previous item in list
Down Arrow	Select next item in list
Home	Select first item in list (All)
End	Select last item in list (NonBlanks)
Enter	Filter list using selected item

Data Form & AutoFilter Keys

TOOLBARS

About Toolbars

Excel has many toolbars, some of which appear automatically as you work. I tell you how to use toolbars in Chapter 1 and how to customize them in Chapter 14. I tell you about toolbar buttons thoughout this book. In this appendix, I illustrate and label the four toolbars you'll see most often.

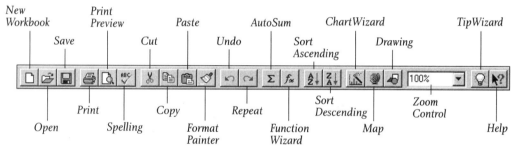

Figure 1. *The Standard toolbar appears, by default, at the top of the screen, right under the menu bar.*

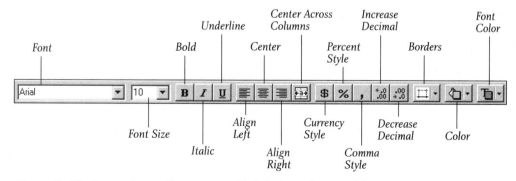

Figure 2. *The Formatting toolbar appears, by default, at the top of the screen, right under the Standard toolbar.*

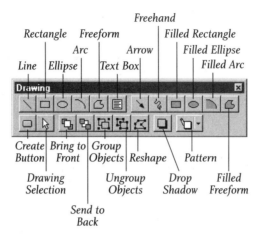

Figure 3. *The Drawing toolbar appears when you click the Drawing button on the Standard toolbar. By default, it's a floating toolbar. See Chapter 7 for details.*

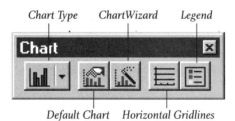

Figure 4. *The Chart toolbar appears when you switch to a chart sheet or click on an embedded chart. By default, it's a floating toolbar. See Chapter 9 for details.*

Drawing & Chart Toolbars

FUNCTIONS

About Functions

Functions are predefined formulas for making specific kinds of calculations. Functions make it quicker and easier to write formulas. I tell you about functions in Chapter 5. In this appendix, I provide a complete list of every Excel function, along with its arguments and a brief description of what it does.

Math & Trig Functions

ABS(number)	Returns the absolute value of a number.
ACOS(number)	Returns the arccosine of a number.
ACOSH(number)	Returns the inverse hyperbolic cosine of a number.
ASIN(number)	Returns the arcsine of a number.
ASINH(number)	Returns the inverse hyperbolic sine of a number.
ATAN(number)	Returns the arctangent of a number.
ATAN2(x_num,y_num)	Returns the arctangent from x- and y-coordinates.
ATANH(number)	Returns the inverse hyperbolic tangent of a number.
CEILING(number,significance)	Rounds a number to the nearest whole number or to the nearest multiple of significance.
COMBIN(number,number_chosen)	Returns the number of combinations for a given number of objects.
COS(number)	Returns the cosine of a number.
COSH(number)	Returns the hyperbolic cosine of a number.
COUNTBLANK(range)	Counts the number of blank cells within a range.
COUNTIF(range,criteria)	Counts the number of non-blank cells within a range which meet the given criteria.
DEGREES(angle)	Converts radians to degrees.
EVEN(number)	Rounds a number up to the nearest even whole number.
EXP(number)	Returns *e* raised to the power of a given number.
FACT(number)	Returns the factorial of a number.
FLOOR(number, significance)	Rounds a number down, toward 0.

Math & Trig Functions

INT(number)	Rounds a number down to the nearest whole number.
LN(number)	Returns the natural logarithm of a number.
LOG(number,base)	Returns the logarithm of a number to a specified base.
LOG10(number)	Returns the base-10 logarithm of a number.
MDETERM(array)	Returns the matrix determinant of an array.
MINVERSE(array)	Returns the matrix inverse of an array.
MMULT(array1,array2)	Returns the matrix product of two arrays.
MOD(number,divisor)	Returns the remainder from division.
ODD(number)	Rounds a number up to the nearest odd whole number.
PI()	Returns the value of pi.
POWER(number,power)	Returns the result of a number raised to a power.
PRODUCT(number 1,number2,...)	Multiplies its arguments
RADIANS(angle)	Converts degrees to radians.
RAND()	Returns a random number between 0 and 1.
ROMAN(number,form)	Converts an Arabic numeral to a Roman numeral, as text.
ROUND(number,num_digits)	Rounds a number to a specified number of digits.
ROUNDDOWN(number,num_digits)	Rounds a number down, toward 0.
ROUNDUP(number,num_digits)	Rounds a number up, away from 0.
SIGN(number)	Returns the sign of a number.
SIN(number)	Returns the sine of a number.
SINH(number)	Returns the hyperbolic sine of a number.
SQRT(number)	Returns a positive square root.
SUBTOTAL(function_num,ref1,...)	Returns a subtotal in a list or database.
SUM(number1,number2,...)	Adds its arguments.
SUMIF(range,criteria, sum_range)	Adds the cells specified by a given criteria.
SUMPRODUCT(array1,array2,array3,...)	Returns the sum of the products of corresponding array components.
SUMSQ(number1,number2,...)	Returns the sum of the squares of its arguments.
SUMX2MY2(array_x,array_y)	Returns the sum of the difference of squares of corresponding values in two arrays.
SUMX2PY2(array_x,array_y)	Returns the sum of the sum of squares of corresponding values in two arrays.
SUMXMY2(array_x,array_y)	Returns the sum of squares of differences of corresponding values in two arrays.
TAN(number)	Returns the tangent of a number.
TANH(number)	Returns the hyperbolic tangent of a number.
TRUNC(number,num_digits)	Truncates a number to a whole number.

Statistical Functions

AVEDEV(number1,number2,...)	Returns the average of the absolute deviations of data points from their mean.
AVERAGE(number1,number2,...)	Returns the average of its arguments.
BETADIST(x,alpha,beta,A,B)	Returns the cumulative beta probability density function.
BETAINV(probability,alpha,beta,A,B)	Returns the inverse of the cumulative beta probability density function.
BINOMDIST(number_s,trials,probability_s,cumulative)	
	Returns the individual term binomial distribution probability.
CHIDIST(x,degrees_freedom)	Returns the one-tailed probability of the chi-squared distribution.
CHIINV(probability,degrees_freedom)	
	Returns the inverse of the one-tailed probability of the chi-squared distribution.
CHITEST(actual_range,expected_range)	
	Returns the test for independence.
CONFIDENCE(alpha,standard_dev,size)	
	Returns the confidence interval for a population mean.
CORREL(array1,array2)	Returns the correlation coefficient between two data sets.
COUNT(value1,value2,...)	Counts how many numbers are in the list of arguments.
COUNTA(value2,value2,...)	Counts how many values are in the list of arguments.
COVAR(array1,array2)	Returns covariance, the average of the products of paired deviations.
CRITBINOM(trials,probability_s,alpha)	
	Returns the smallest value for which the cumulative binomial distribution is greater than or equal to a criterian value.
DEVSQ(number1,number2,...)	Returns the sum of squares of deviations.
EXPONDIST(x,lambda,cumulative)	Returns the exponential distribution.
FDIST(x,degrees_freedom1,degrees_freedom2)	
	Returns the F probability distribution.
FINV(probability,degrees_freedom1,degrees_freedom2)	
	Returns the inverse of the F probability distribution.
FISHER(x)	Returns the Fisher transformation.
FISHERINV(y)	Returns the inverse of the Fisher transformation.
FORECAST(x,known_y's,known_x's)	Returns a value along a linear trend.
FREQUENCY(data_array,bins_array)	Returns a frequency distribution as a vertical array.

FTEST(array1,array2)	Returns the result of an F-test.
GAMMADIST(x,alpha,beta,cumulative)	Returns the gamma distribution.
GAMMAINV(probability,alpha,beta)	Returns the inverse of the gamma cumulative distribution.
GAMMALN(x)	Returns the natural logarithm of the gamma function.
GEOMEAN(number1,number2,...)	Returns the geometric mean.
GROWTH(knowy_y's,known_x's,new_x's,const)	Returns values along an exponential trend.
HARMEAN(number1,number2,...)	Returns the harmonic mean.
HYPGEOMDIST(sample_s,number_sample,population_s,...)	Returns the hypergeometric distribution.
INTERCEPT(known_y's,known_x's)	Returns the intercept of the linear regression line.
KURT(number1,number2,...)	Returns the kurtosis of a data set.
LARGE(array,k)	Returns the k-th largest value in a data set.
LINEST(known_y's,known_x's,const,stats)	Returns the parameters of a linear trend.
LOGEST(known_y's,known_x's,const,stats)	Returns the parameters of an exponential trend.
LOGINV(probability,mean,standard_dev)	Returns the inverse of the lognormal distribution.
LOGNORMDIST(x,mean,standard_dev)	Returns the cumulative lognormal distribution.
MAX(number1,number2,...)	Returns the maximum value in a list of arguments.
MEDIAN(number1,number2,...)	Returns the median of the given numbers.
MIN(number1,number2,...)	Returns the minimum value in a list of arguments.
MODE(number1,number2,...)	Returns the most common value in a data set.
NEGBINOMDIST(number_f,number_s,probability_s)	Returns the negative binomial distribution.
NORMDIST(x,mean,standard_dev,cumulative)	Returns the normal cumulative distribution.
NORMINV(probability,mean,standard_dev)	Returns the inverse of the normal cumulative distribution.
NORMSDIST(z)	Returns the standard normal cumulative distribution.
NORSINV(probability)	Returns the inverse of the standard normal cumulative distribution.
PEARSON(array1,array2)	Returns the Pearson product moment correlation coefficient.

PERCENTILE(array,k)	Returns the k-th percentile of values in a range.
PERCENTRANK(array,x,significance)	Returns the percentage rank of a value in a data set.
PERMUT(number,number_chosen)	Returns the number of permutations for a given number of objects.
POISSON(x,mean,cumulative)	Returns the Poisson distribution.
PROB(x_range,prob_range,lower_limit,upper_limit)	
	Returns the probability that values in a range are between two limits.
QUARTILE(array,quart)	Returns the quartile of a data set.
RANK(number,ref,order)	Returns the rank of a number in a list of numbers.
RSQ(known_y's,known_x's)	Returns the square of the Pearson product moment correlation coefficient.
SKEW(number1,number2,...)	Returns the skewness of a distribution.
SLOPE(known_y's,known_x's)	Returns the slope of the linear regression line.
SMALL(array,k)	Returns the k-th smallest value in a data set.
STANDARDIZE(x,mean,standard_dev)	
	Returns a normalized value.
STDEV(number1,number2,...)	Estimates standard deviation based on a sample.
STDEVP(number1,number2,...)	Calculates standard deviation based on the entire population.
STEYX(known_y's,known_x's)	Returns the standard error of the predicted y-value for each x in the regression.
TDIST(x,degrees_freedom,tails)	Returns the Student's t-distribution.
TINV(probability,degrees_freedom)	Returns the inverse of the Student's t-distribution.
TREND(known_y's,known_x's,new_x's,const)	
	Returns values along a linear trend.
TRIMMEAN(array,percent)	Returns the mean of the interior of a data set.
TTEST(array1,array2,tails,type)	Returns the probability associated with a Student's t-test.
VAR(number1,number2,...)	Estimates variance based on a sample.
VARP(number1,number2,...)	Calculates variance based on the entire population.
WEIBULL(x,alpha,beta,cumulative)	Returns the Weibull distribution.
ZTEST(array,x,sigma)	Returns the two-tailed P-value of a z-test.

Statistical Functions

Financial Functions

DB(cost,salvage,life,period,month)	Returns the depreciation of an asset for a specified period using the fixed-declining balance method.
DDB(cost,salvage,life,period,factor)	Returns the depreciation of an asset for a specified period using the double-declining balance method of some other method you specify.
FV(rate,nper,pmt,pv,type)	Returns the future value of an investment.
IPMT(rate,per,nper,pv,fv,type)	Returns the interest payment for an investment for a given period.
IRR(values,guess)	Returns the internal rate of return for a series of cash flows.
MIRR(values,finance_rate,reinvest_rate)	
	Returns the internal rate of return where positive and negative cash flows are financed at different rates.
NPER(rate,pmt,pv,fv,type)	Returns the number of periods for an investment.
NPV(rate,value1,value2,...)	Returns the net present value of an investment based on a series of periodic cash flows and a discount rate.
PMT(rate,nper,pv,fv,type)	Returns the period payment for an annuity.
PPMT(rate,per,nper,pv,fv,type)	Returns the payment on the principal for an investment for a given period.
PV(rate,nper,pmt,fv,type)	Returns the present value of an investment.
RATE(nper,pmt,pv,fv,type,guess)	Returns the interest rate per period of an annuity.
SLN(cost,salvage,life)	Returns the straight-line depreciation of an asset for one period.
SYD(cost,salvage,life,per)	Returns the sum-of-years'-digits depreciation of an asset for a specified period.
VDB(cost,salvage,life,start_period,end_period,factor,...)	
	Returns the depreciation of an asset for a specified or partial period using a declining balance method.

Logical Functions

AND(logical1,logical2,...)	Returns TRUE if all of its arguments are TRUE.
FALSE()	Returns the logical value FALSE.
IF(logical_test,value_if_true,value_if_false)	
	Specifies a logical test to perform and the value to return based on a TRUE or FALSE result.
NOT(logical)	Reverses the logic of its argument.
OR(logical1,logical2,...)	Returns TRUE if any argument is TRUE.
TRUE()	Returns the logical value TRUE.

Lookup & Reference Functions

ADDRESS(row_num,column_num,abs_num,a1,sheet_text)
Returns a reference as text to a single cell in a worksheet.

AREAS(reference)
Returns the number of areas in a reference.

CHOOSE(index_num,value1,value2,...)
Chooses a value from a list of values.

COLUMN(reference)
Returns the column number of a reference.

COLUMNS(array)
Returns the number of columns in a reference.

HLOOKUP(lookup_value,table_array,row_index_num,...)
Looks in the top row of a table and returns the value of the indicated cell.

INDEX(...)
Uses an index to choose a value from a reference or array.

INDIRECT(ref_text,a1)
Returns a reference indicated by a text value.

LOOKUP(...)
Looks up values in a vector or array.

MATCH(lookup_value,lookup_array,match_type)
Looks up values in a reference or array.

OFFSET(reference,rows,cols,height,width)
Returns a reference offset from a given reference.

ROW(reference)
Returns the row number of a reference.

ROWS(array)
Returns the number of rows in a reference.

TRANSPOSE(array)
Returns the transpose of an array.

VLOOKUP(lookup_value,table_array,col_index_num,...)
Looks in the first column of a table and moves across the row to return the value of a cell.

Information Functions

CELL(info_type,reference)
Returns information about the formatting, location, or contents of a cell.

ERROR.TYPE(error_val)
Returns a number corresponding to an error value.

INFO(type_text)
Returns information about the current operating environment.

ISBLANK(value)
Returns TRUE if the value is blank.

ISERR(value)
Returns TRUE if the value is any error value except #N/A.

ISERROR(value)
Returns TRUE if the value is any error value.

ISLOGICAL(value)
Returns TRUE if the value is a logical value.

ISNA(value)
Returns TRUE if the value is the #N/A error value.

ISNONTEXT(value)	Returns TRUE if the value is not text.
ISNUMBER(value)	Returns TRUE if the value is a number.
ISREF(value)	Returns TRUE if the value is a reference.
ISTECT(value)	Returns TRUE if the value is text.
N(value)	Returns a value converted to a number.
NA()	Returns the error value #N/A.
TYPE(value)	Returns a number indicating the data type of a value.

Date & Time Functions

DATE(year,month,day)	Returns the serial number of a particular date.
DATEVALUE(date_text)	Converts a date in the form of text to a serial number.
DAY(serial_number)	Converts a serial number to a day of the month.
DAYS360(start_date,end_date,method)	
	Calculates the number of days between two dates based on a 360-day year.
HOUR(serial_number)	Converts a serial number to an hour.
MINUTE(serial_number)	Converts a serial number to a minute.
MONTH(serial_number)	Converts a serial number to a month.
NOW()	Returns the serial number of the current date and time.
SECOND(serial_number)	Converts a serial number to a second.
TIME(hour,minute,second)	Returns the serial number of a particular time.
TIMEVALUE(time_text)	Converts a time in the form of text to a serial number.
TODAY()	Returns the serial number of today's date.
WEEKDAY(serial_number,return_type)	
	Converts a serial number to a day of the week.
YEAR(serial_number)	Converts a serial number to a year.

Text Functions

CHAR(number)	Returns the character specified by the code number.
CLEAN(text)	Removes all nonprintable characters from text.
CODE(text)	Returns a numeric code for the first character in a text string.
CONCATENATE(text1,text2,...)	Joins several text items into one text item.
DOLLAR(number,decimals)	Converts a number to text, using currency format.
EXACT(text1,text2)	Checks to see if two text values are identical.

FIND(find_text,within_text,start_num)
Finds one text value within another. This function is case-sensitive.

FIXED(number,decimals,no_commas) Formats a number as text with a fixed number of decimals.

LEFT(text,num_chars) Returns the leftmost characters from a text value.

LEN(text) Returns the number of characters in a text string.

LOWER(text) Converts text to lowercase.

MID(text,start_num,num_chars) Returns a specific number of characters from a text string.

PROPER(text) Capitalizes the first letter in each word of a text value.

REPLACE(old_text,start_num,num_chars,new_text)
Replaces characters within text.

REPT(text,number_times) Repeats text a given number of times.

RIGHT(text,num_chars) Returns the rightmost characters from a text value.

SEARCH(find_text,within_text,start_num)
Finds one text value within another. This function is not case-sensitive.

SUBSTITUTE(text,old_text,new_text,instance_num)
Substitutes new text for old text in a text string.

T(value) Converts its arguments to text.

TEXT(value,format_text) Formats a number and converts it to text.

TRIM(text) Removes spaces from text.

UPPER(text) Converts text to uppercase.

VALUE(text) Converts a text argument to a number.

Database Functions

DAVERAGE(database,field,criteria) Returns the average of selected database entries.

DCOUNT(database,field,criteria) Counts the cells containing numbers from a specified database and criteria.

DCOUNTA(database,field,criteria) Counts nonblank cells from a specified database and criteria.

DGET(database,field,criteria) Extracts from a database a single record that matches the specified criteria.

DMAX(database,field,criteria) Returns the maximum value from selected database entries.

DMIN(database,field,criteria) Returns the minimum value from selected database entries.

DPRODUCT(database,field,criteria) Multiplies the values in a particular field of records that match the criteria in a database.

Text Functions, Database Functions

DSTDEV(database,field,criteria)	Estimates the standard deviation based on a sample of selected database entries.
DSTDEVP(database,field,criteria)	Calculates the standard deviation based on the entire population of selected database entries.
DSUM(database,field,criteria)	Adds the numbers in the field column of records in the database that match the criteria.
DVAR(database,field,criteria)	Estimates the variance based on a sample from selected database entries.
DVARP(database,field,criteria)	Calculates variance based on the entire population of selected database entries.

Database Functions

INDEX

Index

Index